James Harris

Hermes

Or, A philosophical Inquiry concerning universal Grammar

James Harris

Hermes
Or, A philosophical Inquiry concerning universal Grammar

ISBN/EAN: 9783337074340

Printed in Europe, USA, Canada, Australia, Japan

Cover: Foto ©ninafisch / pixelio.de

More available books at **www.hansebooks.com**

HERMES

OR

A PHILOSOPHICAL INQVIRY

CONCERNING

VNIVERSAL GRAMMAR

BY IAMES HARRIS ESQ.

ΕΙΣΙΕΝΑΙ ΘΑΡΡΟΥΝΤΑΣ ΕΙΝΑΙ ΓΑΡ ΚΑΙ ΕΝΤΑΥΘΑ ΘΕΟΥΣ

THE THIRD EDITION
REVISED AND CORRECTED

LONDON

PRINTED FOR IOHN NOVRSE
AND PAVL VAILLAN

M DCC LXXI

To the Right Honourable

PHILIP *Lord* HARDWICKE,

Lord High Chancellor of *Great Britain**.

My Lord,

AS no one has exercised the Powers of Speech with juster and more universal applause, than yourself; I have presumed to inscribe the following Treatise to your Lordship, its End being to investigate the Principles of those Powers. It has a farther claim to your Lordship's Patronage, by being connected in some degree with that politer Literature, which, in the most important scenes

---

* The above Dedication is printed as it originally stood, the Author being desirous that what he intended as real Respect to the noble Lord, when living, should now be considered, as a Testimony of Gratitude to his Memory.

of Buſineſs, you have ſtill found time to cultivate. With regard to myſelf, if what I have written be the fruits of that Security and Leiſure, obtained by living under a mild and free Government; to whom for this am I more indebted, than to your Lordſhip, whether I conſider you as a Legiſlator, or as a Magiſtrate, the firſt both in dignity and reputation? Permit me therefore thus publicly to aſſure your Lordſhip, that with the greateſt gratitude and reſpect I am, My Lord,

Your Lordſhip's moſt obliged,
and moſt obedjent humble Servant,

Cloſe of Saliſbury,
Oct. 1, 1751.

James Harris.

PREFACE.

THE chief End, proposed by the Author of this Treatise in making it public, has been to excite his Readers to curiosity and inquiry; not to teach them himself by prolix and formal Lectures, (from the efficacy of which he has little expectation) but to induce them, if possible, to become Teachers to themselves, by an impartial use of their own understandings. He thinks nothing more absurd than the common notion of Instruction, as if Science were to be poured into the Mind, like water into a cistern, that passively waits to receive all that comes. The growth of Knowlege he rather thinks to resemble the growth of Fruit; however external causes may in some degree co-operate, it is the internal vigour, and virtue of the tree, that muſt ripen the juices to their juſt maturity.

This then, namely, the exciting men to inquire for themſelves into ſubjects worthy of their contemplation, this the Author declares to have been his firſt and principal motive for appearing in print. Next to that, as he has always been a lover of Letters, he would willingly approve his ſtudies to the liberal and ingenuous. He has particularly named theſe, in diſtinction to others; becauſe, as his ſtudies were never proſecuted with the leaſt regard to lucre, ſo they are no way calculated for any lucrative End. The liberal therefore and ingenuous (whom he has mentioned already) are thoſe, to whoſe peruſal he offers what he has written. Should they judge favourably of his attempt, he may not perhaps heſitate to confeſs,

Hoc juvat et melli eſt.———

For tho' he hopes, he cannot be charged with the foolish love of vain Praise, he has no desire to be thought indifferent, or insensible to honest Fame.

From the influence of these sentiments, he has endeavoured to treat his subject with as much order, correctness, and perspicuity as in his power; and if he has failed, he can safely say (according to the vulgar phrase) that the failure has been his misfortune, and not his fault. He scorns those trite and contemptible methods of anticipating pardon for a bad performance, that " it was the hasty " fruits of a few idle hours; written " merely for private amusement; " never revised; published against " consent, at the importunity of " friends, copies (God knows how) " having by stealth gotten abroad;" with other stale jargon of equal falshood and inanity. May we not ask such Prefacers, If what they allege be true, what has the world to do with them and their crudities?

As to the Book itself, it can say this in its behalf, that it does not merely confine itself to what its title promises, but expatiates freely into whatever is collateral; aiming on every occasion to rise in its inquiries, and to pass, as far as possible, from small matters to the greatest. Nor is it formed merely upon sentiments that are now in fashion, or supported only by such authorities as are modern. Many Authors are quoted, that now a-days are but little studied; and some perhaps, whose very names are hardly known.

The Fate indeed of antient Authors (as we have happened to mention them) is not unworthy of our notice. A few of them survive in the Libraries of the learned, where some venerable Folio, that still goes by their name, just

PREFACE.

just suffices to give them a kind of nominal existence. The rest have long fallen into a deeper obscurity, their very names, when mentioned, affecting us as little, as the names, when we read them, of those subordinate Heroes,

Alcandrumque, Haliumque, Noemonaque, Prytanimque.

Now if an Author, not content with the more eminent of antient Writers, should venture to bring his reader into such company as these last, among people *(in the fashionable phrase)* that no body knows; *what usage, what quarter can he have reason to expect?—Should the Author of these speculations have done this (and it is to be feared he has) what method had he best take in a circumstance so critical?—Let us suppose him to apologize in the best manner he can, and in consequence of this, to suggest as follows—*

He

PREFACE.

He hopes there will be found a pleasure in the contemplation of antient sentiments, as the view of antient Architecture, tho' in ruins, has something venerable. Add to this, what from its antiquity is but little known, has from that very circumstance the recommendation of novelty; so that here, as in other instances, Extremes may be said to meet. *Farther still, as the Authors, whom he has quoted, lived in various ages, and in distant countries; some in the full maturity of* Grecian *and* Roman *Literature; some in its declension; and others in periods still more barbarous, and depraved; it may afford perhaps no unpleasing speculation, to see how the* SAME REASON *has at all times prevailed; how there is* ONE TRUTH, *like one Sun, that has enlightened human Intelligence through every age, and saved it from the darkness both of Sophistry and Error.*

Nothing

PREFACE.

Nothing can more tend to enlarge the Mind, than these extensive views of Men, and human Knowlege; nothing can more effectually take us off from the foolish admiration of what is immediately before our eyes, and help us to a juster estimate both of present Men, and present Literature.

It is perhaps too much the case with the multitude in every nation, that as they know little beyond themselves, and their own affairs, so out of this narrow sphere of knowlege, they think nothing worth knowing. As we BRITONS *by our situation live divided from the whole world, this perhaps will be found to be more remarkably our case: And hence the reason, that our studies are usually satisfied in the works of our own Countrymen; that in Philosophy, in Poetry, in every kind of subject, whether serious or ludicrous, whether sacred or profane, we think*

per-

perfection with ourselves, and that it is superfluous to search farther.

The Author of this Treatise would by no means detract from the just honours due to those of his Countrymen, who either in the present, or preceding age, have so illustriously adorned it. But tho' he can with pleasure and sincerity join in celebrating their deserts, he would not have the admiration of these, or of any other few, to pass thro' blind excess into a contempt of all others. Were such Admiration to become universal, an odd event would follow; a few learned Men, without any fault of their own, would contribute in a manner to the extinction of Letters.

A like evil to that of admiring only the authors of our own age, is that of admiring only the authors of one particular Science. There is indeed in this last prejudice something pecu-

PREFACE.

peculiarly unfortunate, and that is, the more excellent the Science, the more likely it will be found to produce this effect.

There are few Sciences more intrinsically valuable, than MATHEMATICS. *It is hard indeed to say, to which they have more contributed, whether to the Utilities of Life, or to the sublimest parts of Science.* They are the noblest Praxis of LOGIC, or UNIVERSAL REASONING. *It is thro'* them *we may perceive, how the stated Forms of Syllogism are exemplified in one Subject, namely the Predicament of* Quantity. *By marking the force of these Forms, as they are applied* here, *we may be enabled to apply them of ourselves* elsewhere. *Nay farther still—by viewing the* MIND, during its process in these syllogistic employments, *we may come to know in part*, what kind of Being it is; since MIND, *like other Powers, can*

be

be only known from its Operations. *Whoever therefore will study* Mathematics *in this view, will become not only by Mathematics a more expert* Logician, *and by Logic a more rational* Mathematician, *but a wiser Philosopher, and an acuter Reasoner, in all the possible subjects either of science or deliberation.*

But when Mathematics, *instead of being applied to this excellent purpose, are used not to exemplify* Logic, *but to supply its place; no wonder if* Logic *pass into contempt, and if* Mathematics, *instead of furthering science, become in fact an obstacle. For when men, knowing nothing of that Reasoning which is* universal, *come to attach themselves for years* to a single Species, *a species wholly involved* in Lines and Numbers only ; *they grow insensibly to believe these last as inseparable from all Reasoning, as the poor* Indians *thought every*

PREFACE.

every horseman to be inseparable from his horse.

And thus we see the use, nay the necessity of enlarging our literary views, lest even Knowlege *itself should obstruct its own growth, and perform in some measure the part of ignorance and barbarity.*

Such then is the Apology made by the Author of this Treatise, for the multiplicity of antient quotations, with which he has filled his Book. If he can excite in his readers a proper spirit of curiosity; if he can help in the least degree to enlarge the bounds of Science; to revive the decaying taste of antient Literature; to lessen the bigotted contempt of every thing not modern; and to assert to Authors of every age their just portion of esteem; if he can in the least degree contribute to these ends, he hopes it may be allowed, that he has done a

service

service to mankind. Should this service be a reason for his Work to survive, he has confest already, it would be no unpleasing event. Should the contrary happen, he must acquiesce in its fate, and let it peaceably pass to those destined regions, whither the productions of modern Wit are every day passing,

―――in vicum vendentem tus et odores.

THE CONTENTS.

BOOK I.

Chapter I. *Introduction. Design of the whole.* page 1

Chap. II. *Concerning the Analyzing of Speech into its smallest Parts.* p. 9

Chap. III. *Concerning the several Species of those smallest Parts.* p. 23

Chap. IV. *Concerning Substantives, properly so called.* p. 37

Chap. V. *Concerning Substantives of the Secondary Order.* p. 63

Chap. VI. *Concerning Attributives, and first concerning Verbs.* p. 87

Chap. VII. *Concerning Time, and Tenses.* p. 100

Chap. VIII. *Concerning Modes.* p. 140

Chap. IX. *Concerning Verbs, as to their Species and other remaining Properties.* p. 173

CONTENTS.

Chap. X. *Concerning Participles and Adjectives.* p. 184
Chap. XI. *Concerning Attributives of the Secondary Order.* p. 192

BOOK II.

Chapter I. *Concerning Definitives.* page 213
Chap. II. *Concerning Connectives, and first those called Conjunctions.* p. 237
Chap. III. *Concerning those other Connectives, called Prepositions.* p. 261
Chap. IV. *Concerning Cases.* p. 275
Chap. V. *Concerning Interjections—Recapitulation—Conclusion.* p. 289

BOOK III.

Chapter I. *Introduction——Division of the Subject into its principal Parts.* page 305
Chap. II. *Upon the Matter or common Subject of Language.* p. 316

Chap.

CONTENTS.

Chap. III. *Upon the Form, or peculiar Character of Language.* p. 327

Chap. IV. *Concerning general or universal Ideas.* p. 350

Chap. V. *Subordination of Intelligence—Difference of Ideas, both in particular Men, and in whole Nations—Different Genius of different Languages——Character of the* English, *the* Oriental, *the* Latin, *and the* Greek *Languages—Superlative Excellence of the Last—Conclusion.* p. 403

HERMES

OR A PHILOSOPHICAL INQUIRY
CONCERNING UNIVERSAL GRAMMAR.

BOOK I.

CHAP. I.

INTRODUCTION.

Defign of the Whole.

IF Men by nature had been framed for Solitude, they had never felt an Impulfe to converfe one with another: And if, like lower Animals, they had been by nature irrational, they could not have recognized the proper Subjects of Difcourfe. Since SPEECH then is the joint Energie of our beft and nobleft Faculties (*a*), (that is to fay, of our *Rea-*

fon

(*a*) See V. I. p. 147 to 169. See alfo Note xv. p. 292, and Note xix. p. 296. of the fame Volume.

Ch. I. *fon* and our *focial Affection)* being withal our *peculiar* Ornament and Diftinction, as *Men*; thofe Inquiries may furely be deemed interefting as well as liberal, which either fearch how SPEECH may be naturally *refolved*; or how, when refolved, it may be again *combined*.

HERE a large field for fpeculating opens before us. We may either behold SPEECH, as divided into *its conftituent Parts*, as a Statue may be divided into its feveral Limbs; or elfe, as refolved into its *Matter* and *Form*, as the fame Statue may be refolved into its Marble and Figure.

THESE different *Analyfings* or *Refolutions* conftitute what we call (*b*) PHILOSOPHICAL, or UNIVERSAL GRAMMAR.

WHEN

(*b*) Grammaticam *etiam bipartitam ponemus, ut alia fit literaria, alia* philofophica *&c.* Bacon. *de Augm. Scient. VI.* 1. And foon after he adds—*Verumtamen hâc ipfâ re moniti, cogitatione complexi fumus Grammaticam quandam, quæ non analogiam verborum ad invicem, fed analogiam inter* verba *et* res *five* rationem *fedulò inquirat.*

Ch. I.

WHEN we have viewed SPEECH thus *analysed*, we may then consider it, as *compounded*. And here in the first place we may contemplate that (*c*) *Synthesis*, which *by combining simple Terms* produces a *Truth*; then *by combining two Truths* produces a *third*; and thus others, and others, in continued Demonstration, till we are led, as by a road, into the regions of SCIENCE.

Now this is that *superior* and most excellent *Synthesis*, which alone applies itself to our *Intellect* or *Reason*, and which to conduct

---

(*c*) *Aristotle* says — τῶν δὲ καλὰ μηδεμίαν συμπλοκὴν λεγομένων ἐδὲν ὅτε ἀληθὲς ὅτε ψευδές ἐστιν· οἷον ἄνθρωπ۞, λεῦκ۞, τρέχει, νικᾷ — *Of those words which are spoken without Connection, there is no one either true or false; as for instance, Man, white, runneth, conquereth.* Cat. C. 4. So again in the beginning of his Treatise *De Interpretatione*, περὶ γὰρ σύνθεσιν κỳ διαίρεσιν ἐστι τὸ ψευδός τε κỳ τὸ ἀληθές. *True and False are seen in Composition and Division.* Composition makes *affirmative* Truth, Division makes *negative*, yet both alike bring Terms together, and so far therefore may be called synthetical.

Ch. I. conduct according to Rule, constitutes the Art of Logic.

AFTER this we may turn to those (*d*) *inferior* Compositions, which are productive

---

(*d*) *Ammonius* in his Comment on the Treatise Περὶ Ἑρμηνείας, p. 53. gives the following Extract from *Theophrastus*, which is here inserted at length, as well for the Excellence of the Matter, as because it is not (I believe) elsewhere extant.

Διτῆς γὰρ ἄσης τᾶ λόγε σχίσεως, (καθ' ἃ διώρισεν ὁ Φιλόσοφ۞ Θεόφρας۞) τῆς τε ΠΡΟΣ ΤΟΥΣ ΑΚΡΟΩΜΕΝΟΥΣ, οἷς κỳ σημαίνει τι, κỳ τῆς ΠΡΟΣ ΤΑ ΠΡΑΓΜΑΤΑ, ὑπὲρ ὧν ὁ λέγων πεῖσαι προσίθηται τὰς ἀκροωμένες, περὶ μὲν ἐν τὴν σχέσιν αὐτὴν τὴν ΠΡΟΣ ΤΟΥΣ ΑΚΡΟΑΤΑΣ καταγίνονται ποιητικὴ κỳ ῥητορικὴ, διότι ἔργον αὐταῖς ἐκλέγεσθαι τὰ σεμνότερα τῶν ὀνομάτων, ἀλλὰ μὴ τὰ κοινὰ κỳ δεδημευμένα, κỳ ταῦτα ἐναρμονίως συμπλέκειν ἀλλήλοις, ὥστε διὰ τύτων κỳ τῶν τύτοις ἑπομένων, οἷον σαφηνείας, γλυκύτητ۞, κỳ τῶν ἄλλων ἰδεῶν, ἔτι τε μακρολογίας, κỳ βραχυλογίας, κατὰ καιρὸν πάντων παραλαμβανομένων, οἷσαί τε τὸν ἀκροατὴν, κỳ ἐκπλῆξαι, κỳ πρὸς τὴν πείθω χειρωθέντα ἔχειν· τῆς δέ γε ΠΡΟΣ ΤΑ ΠΡΑΓΜΑΤΑ τᾶ λόγε σχίσεως ὁ Φιλόσοφ۞ προηγεμένως ἐπιμελήσεται, τό, τε ψεῦδ۞ διελέγχων, κỳ

ductive of the *Pathetic*, and the *Plea-* Ch. I.
fant in all their kinds. These latter Compositions

χ) τὸ ἀληθὲς ἀποδεικνύς. *The Relation of Speech being twofold (as the Philosopher Theophrastus hath settled it) one to the* HEARERS, *to whom it explains something, and one to the* THINGS, *concerning which the Speaker proposes to perfuade his Hearers: With respect to the first Relation, that which regards the* HEARERS, *are employed Poetry and Rhetoric. Thus it becomes the businefs of these two, to select the most respectable Words, and not those that are common and of vulgar ufe, and to connect such Words harmoniously one with another, so as thro' these things and their consequences, such as Perspicuity, Delicacy, and the other Forms of Eloquence, together with Copioufnefs and Brevity, all employed in their proper feafon, to lead the Hearer, and strike him, and hold him vanquifhed by the power of Perfuafion. On the contrary, as to the Relation of Speech to* THINGS, *here the Philofopher will be found to have a principal employ, as well in refuting the Falfe, as in demonftrating the True.*
Sanctius fpeaks elegantly on the fame Subject. *Creavit Deus hominem rationis participem ; cui, quia Sociabilem effe voluit, magno pro munere dedit Sermonem. Sermoni autem perficiendo tres opifices adhibuit. Prima eft* Grammatica, *quæ ab oratione folæcifmos & barbarifmos expellit ; fecunda* Dialectica, *quæ in Sermonis veritate verfatur ;* tertia Rhetorica, *quæ ornatum Sermonis tantum exquirit.* Min. l. 1. c. 2.

Ch. I. positions aspire not to the Intellect, but being addressed to the *Imagination*, the *Affections*, and the *Sense*, become from their different heightnings either RHETORIC or POETRY.

NOR need we necessarily view these Arts distinctly and apart; we may observe, if we please, how perfectly they co-incide. GRAMMAR is equally requisite to every one of the rest. And though LOGIC may indeed subsist without RHETORIC or POETRY, yet so necessary to these last is a sound and correct LOGIC, that without it, they are no better than warbling Trifles.

Now all these Inquiries (as we have said already) and such others arising from them as are of still sublimer Contemplation, (of which in the Sequel there may be possibly not a few) may with justice be deem'd Inquiries both interesting and liberal.

AT present we shall postpone the whole Ch. I. synthetical Part, (that is to say, *Logic* and *Rhetoric*) and confine ourselves to the analytical, that is to say UNIVERSAL GRAMMAR. In this we shall follow the Order, that we have above laid down, first dividing SPEECH, as a WHOLE into its CONSTITUENT PARTS; then resolving it, as a COMPOSITE, into its MATTER and FORM; two Methods of Analysis very different in their kind, and which lead to a variety of very different Speculations.

SHOULD any one object, that in the course of our Inquiry we sometimes descend to things, which appear trivial and low; let him look upon the effects, to which those things contribute, then from the Dignity of the Consequences, let him honour the Principles.

THE following Story may not improperly be here inserted. " When the Fame
" of

"of *Heraclitus* was celebrated through-
"out *Greece*, there were certain perſons,
"that had a curioſity to ſee ſo great a
"Man. They came, and, as it happened,
"found him warming himſelf in a
"Kitchen. The meanneſs of the place
"occaſioned them to ſtop; upon which
"the Philoſopher thus accoſted them—
"ENTER (ſays he) BOLDLY, FOR HERE
"TOO THERE ARE GODS (*e*)."

WE ſhall only add, that as there is no part of Nature too mean for the Divine Preſence; ſo there is no kind of Subject, having its foundation in Nature, that is below the Dignity of a philoſopical Inquiry.

(*e*) See *Ariſtot. de Part. Animal.* l. 1. c. 5.

CHAP. II.

Concerning the Analyſing of Speech into its ſmalleſt Parts.

THOSE things, which are *firſt to Na-*
ture, are not *firſt to Man*. *Nature*
begins from *Cauſes*, and thence deſcends
to *Effects*. *Human Perceptions* firſt open
upon *Effects*, and thence by ſlow degrees
aſcend to *Cauſes*. Often had Mankind
ſeen the Sun in Eclipſe, before they knew
its Cauſe to be the Moon's Interpoſition;
much oftner had they ſeen thoſe unceaſing
Revolutions of Summer and Winter, of
Day and Night, before they knew the
Cauſe to be the Earth's double Motion (*a*).

Even

(*a*) This Diſtinction of *firſt to Man*, and *firſt to*
Nature, was greatly regarded in the Peripatetic Philoſophy. See *Ariſt. Phyſ. Auſcult.* 1. 1. c. 1. *Themiſ-*
tius's Comment on the ſame, *Poſter. Analyt.* l. 1.
c. 2. *De Anima*, l. 2. c. 2. It leads us, when properly regarded, to a very important Diſtinction between

HERMES.

Ch. II. Even in Matters of Art and *human* Creation, if we except a few Artists and critical

---

tween Intelligence *Divine* and Intelligence *Human*. GOD may be said to view the First, as first; and the Last, as last; that is, he views *Effects* thro' *Causes* in their *natural Order*. MAN views the Last, as first; and the First, as last; that is, he views *Causes* thro' *Effects*, in *an inverse Order*. And hence the Meaning of that Passage in *Aristotle:* ὥσπερ γὰρ τὰ τῶν νυκτερίδων ὄμματα πρὸς τὸ φέγγ۞ ἔχει τὸ μεθ' ἡμέραν, ὕτω κὴ τῆς ἡμετέρας ψυχῆς ὁ Νᾶς πρὸς τὰ τῇ φύσει φανερώτατα πάντων. *As are the Eyes of Bats to the Light of the Day, so is Man's Intelligence to those Objects, that are by Nature the brightest and most conspicuous of all Things,* Metaph. l. 2. c. 1. See also l. 7. c. 4. and *Ethic. Nicom.* l. 1. c. 4. *Ammonius,* reasoning in the same way, says very pertinently to the Subject of this Treatise—Ἀγαπητὸν τῇ ἀνθρωπίνῃ φύσει, ἐκ τῶν ἀτελεστέρων κὴ συνθέτων ἐπὶ τὰ ἁπλέστερα κὴ τελειότερα προϊέναι· τὰ γὰρ σύνθετα μᾶλλον συνήθη ἡμῖν, κὴ γνωριμώτερα· Ούτω γᾶν κὴ ὁ παῖς εἴραι μὲν λόγον, κὴ ἐιπεῖν, Σωκράτης περιπατεῖ, οἶδε· τᾶτον δὲ ἀναλῦσαι εἰς ὄνομα κὴ ῥῆμα, κὴ ταῦτα εἰς συλλαβὰς, κἀκεῖνα εἰς στοιχεῖα, ἐκέτι· *Human Nature may be well contented to advance from the more imperfect and complex to the more simple and perfect; for the complex Subjects are more familiar to us, and better known. Thus therefore it is that even a Child knows how to put a Sentence together, and say,* Socrates walketh;

Book the First.

tical Obfervers, the reft look no higher than to the *Practice* and mere *Work*, knowing nothing of thofe *Principles*, on which the whole depends.

Thus in Speech for example—All men, even the loweft, can fpeak their Mother-Tongue. Yet how many of this multitude can neither write, nor even read? How many of thofe, who are thus far literate, know nothing of that Grammar, which refpects the Genius of their own Language? How few then muft be thofe, who know Grammar universal; *that Grammar, which without regarding the feveral Idioms of particular Languages, only refpects thofe Principles, that are effential to them all?*

'Tis our prefent Defign to inquire about this Grammar; in doing which we fhall follow

---

walketh; *but how to refolve this Sentence into a Noun and Verb, and thefe again into Syllables, and Syllables into Letters or Elements, here he is at a lofs.* Am. in Com. de Prædic. p. 29.

Ch. II. follow the Order confonant to *human* Perception, as being for that reafon the more eafy to be underftood.

WE fhall begin therefore firft from a *Period* or *Sentence,* that combination in Speech, which is obvious to all, and thence pafs, if poffible, to thofe its *primary Parts,* which, however effential, are only obvious to a few.

WITH refpect therefore to the different Species of Sentences, who is there fo ignorant, as if we addrefs him in his Mother-Tongue, not to know when 'tis we *affert,* and when we *queftion*; when 'tis we *command,* and when we *pray* or *wifh?*

FOR example, when we read in *Shakefpeare**,
*The Man, that hath no mufic in himfelf,
And is not mov'd with concord of fweet
 founds,
Is fit for Treafons*———
Or

Or in *Milton**,

> *O Friends, I hear the tread of nimble feet,*
> *Hasting this way—*

'tis obvious that these are *assertive Sentences*, one founded upon Judgment, the other upon Sensation.

WHEN the Witch in *Macbeth* says to her Companions,

> *When shall we three meet again*
> *In thunder, lightning, and in rain?*

this 'tis evident is an *interrogative Sentence*.

WHEN *Macbeth* says to the Ghost of *Banquo*,

> ——*Hence, horrible Shadow,*
> *Unreal Mock'ry hence!*——

he speaks an *imperative Sentence*, founded upon the passion of hatred.

---

* P. L. IV. 866.

Ch. II. WHEN *Milton* fays in the character of his *Allegro*,

> *Hafte thee, Nymph, and bring with thee*
> *Jeft and youthful Jollity,*

he too fpeaks an *imperative Sentence*, tho' founded on the paffion, not of hatred but of love.

WHEN in the beginning of the *Paradife Loft* we read the following addrefs,

> *And chiefly thou, O Spirit, that doft prefer*
> *Before all temples th' upright heart, and*
> *pure,*
> *Inftruct me, for thou know'ft—*

this is not to be called an *imperative Sentence*, tho' perhaps it bear the fame Form, but rather (if I may ufe the Word) 'tis a Sentence *precative* or *optative*.

WHAT then fhall we fay? Are Sentences to be quoted in this manner without ceafing, all differing from each other in
    their

their stamp and character? Are they no Ch. II.
way reducible to certain definite Classes?
If not, they can be no objects of *rational*
comprehension.—Let us however try.

'T IS a phrase often apply'd to a man,
when speaking, that *he speaks his* MIND;
as much as to say, that his Speech or Discourse is *a publishing of some Energie or Motion of his Soul.* So it indeed is in every
one that speaks, excepting alone the Dissembler or Hypocrite; and he too, as far
as possible, affects the appearance.

Now the POWERS OF THE SOUL (over
and above the meer † nutritive) may be included all of them in those of PERCEPTION, and those of VOLITION. By the
Powers of PERCEPTION, I mean the
Senses and the *Intellect*; by the Powers of
VOLITION, I mean, in an extended sense,
not only the *Will*, but the several *Passions*
and *Appetites*; in short, *all that moves to
Action, whether rational or irrational.*

IF

---
† Vid. Aristot. de An. II. 4.

Ch. II. IF then the leading Powers of the Soul be thefe two, 'tis plain that every Speech or Sentence, as far as it exhibits the Soul, muſt of courſe reſpect one or other of theſe.

IF we *aſſert*, then is it a Sentence which reſpects the Powers of PERCEPTION. For what indeed is to *aſſert*, if we conſider the examples above alleged, but *to publiſh ſome Perception either of the Senſes or the Intellect?*

AGAIN, if we *interrogate*, if we *command*, if we *pray*, or if we *wiſh*, (which in terms of Art is to ſpeak Sentences *interrogative, imperative, precative,* or *optative)* what do we but publiſh ſo many different VOLITIONS?—For who is it that *queſtions?* He that has *a·Deſire* to be informed.—Who is it that *commands?* He that has *a Will*, which he would have obey'd.—What are thoſe Beings, who either *wiſh* or *pray?* Thoſe, who feel

certain

certain wants either for themselves, or Ch. II. others.

IF then the *Soul's leading Powers* be *the two* above mentioned, and it be true that *all Speech is a publication of these Powers*, it will follow that EVERY SENTENCE WILL BE EITHER A SENTENCE OF ASSERTION, OR A SENTENCE OF VOLITION. And thus, by referring all of them to one of these two classes, have we found an expedient to reduce their infinitude (*b*).

THE

(*b*) Ῥητέον ὖν ὅτι τῆς ψυχῆς τῆς ἡμετέρας διτίας ἐχέσης δυνάμεις, τὰς μὲν γνωςικὰς, τὰς δὲ ζωτικὰς, τὰς κỳ ὀρεκτικὰς λεγομένας· (λέγω δὲ γνωςικὰς μὲν, καθ' ἃς γινώσκομεν ἕκασον τῶν ὄντων, οἷον νῦν, διάνοιαν, δόξαν, φαντασίαν κỳ αἴσθησιν· ὀρεκτικὰς δὲ, καθ' ἃς ὀρεγόμεθα τῶν ἀγαθῶν, ἢ τῶν ὄντων, ἢ τῶν δοκούντων, οἷον βούλησιν λέγω, προαίρεσιν, θυμὸν, κỳ ἐπιθυμίαν) τὰ MEN τέτταρα εἴδη τῦ λόγυ (τὰ παρὰ τὸν ἀποφαντικὸν) ἀπὸ τῶν ὀρεκτικῶν δυνάμεων προέρχονται τῆς ψυχῆς, ἐκ αὐτῆς καθ' αὐτὴν ἐνεργούσης, ἀλλὰ πρὸς ἕτερον ἀποτεινομένης (τὸν συμβάλλεσθαι δοκῦντα πρὸς τὸ τυχεῖν τῆς ὀρέξεως) κỳ ἤτοι λόγον παρ' αὐτῦ
C ζητῦσης

Ch. II. The Extensions of Speech are quite indefinite, as may be seen if we compare the

---

ζητάσης, καθάπερ ἐπὶ τῦ ΠΥΣΜΑΤΙΚΟΥ κ̓
ΕΡΩΤΗΜΑΤΙΚΟΥ καλυμένυ λόγυ, ἢ πρᾶγμα,
κ̓ εἰ πρᾶγμα, ἤτοι αὐτῦ ἐκείνυ τυχεῖν ἐφιεμένης, πρὸς ὃν
ὁ λόγ☉, ὥσπερ ἐπὶ τῦ ΚΛΗΤΙΚΟΥ, ἢ τινὸς παρ᾽
αὐτῦ πράξεως· κ̓ ταύτης, ἢ ὡς παρὰ κρείτον☉, ὡς ἐπὶ
τῆς ΕΥΧΗΣ, ἢ ὡς παρὰ χείρονος, ὡς ἐπὶ τῦ κυρίως
καλυμένης ΠΡΟΣΤΑΞΕΩΣ· μόνον ΔΕ τὸ ΑΠΟ-
ΦΑΝΤΙΚΟΝ ἀπὸ τῶν γνωςικῶν, κ̓ ἔςι τῦτο
ἐξαγγελτικὸν τῆς γενομένης ἐν ἡμῖν γνώσεως τῶν πραγμάτων ἀληθῶς, ἢ φαινομένως, διὸ κ̓ μόνον τῦτο δεκτι-
κόν ἐςιν ἀληθείας ἢ ψεύδυς, τῶν δὲ ἄλλων ὐδέν. The
Meaning of the above paſſage being implied in the
Text, we take its tranſlation from the *Latin* Interpreter. *Dicendum igitur eſt, cum anima noſtra duplicem poteſtatem habeat, cognitionis, & vitæ, quæ etiam appetitionis ac cupiditatis appellatur, quæ vero cognitionis eſt, vis eſt, quâ res ſingulas cognoſcimus, ut mens, cogitatio, opinio, phantaſia, ſenſus: appetitus vero facultas eſt, quâ bona, vel quæ ſunt, vel quæ videntur, concupiſcimus, ut ſunt voluntas, conſilium, ira, cupiditas: quatuor orationis ſpecies, præter enunciantem, a partibus animi proficiſcuntur, quæ concupiſcunt; non cum animus ipſe per ſe agit, ſed cum ad alium ſe convertit, qui ei ad conſequendum id, quod cupit, conducere poſſe videatur; atque etiam vel rationem ab eo exquirit, ut in oratione, quam* Percunctantem,

the Eneid to an Epigram of *Martial*. But the *longeſt Extenſion*, with which Grammar has to do, is the Extenſion here conſider'd, that is to ſay a SENTENCE. The greater Extenſions (ſuch as Syllogiſms, Paragraphs, Sections, and complete Works) belong not to Grammar, but to Arts of higher order; not to mention that all of them are but Sentences repeated.

Now a SENTENCE (*c*) may be ſketch'd in the following deſcription—*a compound Quantity*

---

tem, *aut* Interrogantem *vocant*; *vel rem: ſique rem, vel cum ipſum conſequi cupit, quicum loquitur, ut in* optante oratione, *vel aliquam ejus actionem :* atque in *hâc, vel ut a præſtantiore, ut in* Deprecatione ; *vel ut ab inferiore,* ut *in eo, qvi proprie* Juſſus *nominatur. Scl2 autem* Enuncians *a cognoſcendi facultate proficiſcitur : hæcque nunciat rerum cognitionem, quæ in nobis eſt, aut veram, aut ſimulatam. Itaque* Hæc ſola verum falſumque capit : *præterea vero nulla.* Ammon. in Libr. de Interpretatione.

(*c*) Λόγ⊙ δὲ φωνὴ συνθετὴ σημαντικὴ, ἧς ἔνια μέρη καθ' αὑτὰ σημαίνει τι. Ariſt. Poet. c. 20. See alſo de Interpret. c. 4.

Ch. II. *Quantity of Sound significant, of which certain Parts are themselves also significant.*

THUS when I say [*the Sun shineth*] not only the *whole quantity* of sound has a meaning, but *certain Parts* also, such as [*Sun*] and [*shineth.*]

BUT what shall we say? Have these Parts again other Parts, which are in like manner significant, and so may the progress be pursued to infinite? Can we suppose all Meaning, like Body, to be divisible, and to include within itself other Meanings without end? If this be absurd, then must we necessarily admit, that there is such a thing as *a Sound significant, of which no Part is of itself significant.* And this is what we call the proper character of a (*d*) WORD. For thus, though the Words

---

(*d*) Φωνὴ σημαντικὴ,—ἧς μέρ۞ ἰδέν ἐςι καθ᾽ αὐτὸ σημαντικόν. De Poetic. c. 20. De Interpret. c. 2. & 3. *Priscian's* Definition of a Word (Lib 2.) is as follows

Ch. II.

Words [*Sun*] and [*ſhineth*] have each a Meaning, yet is there certainly no Meaning in any of their Parts, neither in the Syllables of the one, nor in the Letters of the other.

IF therefore ALL SPEECH whether in proſe or verſe, every Whole, every Section, every Paragraph, every Sentence, imply a certain *Meaning, diviſible into other Meanings*, but WORDS imply a *Meaning, which is not ſo diviſible:* it follows that WORDS *will be the ſmalleſt parts of ſpeech*, in as much as nothing leſs has any Meaning at all.

To

---

follows—*Dictio eſt pars minima orationis conſtructæ, id eſt, in ordine compoſitæ. Pars autem, quantum ad totum intelligendum, id eſt, ad totius ſenſus intellectum. Hoc autem ideo dictum eſt, nequis conetur* vires *in duas partes dividere, hoc eſt, in* vi & res; *non enim ad totum intelligendum hæc fit diviſio.* To *Priſcian* we may add *Theodore Gaza.*—Λέξις δὲ, μέρ<g> ἐλάχιστον κατὰ σύνταξιν λόγȣ. Introd. Gram. l. 4. *Plato* ſhewed them this characteriſtic of a Word—See *Cratylus,* p. 385. Edit. Serr.

Ch. II. *To know therefore the species of Words must needs contribute to the knowledge of Speech*, as it implies a knowledge of its *minutest* Parts.

This therefore muſt become our next Inquiry.

CHAP.

CHAP. III.

Concerning the species of Words, the smallest Parts of Speech.

LET us first search for the *Species* of Words among those Parts of Speech, commonly received by Grammarians. For example, in one of the passages above cited.—

The Man, that hath no music in himself,
And is not mov'd with concord of sweet
  sounds,
Is fit for treasons—

Here the Word [*The*] is an ARTICLE;—
[*Man*] [*No*] [*Music*] [*Concord*] [*Sweet*]
[*Sounds*] [*Fit*] [*Treasons*] are all NOUNS,
some *Substantive*, and some *Adjective*—
[*That*] and [*Himself*] are PRONOUNS—
[*Hath*] and [*is*] are VERBS—[*moved*] a
PARTICIPLE—[*Not*] an ADVERB—[*And*]
a CONJUNCTION—[*In*] [*with*] and [*For*]
are

Ch. III. are PREPOSITIONS. In one sentence we have all those Parts of Speech, which the *Greek* Grammarians are found to acknowledge. The *Latins* only differ in having no Article, and in separating the INTERJECTION, as a Part of itself, which the *Greeks* include among the Species of *Adverbs*.

WHAT then shall we determine? why are there not more Species of Words? why so many? or if neither more nor fewer, why these and not others?

To resolve, if possible, these several Queries, let us examine any Sentence that comes in our way, and see what differences we can discover in its Parts. For example, the same Sentence above,

The Man that hath no music, &c.

ONE Difference soon occurs, that some Words are *variable*, and others *invariable*. Thus the Word *Man* may be varied into *Man's* and *Men*; *Hath*, into *Have*, *Hast*, *Had*,

Had, &c. *Sweet* into *Sweeter* and *Sweetest*; Ch. III.
Fit into *Fitter* and *Fittest*. On the contrary the Words, *The, In, And,* and some others, remain as they are, and *cannot be altered.*

AND yet it may be questioned, how far this Difference is essential. For in the first place, there are Variations, which can be hardly called necessary, because only some Languages have them, and others have them not. Thus the *Greeks* have the *dual* Variation, which is unknown both to the Moderns and to the ancient *Latins*. Thus the *Greeks* and *Latins* vary their Adjectives by the *triple Variation* of Gender, Case, and Number; whereas the *English* never vary them in any of those ways, but thro' all kinds of Concord preserve them still the same. Nay even those very Variations, which appear most necessary, may have their places supplied by other methods; some by *Auxiliars*, as when for *Bruti*, or *Bruto* we say, *of Brutus, to Brutus;* some

by

Ch. III. *by mcer Position*, as when for *Brutum amavit Cassius*, we say, *Cassius lov'd Brutus*. For here the *Accusative*, which in *Latin* is known *any where* from its *Variation*, is in *English* only known from its *Position* or place.

IF then the Distinction of Variable and Invariable will not answer our purpose, let us look farther for some other more essential.

SUPPOSE then we should dissolve the Sentence above cited, and view its several *Parts* as they stand *separate* and detached. Some 'tis plain *still preserve a Meaning*, (such as *Man, Music, Sweet*, &c.) others on the contrary *immediately lose it* (such as, *And, The, With*, &c.) Not that these last have no meaning at all, but in fact they never have it, but when *in company*, or *associated*.

Now it should seem that this Distinction, if any, was essential. For if all
Words

Words are significant, or else they would not be Words; and if every thing not *absolute*, is of course *relative*, then will all Words be significant either *absolutely* or *relatively*. Ch. III.

WITH respect therefore to this Distinction, the first sort of Words may be call'd *significant by themselves*; the latter may be call'd *significant by relation*; or if we like it better, the first sort may be call'd *Principals*, the latter *Accessories*. The first are like those stones in the basis of an Arch, which are able to support themselves, even when the Arch is destroyed; the latter are like those stones in its Summit or Curve, which can no longer stand, than while the whole subsists (*e*.)

§ THIS

(*e*) *Appollonius* of *Alexandria* (one of the acutest Authors that ever wrote on the subject of Grammar) illustrates the different power of Words, by the different power of Letters. Ἔτι, ὃν τρόπον τῶν ϛοιχείων τὰ μέν ἐϛι φωνήεντα, ἃ ϰὴ καθ' ἑαυτὰ φωνὴν ἀπoτελεῖ· τὰ

Ch. III.

§ THIS Diſtinction being admitted, we thus purſue our Speculations. All things what-

---

τὰ δὲ σύμφωνα, ἅπερ ἄνευ τῶν φωνηέντων ἐκ ἔχει ῥητὴν τὴν ἐκφώνησιν. τὸν αὐτὸν τρόπον ἐςὶν ἐπινοῆσαι καὶ πὶ τῶν λέξεων. αἱ μὲν γὰρ αὐτῶν, τρόπον τινὰ τῶν φωνηέντων, ῥηταί εἰσι· καθάπερ ἐπὶ τῶν ῥημάτων, ὀνομάτων, ἀντωνυμιῶν, ἐπιρρημάτων·——ἁι δὲ, ὡσπερεὶ σύμφωνα, ἀναμένεσι τὰ φωνήεντα, ἃ δυνάμενα κατ' ἰδίαν ῥητὰ εἶναι——καθάπερ ἐπὶ τῶν προθέσεων, τῶν ἄρθρων, τῶν ςυνδέσμων· τὰ γὰρ τοιαῦτα ἀεὶ τῶν μορίων συσσημαίνει. *In the ſame manner, as of the Elements or Letters ſome are Vowels, which of themſelves complete a Sound; others are Conſonants, which without the help of Vowels have no expreſs Vocality, ſo likewiſe may we conceive as to the nature of Words. Some of them, like Vowels, are of themſelves expreſſive, as is the caſe of Verbs, Nouns, Pronouns, and Adverbs; others, like Conſonants, wait for their Vowels, being unable to become expreſſive by their own proper ſtrength, as is the caſe of Prepoſitions, Articles, and Conjunctions; for thoſe parts of Speech are always Conſignificant, that is, are only ſignificant, when aſſociated to ſomething elſe.* Apollon. de Syntaxi. L. 1. c. 3. *Itaque quibuſdam philoſophis placuit* NOMEN & VERBUM SOLAS ESSE PARTES ORATIONIS; *cætera vero,* ADMINICULA *vel* JUNCTURAS *earum: quomodo navium partes ſunt tabulæ & trabes, cætera autem (id eſt, cera, ſtuppa, & clavi & ſimilia) vincula & conglutinationes*

BOOK THE FIRST. 29

whatever either *exist as the Energies, or* Ch.III. *Affections of some other thing,* or *without being the Energies or Affections of some other thing.* If they exist *as the Energies or Affections of something else,* then are they called ATTRIBUTES. Thus *to think* is the attribute of a Man; *to be white,* of a Swan; *to fly,* of an Eagle; *to be four-footed,* of a Horse. If they exist *not after this manner,* then are they call'd SUBSTANCES*. Thus *Man, Swan, Eagle* and *Horse* are none of them Attributes, but all Substances, because however they may exist in Time and Place, yet neither of these, nor of any thing else do they exist as Energies or Affections.

AND

---

tiones partium navis, (hoc est, tabularum & trabium) non partes navis dicuntur. Prisc L. IX. 913.

* SUBSTANCES] Thus Aristotle. Νῦν μὲν ἐν τύπῳ εἴρηται, τί ποτ' ἐστὶν ἡ οὐσία, ὅτι τὸ μὴ καθ' ὑποκειμένου, ἀλλὰ καθ' οὗ τὰ ἄλλα. Metaph. Z. γ. p. 106. Ed. Sylb.

Ch. III. AND thus all things whatsoever being either (*f*) *Substances* or *Attributes*, it follows of course that all Words, *which are significant as Principals*, must needs be significant of either the one or the other. If they are *significant of Substances*, they are call'd *Substantives*; if *of Attributes*, they are call'd *Attributives*. So that ALL WORDS *whatever, significant as Principals, are either* SUBSTANTIVES *or* ATTRIBUTIVES.

AGAIN, as to Words, which are only significant as *Accessories*, they acquire a Signification either from being associated *to one Word*, or else *to many*. If *to one Word alone*, then as they can do no more than in some manner *define* or *determine*, they may justly for that reason be called DE-

―――――――――

(*f*) This division of things into *Substance* an *Accident* seems to have been admitted by Philosophers of all Sects and Ages. See *Categor.* c. 2. *Metaphys.* L. VII. c. 1. *De Cælo*, L. III. c. 1.

DEFINITIVES. If *to many Words at* Ch.III. *once*, then as they serve to no other purpose than *to connect*, they are called for that reason by the name of CONNECTIVES.

AND thus it is that all WORDS whatever are either *Principals* or *Accessories;* or under other Names, either *significant from themselves*, or *significant by relation*. —If *significant from themselves*, they are either *Substantives* or *Attributives;* if *significant by relation*, they are either *Definitives* or *Connectives.* So that under one of these four Species, SUBSTANTIVES, ATTRIBUTIVES, DEFINITIVES, and CONNECTIVES, *are* ALL WORDS, *however different, in a manner included.*

IF any of these Names seem new and unusual, we may introduce others more usual, by calling the *Substantives*, NOUNS; the *Attributives*, VERBS; the *Definitives*,

ARTI-

Ch. III. ARTICLES; and the *Connectives*, CONJUNCTIONS.

SHOU'D it be aſk'd, what then becomes of *Pronouns, Adverbs, Prepoſitions,* and *Interjections*; the anſwer is, either they muſt be found included within the Species above-mentioned, or elſe muſt be admitted for ſo many Species by themſelves.

§ THERE were various opinions in ancient days, as to the *number* of theſe Parts, or Elements of Speech.

Plato in his * Sophiſt mentions only two, the *Noun* and the *Verb*. *Ariſtotle* mentions no more, where he treats of † Propoſitions. Not that thoſe acute Philoſophers were ignorant of the other Parts, but they ſpoke with reference to *Logic* or *Dia-*

---

* Tom. I. p. 261. Edit. Ser.
† De Interpr. c. 2 & 3.

Dialectic (g), considering the Essence of Ch. III. Speech as contained in these two, because these *alone* combined make a perfect *assertive* Sentence, which none of the rest without them are able to effect. Hence therefore *Aristotle* in his * *treatise of Poetry* (where he was to lay down the elements of

---

(g) *Partes igitur orationis sunt secundum Dialecticos duæ*, NOMEN & VERBUM; *quia hæ solæ etiam per se conjunctæ plenam faciunt orationem; alias autem partes* συγκατηγορήματα, *hoc est, consignificantia appellabant.* Priscian. l. 2. p. 574. Edit. Putschii. *Existit hic quædam quæstio, cur duo tantum*, NOMEN & VERBUM, *se (Aristoteles sc.) determinare promittat, cum plures partes orationis esse videantur. Quibus hoc dicendum est, tantum Aristotelem hoc libro diffinisse, quantum illi ad id, quod instituerat tractare, suffecit. Tractat namque de simplici enuntiativa oratione, quæ scilicet hujusmodi est, ut junctis tantum Verbis & Nominibus componatur.—Quare superfluum est quærere, cur alias quoque, quæ videntur orationis partes, non præposuerit, qui non totius simpliciter orationis, sed tantum simplicis orationis instituit elementa partiri.* Boetius in Libr. de Interpretat. p. 295. *Apollonius* from the above principles elegantly calls the NOUN and VERB, τὰ ἐμψυχότατα μέρη τοῦ λόγου, *the most animated parts of Speech*. De Syntaxi l. 1. c. 3. p. 24. See also *Plutarch. Quæst. Platon.* p. 1009.

* Poet. Cap. 20.

D

Ch. III. of a more variegated speech) adds the *Article* and *Conjunction* to the Noun and Verb, and so adopts the same Parts, with those established in this Treatise. To *Aristotle*'s authority (if indeed better can be required) may be added that also of the elder *Stoics* (*h*).

THE latter *Stoics* instead of four Parts made five, by dividing the Noun into the *Appellative*, and *Proper*. Others increased the number, by detaching the *Pronoun* from the Noun; the *Participle* and *Adverb* from the Verb; and the *Preposition* from the Conjunction. The *Latin Grammarians* went farther, and detached the *Interjection* from the Adverb, within which by the *Greeks* it was always included, as a Species.

WE

(*h*) For this we have the authority of *Dionysius* of *Halicarnassus*, *De Struct. Orat. Sect.* 2. whom *Quintilian* follows, *Inst. l.* 1. *c.* 4. *Diogenes Laertius* and *Priscian* make them always to have admitted five Parts. See *Priscian*, as before, and *Laertius*, *Lib. VII. Segm.* 57.

WE are told indeed by (*i*) *Dionyſius* of Ch. III. *Halicarnaſſus* and *Quintilian*, that *Ariſtotle*, with *Theodectes*, and the more early writers, held but *three Parts* of ſpeech, the *Noun*, the *Verb*, and the *Conjunction*. This, it muſt be owned, accords with the oriental Tongues, whoſe Grammars (we are (*k*) told) admit no other. But as to *Ariſtotle*, we have his own authority to aſſert the contrary, who not only enumerates the *four* Species which we have adopted, but aſcertains them each by a proper Definition *.

(*i*) See the places quoted in the note immediately preceding.

(*k*) *Antiquiſſima eorum eſt opinio, qui tres claſſes faciunt. Eſtque hæc Arabum quoque ſententia.—Hebræi quoque (qui, cum Arabes Grammaticam ſcribere deſinerent, artem eam demum ſcribere cœperunt, quod ante annos contigit circiter quadringentos) Hebræi, inquam hac in re ſecuti ſunt magiſtros ſuos Arabes.—Immo vero trium claſſium numerum aliæ etiam Orientis linguæ retinent. Dubium, utrum eâ in re Orientales imitati ſunt antiquos Græcorum, an hi potius ſecuti ſunt Orientalium exemplum. Utut eſt, etiam veteres Græcos tres tantum partes agnoviſſe, non ſolum auctor eſt Dionyſius,* &c. Voſſ. de Analog. l. 1. c. 1. See alſo *Sanctii Minerv.* l. 1. c. 2.

* Sup. p. 34.

Ch. III. To conclude—the Subject of the following Chapters will be a diſtinct and ſeparate conſideration of the NOUN, the VERB, the ARTICLE, and the CONJUNCTION; which four, the better (as we apprehend) to expreſs their reſpective natures, we chuſe to call SUBSTANTIVES, ATTRIBUTIVES, DEFINITIVES and CONNECTIVES.

CHAP. IV.

Concerning Substantives, properly so called.

SUBSTANTIVES are *all those principal Words, which are significant of Substances, considered as Substances.*

THE first sort of *Substances* are the NATURAL, such as Animal, Vegetable, Man, Oak.

THERE are other Substances *of our own making.* Thus by giving a Figure *not natural* to *natural* Materials we create such Substances, as House, Ship, Watch, Telescope, &c.

AGAIN, by a *more refined operation of our Mind alone,* we *abstract any Attribute* from its necessary subject, and consider it *apart,* devoid of its dependence. For example, from Body we abstract *to Fly;* from Surface,

face, *the being White*; from Soul, *the being Temperate.*

AND thus it is *we convert even Attributes into Substances*, denoting them on this occasion by proper *Substantives*, such as *Flight, Whiteness, Temperance*; or else by others more general, such as *Motion, Colour, Virtue*. These we call ABSTRACT SUBSTANCES; the second sort we call ARTIFICIAL.

Now all those several Substances have their Genus, their Species, and their Individuals. For example in *natural* Substances, *Animal* is a Genus; *Man*, a Species; *Alexander*, an Individual. In *artificial* Substances, *Edifice* is a Genus; *Palace*, a Species; *the Vatican*, an Individual. In *abstract* Substances, *Motion* is a Genus; *Flight*, a Species; *this Flight or that Flight* are Individuals.

As

BOOK THE FIRST. 39

As therefore every (*a*) GENUS may be found *whole and intire in each one of its Species*; (for thus Man, Horfe, and Dog are each of them diftinctly a complete and intire Animal) and as every SPECIES may be found *whole and intire in each one of its Individuals*; (for thus *Socrates, Plato,* and *Xenophon* are each of them completely and diftinctly *a Man*) hence it is, that every *Genus,* tho' ONE, is multiplied into MANY; and every *Species,* tho' ONE, is alfo multiplied into MANY, by *reference to thofe beings, which are their proper fubordinates.* Since then *no Individual has any fuch Subordinates,* it can never in ftrictnefs be confidered as MANY, and fo is truly an INDIVIDUAL as well in *Nature* as in *Name.*

Ch. IV.

(*a*) This is what *Plato* feems to have exprefled in a manner fomewhat myfterious, when he talks of μίαν ἰδέαν διὰ πολλῶν, ἑνὸς ἑκάςῳ κειμένῃ χωρὶς, πάντη διατεταμένην—κ̀ πολλὰς, ἑτέρας ἀλλήλων, ὑπὸ μιᾶς ἔξωθεν περιεχομένας. *Sophift. p.* 253. *Edit. Serrani.* For the common definition of Genus and Species, fee the Ifagoge or Introduction of *Porphyry* to *Ariftotle's* Logic.

Ch. IV. FROM thefe Principles it is, that *Words* following the nature and genius of *Things*, *fuch Subftantives* admit of NUMBER as denote *Genera* or *Species*, while thofe, which denote (*b*) Individuals, in ftrictnefs admit it not.

BESIDES

(*b*) Yet fometimes *Individuals* have plurality or *Number*, from the caufes following. In the firft place the Individuals of the human race are fo large a multitude even in the fmalleft nation, that it would be difficult to invent a new Name for every new born Individual. Hence then inftead of *one* only being call'd *Marcus*, and *one* only *Antonius*, it happens that *many* are called *Marcus* and many called *Antonius*; and thus 'tis the *Romans* had their Plurals, *Marci* and *Antonii*, as we in later days have our *Marks* and our *Anthonies*. Now the Plurals of this fort may be well called *accidental*, becaufe it is meerly by chance that the Names coincide.

There feems more reafon for fuch Plurals, as the *Ptolemies*, *Scipios*, *Catos*, or (to inftance in modern names) the *Howards*, *Pelhams*, and *Montagues*; becaufe a *Race* or Family is like *a fmaller fort of Species*; fo that the *family Name* extends to the Kindred, as the fpecific Name extends to the Individuals.

A third caufe which contributed to make proper Names become Plural, was the *high Character* or *Eminence* of fome one Individual, whofe *Name* became afterwards a kind of *common Appellative*, to denote all thofe,

BESIDES *Number,* another characterCh.IV.
iftic, vifible in Subftances, is that of SEX.
Every Subftance is either *Male* or *Female;*
or *both Male and Female;* or *neither one
nor the other.* So that with refpect to *Sexes*
and their *Negation, all Subftances conceiveable* are comprehended under this *fourfold*
confideration.

Now the exiftence of *Hermaphrodites*
being rare, if not doubtful; hence Language, only regarding thofe diftinctions
which

---

thofe, who had pretenfions to merit in the fame way.
Thus every great *Critic* was call'd an *Ariftarchus;* every
great *Warrior,* an *Alexander;* every great *Beauty,* a *Helen,* &c.

A DANIEL *come to Judgment! yea a* DANIEL,
cries *Shylock* in the Play, when he would exprefs the
wifdom of the young Lawyer.

So *Martial* in that well known verfe,

Sint MÆCENATES, *non deerunt, Flacce,* MARONES.

So *Lucilius,*

ΑΙΓΙΛΙΠΟΙ *montes,* ÆTHNÆ *omnes, afperi* A-
THONES.

πόσοι ΦΑΕΘΟΝΤΕΣ, ἢ ΔΕΥΚΑΛΙΩΝΕΣ. Lucian
in Timon. T. I. p. 108,

Ch. IV. which are more obvious, confiders *Words denoting Subftances* to be either MASCULINE, FEMININE, or NEUTER [*].

As to our own Species and all thofe animal Species, which *have reference to common Life*, or of which the Male and the Female, by their fize, form, colour, &c. are *eminently diftinguifhed*, moft Languages have different Subftantives, to denote the Male and the Female. But as to thofe animal Species, which either *lefs frequently occur*, or of which one Sex is *lefs apparently diftinguifhed* from the other, in thefe a fingle Subftantive commonly ferves for both Sexes.

IN

---

[*] After this manner they are diftinguifhed by *Ariftotle*. Τῶν ὀνομάτων τὰ μὲν ἄρρενα, τὰ δὲ θήλεα, τὰ δὲ μεταξύ. Poet. cap. 21. *Protagoras* before him had eftablifhed the fame Diftinction, calling them ἄρρενα, θήλεα, ϗ σκεύη. Ariftot. Rhet. L. III. c. 5. Where mark what were afterwards called ἑδέτερα, or Neuters, were by thefe called τὰ μεταξὺ ϗ σκεύη.

† In the *English* Tongue it seems a general rule (except only when infringed by a figure of Speech) that no Substantive is *Masculine*, but what denotes a *Male animal Substance*; none *Feminine*, but what denotes a *Female animal Substance*; and that where the Substance *has no Sex*, the Substantive is always *Neuter*.

Ch.IV.

But 'tis not so in *Greek*, *Latin*, and many of the *modern* Tongues. These all of them have Words, some masculine, some feminine (and those too in great multitudes) which have reference to Substances, where Sex never had existence. To give one instance for many. MIND is surely neither male, nor female; yet is ΝΟΥΣ, in *Greek*, masculine, and MENS, in *Latin*, feminine.

In

---

† *Nam quicquid per Naturam Sexui non adsignatur, neutrum haberi oportet, sed id Ars* &c. Consent apud Putsch. p. 2023, 2024.

The whole Passage from *Genera Hominum, quæ naturalia sunt* &c. is worth perusing.

Ch. IV. IN some Words these distinctions seem owing to nothing else, than to the mere casual structure of the Word itself: It is of such a Gender, from having such a Termination; or from belonging perhaps to such a Declension. In others we may imagine a more subtle kind of reasoning, a reasoning which discerns even *in things without Sex* a distant analogy to that great NATURAL DISTINCTION, *which* (according to *Milton*) *animates the World* ‡.

IN this view we may conceive such SUBSTANTIVES to have been considered, as MASCULINE, which were " conspicuous
" for the Attributes of imparting or com-
" municating; or which were by nature
" active, strong, and efficacious, and that
" indiscriminately whether to good or to
" ill; or which had claim to Eminence,
" either laudable or otherwise."

THE

---

‡ Mr. *Linnæus*, the celebrated Botanist, has traced the *Distinction of Sexes* throughout the whole *Vegetable World*, and made it the Basis of his Botanic Method.

The Feminine on the contrary were "such, as were conspicuous for the At- "tributes either of receiving, of contain- "ing, or of producing and bringing forth; "or which had more of the passive in "their nature, than of the active; or "which were peculiarly beautiful and "amiable; or which had respect to such "Excesses, as were rather Feminine, than "Masculine."

Ch.IV.

Upon these Principles the two greater Luminaries were considered, one as Masculine, the other as Feminine; the Sun ('Ηλι☉, *Sol*) as *Masculine*, from communicating Light, which was native and original, as well as from the vigorous warmth and efficacy of his Rays; the Moon (Σελήνη, *Luna*) as *Feminine*, from being the Receptacle only of another's Light, and from shining with rays more delicate and soft.

Thus

Ch. IV. THUS *Milton*,

First in HIS *East the glorious Lamp was seen,
Regent of Day, and all th' Horizon round
Invested with bright rays; jocund to run*
HIS *longitude thro' Heav'ns high road:
   the gray
Dawn, and the Pleiades before* HIM *danc'd,
Shedding sweet influence. Less bright the
   Moon
But opposite, in levell'd West was set,*
HIS *mirrour, with full face borrowing* HER
   *Light
From* HIM; *for other light* SHE *needed none.*
                                    P. L. VII. 370.

BY *Virgil* they were considered as *Brother* and *Sister*, which still preserves the same distinction.

Nec FRATRIS *radiis obnoxia surgere* LUNA.
                                    G. I. 396.

THE SKY or ETHER is in *Greek* and *Latin Masculine*, as being the source of those showers, which impregnate the Earth.
                                                    The

* The EARTH on the contrary is universally *Feminine,* from being the grand *Receiver,* the grand *Container,* but above all from being the *Mother* (either mediately or immediately) of every sublunary Substance, whether animal or vegetable.

Ch.IV.

THUS *Virgil,*

Tum PATER OMNIPOTENS *fœcundis imbribus* ÆTHER
CONJUGIS *in gremium* LÆTÆ *defcendit,*
& *omnes*
Magnus alit magno commixtus corpore fœtus.
G. II. 325.

THUS *Shakefpear,*

——‡ COMMON MOTHER, *Thou*
Whofe Womb unmeafurable, and infinite Breaft
Teems and feeds all— Tim. of Athens.

So *Milton,*

Whatever Earth, ALL-BEARING MOTHER, *yields.* P. L. V.

So

---

* Senecæ Nat. *Quæſt. III.* 14.
‡ Παμμῆτορ γῆ χαῖρε— Græc. Anth. p. 281.

Ch. IV.   So *Virgil*,

Non jam MATER *alit* TELLUS, *virefque miniſtrat* (c).   Æn. XI. 71.

AMONG *artificial* Subſtances the SHIP (Ναῦς, *Navis*) is *feminine*, as being ſo eminently a *Receiver* and *Container* of various things, of Men, Arms, Proviſions, Goods, &c. Hence Sailors, ſpeaking of their Veſſel, ſay always, " SHE *rides at* " *anchor*," " SHE *is under ſail*."

A CITY (Πόλις, *Civitas*) and a COUNTRY (Πάτρις, *Patria*) are *feminine* alſo, by being (like the Ship) *Containers* and *Receivers*, and farther by being as it were the *Mothers* and *Nurſes* of their reſpective Inhabitants.

THUS

(c) —διὸ ϗ ἐν τῷ ὅλῳ τὴν ΓΗΣ φύσιν, ὡς ΘΗΛΥ ϗ ΜΗΤΕΡΑ νομίζυσιν· ΟΥΡΑΝΟΝ δὲ ϗ ΗΛΙΟΝ, ϗ ἔι τι τῶν ἄλλων τῶν τοιύτων, ὡς ΓΕΝΩΝΤΑΣ ϗ ΠΑΤΕΡΑΣ προσαγορεύυσι. Ariſt. de Gener. Anim. l. 1. c. 2.

THUS *Virgil*,   Ch.IV.
Salve, MAGNA PARENS FRUGUM, *Saturnia Tellus,*
MAGNA VIRUM——   Geor. II. 173.

So, in that Heroic Epigram on those brave *Greeks,* who fell at *Chæronea,*

Γαῖα δὲ Πάτρις ἔχει κόλποις τῶν πλεῖςα κα-
μόντων
Σώματα—
Their PARENT COUNTRY *in* HER *bosom holds
Their wearied bodies.*—*

So *Milton,*
*The City, which Thou seest, no other deem
Than great and glorious Rome,* QUEEN *of the Earth.*   Par. Reg. L. IV.

As to the OCEAN, tho' from its being the *Receiver* of all Rivers, as well as the
Container

---

* Demoſt. in Orat. de Coronà.

E

Ch. IV. *Container* and *Productress* of so many Vegetables and Animals, it might justly have been made (like the Earth) *Feminine*; yet its *deep Voice* and *boisterous Nature* have, in spight of these reasons, prevailed to make it *Male*. Indeed the very sound of *Homer's*

———μέγα σθένΘ- 'Ωκεανοῖο,

would suggest to a hearer, even ignorant of its meaning, that the Subject was incompatible with *female* delicacy and softness.

TIME (ΧρόνΘ-) *from his mighty Efficacy upon every thing around us*, is by the *Greeks* and *English* justly considered as *Masculine*. Thus in that elegant distich, spoken by a decrepit old Man,

* Ὁ γὰρ ΧρόνΘ- μ᾽ ἔκαμψε, τέκτων ἇ σοφὸς,
Ἅπαντα δ᾽ ἐργαζόμενΘ- ἀσθενέστερα †.

Me TIME *hath bent, that sorry Artist,* HE
That surely makes, whate'er he handles, worse.

So

---

* Ὦ Χρόνε, παντοίων θνητῶν πανεπίσκοπε Δαῖμον.
Græc. Anth. p. 290.
† Stob. Ecl. p. 591.

So too *Shakespear,* speaking likewise of Ch.IV.
Time, ⎫
          ⎬
          ⎭

Orl. *Whom doth* HE *gallop withal?*
Ros. *With a thief to the gallows.—*
As you like it.

The *Greek* Θάνατ⊕ or Άΐδης and the *English* Death, seem from the same irresistible Power to have been considered as *Masculine.* Even the Vulgar with us are so accustomed to this notion, that a Female Death they would treat as ridiculous *(d).*

Take a few Examples of the masculine Death.

E 2   *Calli-*

(d) Well therefore did *Milton* in his Paradise Lost not only adopt Death as a *Person,* but consider him as *Masculine:* in which he was so far from introducing a Phantom of his own, or from giving it a *Gender not supported by Custom*; that perhaps he had as much *the Sanction of national Opinion* for his *Masculine Death,* as the ancient Poets had for many of their Deities.

Ch. IV. *Callimachus* upon the Elegies of his Friend *Heraclitus*—

Ἀι δὲ τεαὶ ζώɛσιν ἀηδόνες, ᾗσιν ὁ πάντων
Ἀρπάκ]ηρ Ἀίδης ἐκ ἐπὶ χεῖρα βαλεῖ.

———*yet thy sweet warbling strains
Still live immortal, nor on them shall* DEATH
HIS *hand e'er lay, tho' Ravager of all.*

IN the *Alcestis* of *Euripides*, Θάνατ☉ or DEATH is one of the Persons of the drama; the beginning of the play is made up of dialogue between *Him* and *Apollo*; and towards its end, there is a fight between *Him* and *Hercules*, in which *Hercules* is conqueror, and rescues *Alcestis* from his hands.

IT is well known too, that SLEEP and DEATH are made *Brothers* by *Homer*. It was to this old *Gorgias* elegantly alluded, when at the extremity of a long life he lay slumbering on his Death-bed. A Friend asked him, " *How he did?*"———
" SLEEP

"SLEEP (replied the old Man) *is juſt upon* Ch. IV.
"*delivering me over to the care of his*
"BROTHER (*e*)."

THUS *Shakeſpear*, ſpeaking of Life,
——*merely Thou art Death's Fool*;
For HIM *Thou labour'ſt by thy flight to
    ſhun,
And yet run'ſt towards* HIM *ſtill.*
                    Meaſ. for Meaſ.

So *Milton*,

*Dire was the toſſing, deep the groans;
    Deſpair
Tended the ſick, buſieſt from couch to couch:
And over them triumphant* DEATH HIS
    *dart
Shook; but delay'd to ſtrike*——
                    P. L. XI. 489 *(f)*.

(*e*) Ἤδη με Ο ὝΠΝΟΣ ἄρχεται παρακατατί-
θεσθαι Τ'ΑΔΕΛΦΩΙ. Stob. Ecl. p. 600.

(*f*) Suppoſe in any one of theſe examples we introduce *a female Death*; ſuppoſe we read,
            E 3   *And*

Ch. IV. THE supreme Being (GOD, Θεὸς, *Deus*, *Dieu*, &c.) is in all languages *Masculine*, in as much as the masculine Sex is the superior and more excellent; and as He is the Creator of all, the Father of Gods and Men. Sometimes indeed we meet with such words as Τὸ Πρῶτον, Τὸ Θεῖον, *Numen*, DEITY (which last we *English* join to a neuter, saying *Deity itself*) sometimes I say we meet with these *Neuters*. The reason in these instances seems to be, that as GOD is prior to all things, both in dignity and in time, this Priority is better characterized and exprest by a *Negation*, than by any of those Distinctions which are *co-ordinate with some Opposite*, as Male

for

And over them triumphant Death HER *dart
Shook,* &c.

What a falling off? How are the nerves and strength of the whole Sentiment weakened?

for example is co-ordinate with Female, Ch.IV.
Right with Left, &c. &c. (g).

VIRTUE ('Ἀρετὴ, *Virtus*) as well as most
of its Species are all *Feminine*, perhaps
from their Beauty and amiable Appearance,
which are not without effect even upon
the most reprobate and corrupt.

E 4 ———*abash'd*

(g) Thus *Ammonius*, speaking on the same Subject
—ΤΟ ΠΡΩΤΟΝ λέγομεν, ἐφ' ᾧ μὴ δὲ τῶν διὰ
μυθολογίας παραδόντων ἡμῖν τὰς θεολογίας ἐτόλμησέ
τις ἢ ἀρρενωπὸν, ἢ θυληπρεπῆ (lege θηλυπρεπῆ) δια-
μόρφωσιν φέρειν· καὶ τοῦτο εἰκότως· τῷ μὲν γὰρ ἄρ-
ρενι τὸ θῆλυ σύςοιχον· τὸ (lege τῷ) δὲ ΠΑΝΤΗΙ
ΑΠΛΩΣ ΑΙΤΙΩΙ σύςοιχον ὐδέν. ἀλλὰ καὶ
ὅταν ἀρσενικῶς ΤΟΝ ΘΕΟΝ ὀνομάζομεν, [πρὸς]
τὸ σεμνότερον τῶν γενῶν τὸ ὑφειμένον προτιμῶντες, ἕτως
αὐτὸν προσαγορεύομεν. PRIMUM *dicimus, quod rerum
etiam eorum, qui theologiam nobis fabularum integumentis
obvolutam tradiderunt, vel maris vel fœminæ specie fingere
ausus est: idque merito:* conjugatum enim mari *fœmini-
num est.* CAUSÆ *autem omnino* ABSOLUTÆ AC SIM-
PLICI *nihil est conjugatum. Immo vero cum* DEUM
*masculino genere appellamus, ita ipsum nominamus, genus
præstantius submisso atque humili præferentes.* Ammon.
in Lib. de Interpr p. 30. b.—ἐ γὰρ ἐναντίον τῷ Πρώτῳ
ὐδέν. Aristot. Metaph. Λ. p. 210. Sylb.

Ch. IV. ——*abash'd the Devil stood,*
And felt, how awful Goodness is, and saw
VIRTUE *in her shape how lovely; saw,*
and pin'd
His loss——

P. L. IV. 846.

THIS being allowed, VICE (Κακία) becomes *Feminine* of course, as being, in the συςοιχία or Co-ordination of things, Virtue's natural Opposite (*h*).

THE Fancies, Caprices, and fickle Changes of FORTUNE would appear but awkwardly under a Character, that was Male: but taken together they make a

very

(*h*) They are both reprefented as *Females* by *Xenophon*, in the celebrated Story of *Hercules*, taken from *Prodicus*. See *Memorab*. L. II. c. 1. As to the συςοιχία here mentioned, thus *Varro*.——*Pythagoras Samius ait omnium rerum initia esse bina: ut finitum & infinitum, bonum & malum, vitam & mortem, diem & noctem*. De Ling. Lat. L. IV. See also *Arist. Metaph*. L. 1. c. 5. and *Ecclesiasticus*, Chap. lxii. ver. 24.

very natural *Female*, which has no small Ch.IV.
resemblance to the Coquette of a modern
Comedy, bestowing, withdrawing, and
shifting her favours, as different Beaus
succeed to her good graces.

Transmutat incertos honores,
Nunc mihi, nunc alii benigna.   Hor.

WHY the FURIES were made *Female*,
is not so easy to explain, unless it be that
female Passions of all kinds were considered as susceptible of greater excess, than
male Passions; and that the *Furies* were
to be represented, as Things superlatively
outrageous.

Talibus Alecto dictis exarsit in iras.
At Juveni oranti subitus tremor occupat
    artus:
Diriguere oculi: tot Erinnys sibilat Hydris,
Tantaque se facies aperit: tum flammea
    torquens

                            Lumina

Ch. IV. *Lumina cunctantem & quærentem dicere
plura
Reppulit, & geminos erexit crinibus angues,
Verberaque infonuit, rabidoque hæc addidit ore:
En! Ego victa fitu,* &c.
Æn. VII. 455 (i).

HE

(i) The Words above mentioned, *Time, Death, Fortune, Virtue,* &c. in *Greek, Latin, French,* and moſt modern Languages, though they are diverſified with Genders in the manner deſcribed, yet never vary the Gender, which they have once acquired, except in a few inſtances, where the Gender is doubtful. We cannot ſay ή ἀρετὴ or ὁ ἀρετή, *hæc Virtus* or *hic Virtus, la Vertu* or *le Vertu,* and ſo of the reſt. But it is otherwiſe in *Engliſh*. We in our own language ſay, Virtue is *its* own Reward, or Virtue is *her* own Reward; Time maintains *its* wonted Pace, or Time maintains *his* wonted Pace.

There is a ſingular advantage in this liberty, as it enables us to mark, with a peculiar force, the Diſtinction between the ſevere or *Logical* Stile, and the ornamental or *Rhetorical*. For thus when we ſpeak of the above Words, and of all others naturally devoid of Sex,

as

HE, that would see more on this Sub- Ch.IV.
ject, may consult *Ammonius* the Peripatetic

---

as *Neuters*, we speak of them *as they are*, and as becomes a *logical* Inquiry. When we give them *Sex*, by
making them Masculine or Feminine, they are from
thenceforth *personified*; are a kind of *intelligent Beings*,
and become, as such, the proper ornaments either of
Rhetoric or of *Poetry*.

Thus *Milton*,

―――*The Thunder*
Wing'd with red light'ning and impetuous rage,
Perhaps hath spent HIS *shafts*――― P. Lost. I. 174.

The Poet, having just before called the *Hail*, and
Thunder, God's *Ministers of Vengeance*, and so personified them, had he afterwards said *its* shafts for *his*
Shafts, would have destroyed his own Image, and ap-
proached withal so much nearer to Prose.

The following Passage is from the same Poem.

Should intermitted Vengeance arm again
*H*IS *red right hand*――― P. L. II. 174.

In this Place *His* Hand is clearly preferable either to
Her's or *Its*, by immediately referring to God himself the Avenger.

tic in his Commentary on the Treatise *de Interpretatione*, where the Subject is treated at large with respect to the *Greek* Tongue. We shall only observe, that as all such Speculations are at best but Conjectures, they should therefore be received with

---

I shall only give one instance more, and quit this Subject.

At his command th' up-rooted Hills retir'd
Each to HIS *place: they heard his voice and went*
Obsequious: Heav'n HIS *wonted face renew'd,*
And with fresh flourets Hill and Valley smil'd.
P. L. VI.

See also ver. 54, 55, of the same Book.

Here all things are personified; the Hills *hear*, the Valleys *smile*, and the *Face* of Heaven is renewed. Suppose then the Poet had been necessitated by the laws of his Language to have said—*Each Hill retir'd to* ITS *Place—Heaven renewed its wonted face*—how prosaic and lifeless would these Neuters have appeared; how detrimental to the *Prosopopeia*, which he was aiming to establish? In this therefore he was happy, that the Language, in which he wrote, imposed no such necessity; and he was too wise a Writer, to impose it on himself. It were to be wished, his Correctors had been as wise on their parts.

with candour, rather than scrutinized Ch.IV.
with rigour. *Varro's* words on a Subject
near akin are for their aptness and elegance
well worth attending. *Non mediocres enim
tenebræ in silvâ, ubi hæc captanda; neque
eò, quò pervenire volumus, semitæ tritæ;
neque non in tramitibus quædam objecta,
quæ euntem retinere possunt* *.

To conclude this Chapter. We may
collect, from what has been said, that
both NUMBER and GENDER appertain to
WORDS, because in the first place they
appertain to THINGS; that is to say, *because Substances are Many, and have either
Sex, or no Sex; therefore Substantives have
Number, and are Masculine, Feminine, or
Neuter.* There is however this difference between the two Attributes: NUMBER in strictness descends no lower, than

to

---

* De Ling. Lat. L.IV.

Ch. IV. to *the laſt Rank of Species* (*k*) : GENDER on the contrary ſtops not here, but deſcends to *every Individual,* however diverſified. And ſo much for SUBSTANTIVES, PROPERLY SO CALLED.

(*k*) The reaſon, why *Number* goes no lower, is, that it does not naturally appertain to *Individuals*; the cauſe of which ſee before, p. 39.

CHAP. V.

Concerning Substantives of the Secondary Order.

WE are now to proceed to a SECON-DARY RACE of SUBSTANTIVES, a Race quite different from any already mentioned, and whose Nature may be explained in the following manner.

EVERY Object, which presents itself to the Senses or the Intellect, is either then perceived for the *first time*, or else is recognized, as having been perceived *before*. In the former case it is called an Object τῆς πρώτης γνώσεως, *of the first knowledge* or *acquaintance* (*a*); in the latter
ter

(*a*) See *Apoll. de Syntaxi*, l. 1. c. 16. p. 49. l. 2. c. 3. p. 103 Thus *Priscian—Interest autem inter demonstrationem & relationem hoc; quod demonstratio, interrogationi reddita,* Primam Cognitionem *ostendit;*
Quis

Ch. V. ter it is called an Object τῆς δευτέρας γνώσεως, *of the second knowledge* or *acquaintance*.

Now as all Conversation passes between *Particulars* or *Individuals*, these will often happen to be reciprocally Objects τῆς πρώτης γνώσεως, that is to say, *till that instant unacquainted with each other*. What then is to be done? How shall the Speaker address the other, when he knows not his Name? or how explain himself by his own Name, of which the other is wholly ignorant? Nouns, as they have been described, cannot answer the purpose. The first expedient upon this occasion seems to have been Δεῖξις, that is, *Pointing*, or *Indication by the Finger or Hand*, some traces of which are still to be observed, as a part of that Action, which naturally attends our speaking. But the Authors of Language were

---

Quis fecit? Ego: *relatio vero* Secundam Cognitionem *significat, ut,* Is, de quo jam dixi. *Lib. XII.* p. 936. *Edit. Putschii.*

BOOK THE FIRST. 65

were not content with this. They in- Ch. V.
vented a race of *Words to supply this*
Pointing; which Words, *as they always
stood for Substantives or Nouns*, were characterized by the Name of Ἀντωνυμίαι, or
PRONOUNS (*b*). These also they distinguished into three several sorts, calling
them *Pronouns* of the *First*, the *Second*,
and the *Third Person*, with a view to certain distinctions, which may be explained
as follows.

SUPPOSE the Parties conversing to be
wholly unacquainted, neither Name nor
Countenance on either side known, and
the

(*b*) Ἐκεῖνο ἓν Ἀντωνυμία, τὸ μετὰ ΔΕΙΞΕΩΣ
ἢ ἀναφορᾶς 'ANTONOMAZOMENON. Apoll.
de Synt. L. II. c. 5. p. 106. *Priscian* seems to consider them so peculiarly destined to the expression of *Individuals*, that he does not say they supply the place of
any Noun, but that of the *proper* Name only. And
this undoubtedly was their original, and still is their
true and natural use. PRONOMEN *est pars orationis,
quæ pro* nomine proprio uniuscujusque *accipitur*. Prisc.
L. XII. See also *Apoll*. L. II. c. 9. p. 117, 128.

F

Ch. V. the Subject of the Conversation to be *the Speaker himself*. Here, to supply the place of Pointing by a Word of *equal* Power, they furnished the Speaker with the *Pronoun*, I. *I write, I say, I desire,* &c. and as the Speaker is always principal with respect to his own discourse, this they called for that reason *the Pronoun of the First Person*.

AGAIN, suppose the Subject of the Conversation to be *the Party addrest*. Here for similar reasons they invented the *Pronoun*, THOU. *Thou writest, Thou walkest*, &c. and as the Party addrest is next in dignity to the Speaker, or at least comes next with reference to the discourse; this Pronoun they therefore called *the Pronoun of the Second Person*.

LASTLY, suppose the Subject of Conversation neither the Speaker, nor the Party addrest, but *some third Object, different from both*. Here they provided another *Pronoun*, HE, SHE, or IT, which

in

BOOK THE FIRST. 67

in diſtinction to the two former was called Ch. V.
the *Pronoun of the Third Perſon.*

AND thus it was that *Pronouns* came to
be diſtinguiſhed by their reſpective PER-
SONS (c).

As

(c) The Deſcription of the different PERSONS here
given is taken from *Priſcian,* who took it from *Apollonius.* *Perſonæ Pronominum ſunt tres ; prima, ſecunda,
tertia.* Prima *eſt, cum ipſa, quæ loquitur,* de ſe pronun-
tiat; Secunda, *cum de eâ pronunciat,* ad quam directo
ſermone loquitur ; Tertia, *cum de eâ,* quæ nec loquitur, nec ad ſe directum accipit Sermonem. L. XII.
p. 940. *Theodore Gaza* gives the ſame Diſtinctions.
Πρῶτον (πρόσωπον ſc.) ᾧ περὶ ἑαυτᾶ Φράζει ὁ λέγων·
δεύτερον, ᾧ περὶ τᾶ, πρὸς ὃν ὁ λόγ☉· τρίτον, ᾧ περὶ
ἑτέρᾶ. Gaz. Gram. L. IV. p. 152.

This account of *Perſons* is far preferable to the common one, which makes the Firſt the *Speaker* ; the Second, the Party *addreſt* ; and the Third, the *Subject.*
For tho' the Firſt and Second be as commonly deſcribed, one the Speaker, the other the Party addreſt ; yet
till they become *ſubjects of the diſcourſe,* they have no
exiſtence Again as to the Third Perſon's being the
ſubject, this is a character, which it *ſhares in common*
F 2 with

Ch. V. As to NUMBER, the Pronoun of each Perſon has it: (I) has the plural (WE), becauſe

---

with both the other Perſons, and which can never therefore be called a peculiarity of its own. To explain by an inſtance or two. When *Eneas* begins the narrative of his adventures, *the ſecond Perſon* immediately appears, becauſe he makes *Dido*, whom he *addreſſes*, the immediate ſubject of his Diſcourſe.

Infandum, Regina, jubes, *renovare dolorem.*

From hence forward for 1500 Verſes (tho' ſhe be all that time the party addreſt) we hear nothing farther of this *Second Perſon*, a variety of other Subjects filling up the Narrative.

In the mean time the *Firſt Perſon* may be ſeen every where, becauſe the *Speaker* every where is himſelf the *Subject*. They were indeed Events, as he ſays himſelf,

—*quæque ipſe miſerrima vidi,*
Et quorum pars magna fui——

Not that the Second Perſon does not often occur in the courſe of this Narrative; but then it is always by a Figure of Speech, when thoſe, who by their abſence are in fact ſo many Third Perſons, are converted into Second

because there may be many Speakers at Ch. V. once of the same Sentiment; as well as one, who, including himself, speaks the Sentiment of many. (THOU) has the plural (YOU), because a Speech may be spoken to many, as well as to one. (HE) has the plural (THEY) because the Subject of discourse is often many at once.

BUT tho' all these Pronouns have *Number*, it does not appear either in *Greek*, or *Latin*, or any modern Language, that those of the first and second Person carry the distinctions of SEX. The reason seems to

---

cond Persons by being introduced as *present*. The real Second Person (*Dido*) is never once hinted.

Thus far as to *Virgil*. But when we read *Euclid*, we find neither *First* Person, nor *Second* in any part of the whole Work. The reason is, that neither Speaker nor Party addrest (in which light we may always view the Writer and his Reader) can possibly become the Subject of pure Mathematics, nor indeed can any thing else, except abstract Quantity, which neither speaks itself, nor is spoken to by another.

Ch. V. to be, that the Speaker and Hearer being generally prefent to each other, it would have been fuperfluous to have marked a diftinction by Art, which from Nature and even Drefs was commonly (*d*) apparent on both fides. But this does not hold with refpect to the third Perfon, of whofe Character and Diftinctions, (including Sex among the reft) we often know no more, then what we learn from the difcourfe. And hence it is that in moft Languages *the third Perfon* has its *Genders*, and that even *Englifh* (which allows its Adjectives no Genders at all) has in this Pronoun the triple (*e*) diftinction of *He*, *She*, and *It*.

HENCE

(*d*) *Demonftratio ipfa fecum genus oftendit.* Prifcian. L. XII. p. 942. See *Apoll. de Syntax.* L. II. c. 7. p. 109.

(*e*) The Utility of this Diftinction may be better found in fuppofing it away. Suppofe for example we fhould read in hiftory thefe words—*He caufed him*

to

HENCE too we see the reason why *a single Pronoun (f) to each Person, an I to*   Ch. V.

to destroy him—and that we were to be informed the [He], which is here thrice repeated, stood each time for something different, that is to say, for a Man, for a Woman, and for a City, whose Names were *Alexander*, *Thais*, and *Persepolis*. Taking the Pronoun in this manner, divested of its Genders, how would it appear, which was destroyed; which was the destroyer; and which the cause, that moved to the destruction? But there are not such doubts, when we hear the Genders distinguished; when instead of the ambiguous Sentence, *He caused him* to destroy *him*, we are told with the proper distinctions, that SHE *caused* HIM *to destroy* IT. Then we know with certainty, what before we could not: that the Promoter was the Woman; that her Instrument was the Hero; and that the Subject of their Cruelty was the unfortunate City.

(*f*) *Quæritur tamen cur prima quidem Persona & secunda* singula *Pronomina habeant, tertiam vero* sex *diversæ indicent voces? Ad quod respondendum est, quod prima quidem & secunda Persona ideo non egent diversis vocibus, quod* semper præsentes inter se sunt, *& demonstrativæ; tertia vero Persona modo demonstrativa est, ut,* Hic, Iste; *modo relativa, ut* Is, Ipse, &c. Priscian, L. XII. p. 933.

Ch. V. to the *First*, and a *Thou* to the *Second*, are abundantly sufficient to all the purposes of Speech. But it is not so with respect to the *Third* Person. The various relations of the various Objects exhibited by this (I mean relations of near and distant, present and absent, same and different, definite and indefinite, *&c.*) made it necessary that here there should not be one, but *many* Pronouns, such as *He*, *This*, *That*, *Other*, *Any*, *Some*, &c.

It must be confest indeed, that all these Words do not always appear as *Pronouns*. When they stand by themselves, and represent some Noun, (as when we say, This *is Virtue*, or δεικ]ικῶς, *Give me* That) then are they *Pronouns*. But when they are associated to some Noun (as when we say, This *Habit* is Virtue; or δεικ]ικῶς, That *Man* defrauded me) then as they supply not the place of a Noun, but only serve to ascertain one, they fall rather into the Species of *Definitives* or *Articles*. That there is indeed

deed a near relation between *Pronouns* Ch. V. and *Articles*, the old Grammarians have all acknowledged, and some words it has been doubtful to which Class to refer. The best rule to distinguish them is this —The genuine PRONOUN *always stands by itself*, assuming the *Power* of a Noun, and supplying its *place*—The genuine ARTICLE *never stands* by itself, but appears at all times associated to something else, requiring a Noun for its support, as much as Attributives or (*g*) Adjectives.

As

(*g*) Τὸ Ἄρθρον μἑτὰ ὀνόμαΘ‑, ϗ ἡ Ἀνlωνυμία ἀνl' ὀνόμαlΘ‑. THE ARTICLE *stands* WITH *a Noun*; *but* THE PRONOUN *stands* FOR *a Noun*. Apoll. L. I. c. 3. p. 22. Ἀυlὰ ἐν τὰ ἄρθρα, τῆς πρὸς τὰ ὀνόμαlα συναρτήσεως ἀποςάντα, εἰς τὴν ὑποτεταγμένην ἀντωνυμίαν μεταπίπlει. *Now Articles themselves, when they quit their Connection with Nouns, pass into such Pronoun, as is proper upon the occasion.* Ibid. Again—Ὅταν τὸ Ἄρθρον μὴ μετ' ὀνόματΘ‑ παραλαμβάνηται, ποιήσlαι δὲ σύνταξιν ὀνόματΘ‑ ἠν

προ-

Ch. V. As to the *Coalescence* of thefe Pronouns, it is, as follows. The Firſt or Second

---

προεκ]εθείμεθα, ἐκ πάσης ἀνάγκης εἰς ἀνωνυμίαν μεταληφθήσεται, εἴγε ἐκ ἐγγινόμενον μετ᾽ ὀνόματΘ δυνάμει ἀντὶ ὀνόματΘ παρελήφθη. *When the Article is aſſumed without the Noun, and has (as we explained before) the ſame Syntax, which the Noun has; it muſt of abſolute neceſſity be admitted for a Pronoun, becauſe it appears without a Noun, and yet is in power aſſumed for one.* Ejuſd. L. II. c. 8. p. 113. L. I. c. 45. p. 96. *Inter Pronomina & Articulos hoc intereſt, quod Pronomina ea putantur, quæ, cum ſola ſint, vicem nominis complent, ut* QUIS, ILLE, ISTE: *Articuli vero cum Pronominibus, aut Nominibus, aut Participiis adjunguntur.* Donat. Gram. p. 1753.

Priſcian, ſpeaking of the *Stoics*, ſays as follows: ARTICULIS *autem* PRONOMINA *connumerantes,* FINITOS *ea* ARTICULOS *appellabant; ipſos autem Articulos, quibus nos caremus,* INFINITOS ARTICULOS *dicebant. Vel, ut alii dicunt, Articulos connumerabant Pronominibus, &* ARTICULARIA *eos* PRONOMINA *vocabant,* &c. Priſc. L. I. p. 574. *Varro*, ſpeaking of *Quiſque* and *Hic*, calls them both ARTICLES, the firſt *indefinite*, the ſecond *definite.* De Ling. Lat. L. VII. See alſo L. IX p. 132. *Voſſius* indeed in his Analogi *(L. I. c. 1)* oppoſes this Doctrine, becauſe *Hic* has not the ſame power with the *Greek* Article,

Book the First.

Ch. V.

Second will, either of them, by themselves coalesce with the Third, but not with each other. For example, it is good sense, as well as good Grammar, to say in any Language—I AM HE—THOU ART HE—but we cannot say—I AM THOU—nor THOU ART I. The reason is, there is no absurdity for the *Speaker* to be the *Subject* also of the Discourse, as when we say, *I am He*; or for the *Person addrest*; as when we say, *Thou art He*. But for the same Person, in the same circumstances, to be at once the Speaker, and the Party addrest, this is impossible; and so therefore is the Coalescence of the First and Second Person.

AND now perhaps we have seen enough of *Pronouns*, to perceive how they differ from

---

ticle, ὅ. But he did not enough attend to the antient Writers on this Subject, who considered all Words, as ARTICLES, which *being associated to Nouns (and not standing in their place) served in any manner to ascertain, and determine their Signification.*

Ch. V. from others Substantives. The others are *Primary*, these are their *Substitutes*; a kind of secondary Race, which were taken in aid, when for reasons already *(h)* mentioned the others could not be used. It is moreover by means of these, and of *Articles*, which are nearly allied to them, that

---

(*h*) See these reasons at the beginning of this chapter, of which reasons the principal one is, that " no
" Noun, properly so called, implies its own Presence.
" It is therefore *to ascertain such Presence*, that the Pro-
" noun is taken in aid; and hence it is it becomes
" equivalent to δεῖξις, that is, to *Pointing or Indication*
" *by the Finger*." It is worth remarking in that Verse of *Persius*,

    Sed pulchrum est DIGITO MONSTRARI, *& dicier*,
    HIC EST,

how *the* δεῖξις, and *the Pronoun* are introduced together, and made to co-operate to the same end.

Sometimes by virtue of δεῖξις the Pronoun of the *third* Person stands for the *first*.

    Quod si militibus parces, erit HIC *quoque Miles*.
    That is, *I also will be a Soldier*.
    Tibul. L. II. El. 6. v. 7. See *Vulpius*.

Book the First.

that "LANGUAGE, tho' in itself only fig-
"nificant of *general Ideas*, is brought down
"to denote *that infinitude of Particulars*,
"which are for ever arising, and ceasing
"to be." But more of this hereafter in
a proper place.

As to the three orders of Pronouns already mentioned, they may be called *Prepositive,* as may indeed all Substantives, because they are capable of introducing or leading a Sentence, without having reference to any thing previous. But besides those there is ANOTHER PRONOUN

(in

It may be observed too, that even in Epistolary Correspondence, and indeed in all kinds of Writing, where the Pronouns I and You make their appearance, there is a sort of *implied Presence*, which they are supposed to indicate, though the parties are in fact at ever so great a distance. And hence the rise of that distinction in *Apollonius*, τὰς μὲν τῆς ὄψεως εἶναι δείξεις, τὰς δὲ τῦ νῦ, *that some Indications are ocular, and some are mental.* De Syntaxi, L. II. c. 3. p. 104.

Ch. V. (in *Greek* ὃς, ὅστις *(i)*; in *Latin*, *Qui*; in *English*, *Who*, *Which*, *That*) a Pronoun having a character peculiar to itself, the nature of which may be explained as follows.

SUPPOSE I was to say—LIGHT *is a Body*, LIGHT *moves with great celerity.*— These

---

(*i*) The *Greeks*, it must be confest, call this Pronoun ὑποτακτικὸν ἄρθρον, *the subjunctive Article.* Yet, as it should seem, this is but an improper Appellation. *Apollonius*, when he compares it to the προτακτικὸν or true *prepositive Article*, not only confesses it to differ, as being exprest by a different Word, and having a different place in every Sentence; but in Syntax he adds, *it is wholly different.* De Syntax. L. I. c. 43. p. 91. *Theodore Gaza* acknowledges the same, and therefore adds——ὅθεν δὴ κȷ̀ ȣ̓ κυρίως ἂν ἔιη ἄρθρον ταυτὶ——*for these reasons this (meaning the Subjunctive) cannot properly be an Article.* And just before he says, κυρίως γεμὴν ἄρθρον τὸ προτακτικὸν——*however properly speaking it is the Prepositive is the Article.* Gram. Introd. L. IV. The Latins therefore have undoubtedly done better in ranging it with the Pronouns.

These would apparently be two distinct Ch. V.
Sentences. Suppose, instead of the Second, LIGHT, I were to place the prepositive Pronoun, IT, and say—LIGHT *is a Body*; IT *moves with great celerity*—the Sentences would still be distinct and two. But if I add *a Connective* (as for Example an AND) saying—LIGHT *is a Body*, AND *it moves with great celerity*—I then by Connection make the two into one, as by cementing many Stones I make one Wall.

Now it is *in the united Powers of a Connective, and another Pronoun*, that we may see the force, and character of the Pronoun here treated. Thus therefore, if in the place of AND IT, we substitute THAT, or WHICH, saying LIGHT *is a Body*, WHICH *moves with great celerity*—the Sentence still retains its *Unity* and *Perfection*, and becomes if possible more compact than before. We may with just reason therefore call this Pronoun the SUBJUNCTIVE, because it cannot (like
the

Ch. V. the Prepofitive) introduce an original Sentence, but only *ferves to fubjoin one to fome other, which is previous* (*k*).

THE

(*k*) Hence we fee why the Pronoun here mentioned is always *neceffarily* the Part of fome *complex* Sentence, which Sentence contains, either expreft or underftood, *two* Verbs, and *two* Nominatives.

Thus in that Verfe of *Horace*,

QUI *metuens vivit, liber mihi non erit unquam.*

Ille non erit liber—is one Sentence; *qui metuens vivit*— is another. *Ille* and *Qui* are the *two Nominatives*; *Erit* and *Vivit*, the *two Verbs*; and fo in all other inftances.

The following paffage from *Apollonius* (though fomewhat corrupt in more places than one) will ferve to fhew, whence the above Speculations are taken. Τὸ ὑποτακ]ικὸν ἄρθρον ἐπὶ ῥῆμα ἴδιον φέρεται, συνδεδεμένον διὰ τῆς ἀναφορᾶς τῷ προκειμένῳ ὀνόματι· κỳ ἐντεῦθεν ἁπλῶ λόγου ἀ παρισάνει καλὰ τὴν τῶν δύο ῥημάτων σύνταξιν (λέγω τὴν ἐν τῷ ὀνόματι, κỳ τὴν ἐν αὑτῷ τῷ ἄρθρῳ) ὅπερ πάλιν παρείπετο τῷ ΚΑΙ συνδέσμῳ. Κοινὸν μὲν (lege ΤΟ ΚΑΙ γὰρ κοινὸν μὲν) παρελάμβανε

THE Application of this SUBJUNCTIVE, Ch. V.
like the other Pronouns, is univerſal. It
may

Ἔλαβε τὸ ὄνομα τὸ προκείμενον, σύμπλεκον δὲ ἕτερον λόγον πάντως ᾧ ἕτερον ῥῆμα παρελάμβανε, ᾧ ὕτω τὸ, ΠΑΡΕΓΕΝΕΤΟ Ο ΓΡΑΜΜΑΤΙΚΟΣ, ΟΣ ΔΙΕΛΕΞΑΤΟ, δυνάμει τὸν αὐτὸν ἀποτελεῖ τᾶ (forſ. τῳ) Ο ΓΡΑΜΜΑΤΙΚΟΣ ΠΑΡΕΓΕΝΕΤΟ, ΚΑΙ ΔΙΕΛΕΞΑΤΟ. *The ſubjunctive Article, (that is, the Pronoun here mentioned) is applied to a Verb of its own, and yet is connected withal to the antecedent Noun. Hence it can never ſerve to conſtitute a ſimple Sentence, by reaſon of the Syntax of the two Verbs, I mean that which reſpects the Noun or Antecedent, and that which reſpects the Article or Relative. The ſame too follows as to the Conjunction,* AND. *This Copulative aſſumes the Antecedent Noun, which is capable of being applied to many Subjects, and by connecting to it a new Sentence, of neceſſity aſſumes a new Verb alſo. And hence it is that the Words—*the Grammarian came, WHO *diſcourſed—form in power nearly the ſame ſentence, as if we were to ſay—*the Grammarian came, AND *diſcourſed. Apoll. de Syntaxi, L. I. c* 43. *p.* 92. See alſo an ingenious *French* Treatiſe, called *Grammaire generale & raiſonnée,* Chap. IX.

The *Latins,* in their Structure of this Subjunctive, ſeem to have well repreſented its *compound* Nature of part *Pronoun,* and part *Connective,* in forming their

G   QUI

Ch. V. may be the Subſtitute of all kinds of Subſtantives, natural, artificial, or abſtract; as well as general, ſpecial, or particular. We may ſay, the *Animal, Which,* &c. the *Man, Whom,* &c. the *Ship, Which,* &c. *Alexander, Who,* &c. *Bucephalus, That,* &c. *Virtue, Which,* &c. &c.

NAY, it may even be the Subſtitute of all the other Pronouns, and is of courſe therefore expreſſive of all three Perſons. Thus we ſay, I, WHO *now read, have near finiſhed this Chapter;* THOU, WHO *now readeſt*: HE, WHO *now readeth,* &c. &c.

AND thus is THIS SUBJUNCTIVE truly a *Pronoun* from its *Subſtitution,* there being

---

QUI & QUIS from QUE and IS, or (if we go with *Scaliger* to the *Greek)* from ΚΑΙ and 'ΟΣ, ΚΑΙ and 'Ο. *Scal. de Cauſ. Ling. Lat. c.* 127.

HOMER alſo expreſſes the Force of this *Subjunctive, Pronoun* or *Article,* by help of the *Prepoſitive* and a *Connective,* exactly conſonant to the Theory here eſtabliſhed, See *Iliad.* Λ. ver. 270, 553. N. 571. Π. 54, 157, 158.

BOOK THE FIRST.

ing no Subſtantive exiſting, in whoſe place Ch. V.
it may not ſtand. At the ſame time, it is
eſſentially diſtinguiſhed from the other Pronouns, by this peculiar, that it is not only
a *Subſtitute*, but withal *a Connective (1)*.

AND

---

(1) Before we quit this Subject, it may not be improper to remark, that in the *Greek* and *Latin* Tongues
the two principal Pronouns, that is to ſay, the Firſt
and Second Perſon, the *Ego* and the *Tu* are *implied* in
the very Form of the Verb itſelf (γράφω, γράφεις,
ſcribo, ſcribis) and are for that reaſon never *expreſt*,
unleſs it be to mark a Contradiſtinction; ſuch as in
Virgil,

Nos *patriam fugimus* ; Tu, *Tityre, lentus in umbrâ
Formoſam reſonare doces*, &c.

This however is true with reſpect only to the *Caſus
rectus,* or *Nominative* of theſe Pronouns, but not with
reſpect to their *oblique Caſes*, which muſt always be
added, becauſe tho' we ſee the Ego in *Amo*, and the
Tu in *Amas*, we ſee not the Te or Me in *Amat*, or
Amant.

Yet even theſe *oblique Caſes* appear in a different
manner, according as they mark Contradiſtinction,
or not. If they contradiſtinguiſh, then are they *commonly* placed at the beginning of the Sentence, or at
leaſt before the Verb, or leading Subſtantive.

Thus

Ch. V. And now to conclude what we have said concerning Substantives. All Sub-
STANTIVES

Thus *Virgil*,

——*Quid Thesea, magnum
Quid memorem Alciden? Et* MI *genus ab Jove summo.*

Thus *Homer*,

ΎMIN μὲν θεοὶ δοῖεν——
Παῖδα δὲ MOI λύσατε φίλην—— Ἰλ. A.

where the Ὑμῖν and the Μοὶ stand, as contradistinguished, and both have precedence of their respective Verbs, the Ὑμῖν even leading the whole Sentence. In other instances, these Pronouns commonly take their place behind the Verb, as may be seen in examples every where obvious. The *Greek* Language went farther still. When the oblique Case of these Pronouns happened to contradistinguish, they assumed a peculiar Accent of their own, which gave them the name of ὀρθοτονεμέναι, or *Pronouns uprightly accented.* When they marked no such opposition, they not only took their place behind the Verb, but even *gave it their Accent,* and (as it were) *inclined themselves upon it.* And hence they acquired the name of Ἐγκλιτικαὶ, that is, *Leaning* or *Inclining* Pronouns. The *Greeks* too had in the first person Ἐμῦ, Ἐμοί, Ἐμέ for *Contradistinctives,* and Μῦ, Μοὶ, Μὲ for *Enclitics.* And hence it was that *Apollonius* contended, that in the passage above quoted from the first Iliad, we should read παῖδα δ' ΕΜΟΙ,

for

STANTIVES are either *Primary*, or *Secondary*, that is to say, according to a Language more familiar and known, are either NOUNS or PRONOUNS. The NOUNS denote *Substances*, and those either *Natural*, *Artificial*, or *Abstract* *. They moreover denote Things either *General*, or *Special*, or *Particular*. The PRONOUNS, their Substitutes, are either *Prepositive*, or *Subjunctive*. THE PREPOSITIVE is distinguished into *three* Orders called the *First*, the *Second*, and the *Third* Person. THE SUBJUNCTIVE includes the powers

---

for παῖδα δὲ MOI, on account of the Contradistinction, which there occurs between the *Grecians* and *Chryses*. See *Apoll. de Syntaxi L. I. c. 3. p. 20. L. II. c. 2. p. 102, 103.*

This Diversity between the Contradistinctive Pronouns, and the Enclitic, is not unknown even to the *English* Tongue. When we say, *Give me Content,* the (*Me*) in this case is a perfect Enclitic. But when we say, *Give Me Content, Give Him his thousands,* the (*Me*) and (*Him*) are no Enclitics, but as they stand in opposition, assume an Accent of their own, and so become the true ὀρθοτονούμεναι.

* See before p. 37, 38.

Ch. V. of all thofe three, having *fuperadded*, as of its own, the peculiar force of a *Connective*.

HAVING done with SUBSTANTIVES, we now proceed to ATTRIBUTIVES.

CHAP. VI.

Concerning Attributives.

ATTRIBUTIVES are *all those princi- pal Words, that denote Attributes, considered as Attributes.* Such for example are the Words, *Black, White, Great, Little, Wise, Eloquent, Writeth, Wrote, Writing,* &c. (*a*).

How-

(*a*) In the above list of Words are included what Grammarians called *Adjectives, Verbs,* and *Participles,* in as much as *all of them equally* denote the *Attributes of Substance.* Hence it is, that as they are all from their very nature the Predicates in a Proposition (being all predicated of some Subject or Substance, *Snow is white,* Cicero *writeth,* &c.) hence I say the Appellation PHMA or VERB is employed by Logicians in an extended Sense *to denote them all.* Thus *Ammonius* explaining the reason, why *Aristotle* in his Tract *de Interpretatione* calls λευκὸς *a Verb,* tells us πᾶσαν φωνὴν, κακηγορέμενον ὅρον ἐν προτάσει ποιῆσαν, 'PHMA καλεῖσθαι, *that every Sound articulate, that forms the*

Pre-

Ch. VI. However, previously to these, and to every other possible Attribute, whatever a thing may be, whether black or white, square or round, wise or eloquent, writing or thinking, it must *first* of necessity EXIST, before it can possibly be any thing else. For EXISTENCE may be considered as *an universal Genus*, to which all things of all kinds are at all times to be referred. The Verbs therefore, which denote it, claim precedence of all others, as being essential to the very being of every Proposition, in which they may still be found, either *exprest*, or by *implication*; exprest, as when we say, *The Sun* is *bright*; by

im-

Predicate in a Proposition, is called a VERB. p. 24. Edit. Ven. *Priscian's* observation, though made on another occasion, is very pertinent to the present. *Non Declinatio, sed proprietas excutienda est significationis.* L. II. p. 576. And in another place he says——*non similitudo declinationis omnimodo conjungit vel discernit partes orationis inter se, sed vis ipsius significationis.* L. XIII. p. 970.

implication, as when we fay, *The Sun rifes*, which means, when refolved, *The Sun is rifing* (b).

THE Verbs, *Is, Groweth, Becometh, Eſt, Fit,* ὑπάρχει, ἐςὶ, πέλει, γίγνεται, are all of them uſed to expreſs this *general Genus*. The *Latins* have called them *Verba Subſtantiva, Verbs Subſtantive,* but the *Greeks* Ῥήματα Ὑπαρκ]ικὰ, *Verbs of Exiſtence,* a Name more apt, as being of greater latitude, and comprehending equally as well Attribute, as Subſtance. The principal of thoſe Verbs, and which we ſhall here particularly conſider, is the Verb, Ἐςὶ, *Eſt, Is*.

Now all EXISTENCE is either abſolute or qualified—*abſolute,* as when we fay, B IS; *qualified,* as when we fay, B IS AN ANIMAL; B IS BLACK, IS ROUND, &c.

WITH

(b) See *Metaphyſ. Ariſtot.* L. V. c. 7. Edit. *Du-Vail.*

Ch. VI. WITH refpect to this difference, the Verb (IS) can by itfelf exprefs *abfolute Exiftence*, but never the *qualified*, without fubjoining the particular Form, becaufe the Forms of Exiftence being in number infinite, if the particular Form be not expreft, we cannot know which is intended. And hence it follows, that when (IS) only ferves to fubjoin fome fuch Form, it has little more force, than that of *a mere Affertion*. It is under the fame character, that it becomes a latent part in every other Verb, by expreffing that Affertion, which is one of their Effentials. Thus, as was obferved juft before, *Rifeth* means, IS *rifing* ; *Writeth*, IS *writing*.

AGAIN—As to EXISTENCE in general, it is either *mutable*, or *immutable*; *mutable*, as in the *Objects of Senfation*; *immutable*, as in the *Objects of Intellection and Science*. Now *mutable* Objects exift all in *Time*, and admit the feveral Diftinctions

stinctions of present, past, and future. Ch. VI.
But *immutable Objects know no such Distinctions*, but rather stand opposed to all
things temporary.

AND hence two different Significations
of the substantive Verb (IS) according
as it denotes *mutable*, or *immutable* Being.

FOR example, if we say, *This Orange
is ripe*, (IS) meaneth, *that it existeth so
now at this present*, in opposition to *past*
time, when it was green, and to *future*
time, when it will be rotten.

BUT if we say, *The Diameter of the
Square is incommensurable with its side*,
we do not intend by (IS) that it is incommensurable *now*, having been *formerly*
commensurable, or being to become so
hereafter; on the contrary we intend that
Perfection of Existence, to which *Time*
and *its Distinctions* are utterly unknown.
It is under the same meaning we employ
this

Ch. VI. this Verb, when we say, TRUTH IS, or, GOD IS. The opposition is not of *Time present* to *other Times*, but of *necessary Existence* to *all temporary Existence whatever* (c). And so much for *Verbs of Existence,* commonly called *Verbs Substantive.*

WE are now to descend to the common Herd of Attributives, such as *black* and *white, to write, to speak, to walk.* &c. among which when compared and opposed to each other, one of the most eminent distinctions appears to be this. Some, by being joined to a proper Substantive

---

(c) *Cum enim dicimus,* DEUS EST, *non eum dicimus* NUNC ESSE, *sed tantum* IN SUBSTANTIA ESSE, *ut hoc ad immutabilitatem potius substantiæ, quam ad tempus aliquod referatur. Si autem dicimus,* DIES EST, *ad nullam diei substantiam pertinet, nisi tantum ad temporis constitutionem; hoc enim, quod significat, tale est, tanquam si dicamus,* NUNC EST. *Quare cum dicimus* ESSE, *ut substantiam designemus, simpliciter* EST *addimus; cum vero ita ut aliquid præsens significetur, secundum Tempus,* Boeth. in Lib. de Interpr. p. 307. See also *Plat. Tim.* p. 37, 38. *Edit. Serrani.*

stantive *make* without farther help *a per-* Ch. VI.
fect assertive Sentence; while the rest,
tho' otherwise perfect, are *in this respect*
deficient.

To explain by an example. When
we say, *Cicero eloquent, Cicero wise,* these
are imperfect Sentences, though they denote a Substance and an Attribute. The
reason is, that they want an *Assertion,*
to shew that such Attribute appertains to
such Substance. We must therefore call
in the help of an Assertion elsewhere, an
(IS) or a (WAS) to complete the Sentence,
saying, *Cicero* IS *wise, Cicero* WAS *eloquent.* On the contrary, when we say,
Cicero writeth, Cicero walketh, in instances like these there is no such occasion,
because the Words *(writeth)* and *(walketh)* imply in their own Form not an Attribute only, but an Assertion likewise.
Hence it is they may be resolved, the one
into *Is* and *Writing,* the other into *Is*
and *Walking.*

Now

Ch. VI. Now all those Attributives, which have this complex Power of denoting both an Attribute and an Assertion, make that Species of Words, which Grammarians call VERBS. If we resolve this complex Power into its distinct Parts, and take *the Attribute alone* without the Assertion, then have we PARTICIPLES. All other Attributives, besides the two Species before, are included together in the general Name of ADJECTIVES.

AND thus it is, that ALL ATTRIBUTIVES are either VERBS, PARTICIPLES, or ADJECTIVES.

BESIDES the Distinctions abovementioned, there are others, which deserve notice. Some Attributes have their Essence in *Motion*; such are *to walk, to fly, to strike, to live.* Others have it in the *privation of Motion*; such are *to stop, to rest, to cease, to die.* And lastly, others have it in subjects, *which have nothing to*
do

do *with either Motion or its Privation*; such are the Attributes of, *Great* and *Little*, *White* and *Black*, *Wise* and *Foolish*, and in a word the several *Quantities*, and *Qualities* of all Things. Now these last are ADJECTIVES; those which denote *Motions*, or their *Privation*, are either VERBS or PARTICIPLES.

AND this Circumstance leads to a farther Distinction, which may be explained as follows. That *all Motion is in Time,* and therefore, wherever it exists, implies *Time* as its concomitant, is evident to all and requires no proving. But besides this, *all Rest or Privation of Motion implies Time likewise.* For how can a thing be said to rest or stop, by being in *one* Place for *one* Instant only?—so too is that thing, which moves with the greatest velocity. † To stop therefore or rest, is to be in *one* Place for *more than one* Instant, that is to say,

during

---

† Thus *Proclus* in the Beginning of his Treatise concerning *Motion*. Ἠρεμοῦν ἐςὶ τὸ πρότερον ἢ ὕςερον ἐν τῷ αὐτῷ τόπῳ ὄν, ᾧ αὐτὸ, ᾧ τὰ μέρη.

Ch. VI. *during an Extenſion between two Inſtants,* and *this* of courſe gives us the Idea of TIME. As therefore *Motions* and their *Privation* imply *Time* as their concomitant, ſo VERBS, which denote them, come to denote TIME alſo (*d*). And hence the origin and uſe of TENSES, " which are ſo many " different forms, aſſigned to each Verb, " to ſhew, without altering its principal " meaning the various TIMES in which " ſuch meaning may exiſt." Thus *Scribit, Scripſit, Scripſerat,* and *Scribet,* denote all equally the Attribute, *To Write,* while the difference between them, is, that they denote *Writing in different Times.*

SHOULD

(*d*) The antient Authors of Dialectic or Logic have well deſcribed this Property. The following is part of their Definition of a Verb——ῥῆμα δέ ἐστι τὸ προσσημαῖνον χρόνον, *a Verb is ſomething, which ſignifieſ Time* OVER AND ABOVE (for ſuch is the force of the Propoſition, Πρὸς.) If it ſhould be aſked, *over and above what?* It may be anſwered over and above its *principal* Signification, which is to denote ſome *moving* and *energizing* Attribute. See *Ariſt. de Interpret.* c. 3. together with his Commentators *Ammonius* and *Boethius.*

SHOULD it be afked, whether *Time* it- Ch.VI.
felf may not become upon occafion the
Verb's *principal* Signification; it is anfwered,
No. And this appears, becaufe *the
fame Time* may be denoted by different
verbs (as in the words, *writeth* and *fpeaketh*)
and *different Times* by the fame Verb
(as in the words, *writeth* and *wrote*) neither
of which could happen, were *Time*
any thing more, than a mere *Concomitant*.
Add to this, that when words denote
Time, not collaterally, but principally,
they ceafe to be verbs, and become either
adjectives, or fubftantives. Of the adjective
kind are *Timely, Yearly, Dayly,
Hourly,* &c. of the fubftantive kind are
Time, Year, Day, Hour, &c.

THE moft obvious divifion of TIME is
into Prefent, Paft, and Future, nor is any
language complete, whofe verbs have
not TENSES, to mark thefe diftinctions.
But we may go ftill farther. Time paft
and future are both *infinitely* extended.
H   Hence

Ch. VI. Hence it is that in *univerſal Time paſt* we may aſſume *many particular Times paſt*, and in *univerſal Time future*, *many particular Times future*, ſome more, ſome leſs remote, and correſponding to each other under different relations. Even *preſent Time itſelf* is not exempt from theſe differences, and as neceſſarily implies *ſome degree of Extenſion*, as does every given line, however minute.

HERE then we are to ſeek for the reaſon, which firſt introduced into language that variety of Tenſes. It was not it ſeems enough to denote *indefinitely* (or by Aoriſts) mere Preſent, Paſt, or Future, but it was neceſſary on many occaſions to define with more preciſion, *what kind* of Paſt, Preſent, or Future. And hence the multiplicity of Futures, Præterits, and even Preſent Tenſes, with which all languages are found to abound, and without which it would be difficult to aſcertain our Ideas.

How-

However as the knowledge of TENSES Ch.VI. depends on the theory of TIME, and this is a subject of no mean speculation, we shall reserve it by itself for the following chapter.

CHAP. VII.

Concerning Time, and Tenses.

TIME and SPACE have this in common, that they are both of them by nature things *continuous*, and as such they both of them imply *Extension*. Thus between *London* and *Salisbury* there is the Extension of *Space*, and between *Yesterday* and *To-morrow*, the Extension of *Time*. But in this they differ, that all the parts of Space exist *at once* and *together*, while those of Time only exist *in Transition* or *Succession* (*a*). Hence then we may gain some Idea of TIME, by considering it under the notion

---

(*a*) See Vol. I. p. 275. Note XIII. To which we may add, what is said by *Ammonius*—οὐδὲ γὰρ ὁ χρόνος ὅλος ἅμα ὑφίσταται, ἀλλ᾽ ἢ κατὰ μόνον τὸ ΝΥΝ· ἐν γὰρ τῷ γίνεσθαι κὴ φθείρεσθαι τὸ εἶναι ἔχει. TIME *doth not subsist the whole at once, but only in a single* NOW *or* INSTANT; *for it hath its Existence in becoming and in ceasing to be.* Amm in Predicam. p. 82. b.

notion of *a tranſient Continuity.* Hence also, as far as the affections and properties of *Tranſition* go, Time is *different* from Space; but as to thoſe of *Extenſion* and *Continuity,* they perfectly coincide.

C. VII.

LET us take, for example, ſuch a part of Space, as a Line. In every given LINE we may aſſume any where *a Point,* and therefore in every given *Line* there may be aſſumed infinite *Points.* So in every given TIME we may aſſume any where *a Now* or *Inſtant,* and therefore in every given *Time* there may be aſſumed infinite *Nows* or *Inſtants.*

FARTHER ſtill—A POINT is the *Bound* of every finite *Line*; and A NOW or INSTANT, of every finite *Time.* But altho' they are *Bounds,* they are neither of them *Parts,* neither the *Point* of any *Line,* nor the *Now* or *Inſtant* of any *Time.* If this appear ſtrange, we may remember, that the *parts* of any thing *extended* are *neceſ-*

H 3   *ſarily*

C. VII. *sarily extended* also, it being essential to their character, *that they should measure their Whole.* But if a *Point* or *Now* were *extended,* each of them would contain within itself *infinite other Points,* and *infinite other Nows* (for these may be assumed infinitely within the minutest Extension) and this, it is evident, would be absurd and impossible.

THESE assertions therefore being admitted, and both *Points* and *Nows* being taken as *Bounds,* but not as *Parts* (*b*), it will follow,

---

(*b*) —Φανερὸι ὅτι ἐδὲ μόριον τὸ ΝΥΝ τῦ χρόνυ, ὥσπερ ἐδ' ἀι στιγμαὶ τῆς γραμμῆς· αἱ δὲ γραμμαὶ δύο τῆς μίας μόρια. *It is evident that* A Now *or Instant is no more a part of Time, than* POINTS *are of a Line. The parts indeed of one Line are two other Lines.* Natur. Ausc. L. IV. c. 17. And not long before—Τὸ δὲ ΝΥΝ ἀ μέρ⊕· μετρεῖ, τε γὰρ τὸ μερ⊕, ᾗ σύγκεισθαι δεῖ τὸ ὅλον ἐκ τῶν μερῶν· ὁ δὲ ΧΡΟΝΟΣ ἐ δοκεῖ σύγκεισθαι ἐκ τῶν ΝΥΝ. *A* Now *is no Part of Time; for a Part is able to measure its Whole, and the Whole is necessarily made up of its Parts; but* TIME *doth not appear to be made up of* Nows. Ibid. c. 14.

follow, that in the same manner as *the same* C. VII.
Point may be the *End* of one Line, and the
Beginning of another, so the *same Now* or
Instant may be the *End* of one Time,
and the *Beginning* of another. Let us
suppose for example, the Lines, A B, B C.

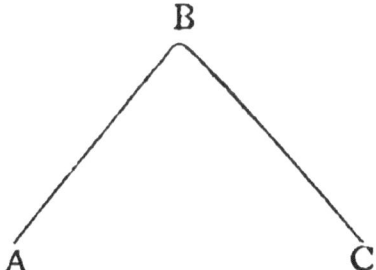

I say that the Point B, is the End of the
Line A B, and the Beginning of the Line,
B C. In the same manner let us suppose
A B, B C to represent certain Times, and
let B be a *Now* or *Instant*. In such case
I say that the *Instant* B is the End of the
Time A B, and the Beginning of the Time,
B C. I say likewise of these two Times,
that with respect to the *Now* or *Instant*,
which they include, the first of them is
necessarily PAST TIME, as being *previous*
to it; the other is necessarily FUTURE, as
being *subsequent*. As therefore every Now

C. VII. or INSTANT always exists in Time, and without being Time, is *Time's Bound*; the Bound of *Completion* to the *Past*, and the Bound of *Commencement* to the *Future:* from hence we may conceive its nature or end, which is *to be the Medium of Continuity between the Past and the Future, so as to render Time, thro' all its Parts, one Intire and Perfect Whole* (*c*).

FROM the above speculations, there follow some conclusions, which may be perhaps called paradoxes, till they have been attentively considered. In the first place *there cannot* (strictly speaking) *be any such*

(*c*) Τὸ δὲ ΝΥΝ ἐςι συνέχεια χρόνε, ὥσπερ ἐλέχθη. συνέχει γὰρ τὸν χρόνον, τὸν παρελθόντα κỳ ἐσόμενον, κỳ ὅλως πέρας χρόνε ἐςίν· ἔςι γὰρ τᾶ μὲν ἀρχὴ, τᾶ δὲ τελευτή. *A Now or Instant is (as was said before) the Continuity or holding together of Time; for it makes Time continuous, the past and the future, and is in general its boundary, as being the beginning of one Time and the ending of another.* Natur. Auscult. L IV. c. 19. Συνέχεια in this place means not *Continuity*, as standing for *Extension*, but rather that *Junction* or *Holding together*, by which Extension is imparted to other things.

such thing as Time present. For if all Time C. VII.
be *transient* as well as *continuous*, it cannot
like a Line be present all together, but part
will necessarily be gone, and part be coming. If therefore any portion of its continuity were to be present *at once*, it would
so far quit its *transient* nature, and be *Time*
no longer. But if no portion of its continuity can be thus present, how can *Time*
possibly be *present*, to which such Continuity is essential?

FARTHER than this—If there be no
such thing as *Time Present*, there can be *no
Sensation of Time* by any one of the senses.
For ALL SENSATION *is of the*† *Present only,*
the Past being preserved not by *Sense* but by
Memory, and the Future being anticipated
by *Prudence* only and wise *Foresight*.

BUT if *no Portion* of Time be the object of *any Sensation*; farther, if the Present

---

† Ταυτῇ γὰρ (αἰσθήσει sc.) οὔτε τὸ μέλλον, οὔτε
τὸ γιγνόμενον γνωρίζομεν, ἀλλὰ τὸ παρὸν μόνον.
Αρις. περὶ Μνημ. A. α.

C. VII. sent *never* exist; if the Past be *no more*; if the Future be not *as yet*; and if these are all the parts, out of which TIME is compounded: how strange and shadowy a Being do we find it? How nearly approaching to a perfect Non-entity (*d*)? Let us try however, since the senses fail us, if we have not faculties of higher power, to seize this fleeting Being.

THE World has been likened to a variety of Things, but it appears to resemble no one more, than some moving spectacle

---

(*d*) Ὅτι μὲν ἂν ὅλως ἐκ ἔστιν, ἢ μόγις κ᾽ ἀμυδρῶς, ἐκ τῶν δέ τις ἂν ὑποπλεύσειε· τὸ μὲν γὰρ αὐτᾶ γέγονε, κ᾽ ἂκ ἔστι· τὸ δὲ μέλλει, κ᾽ ἄπω ἐστίν· ἐκ δὲ τέτων κ᾽ ὁ ἄπειρος κ᾽ ὁ ἀεὶ λαμβανόμενος χρόνος σύγκειται· τὸ δ᾽ ἐκ μὴ ὄντων συγκείμενον, ἀδύνατον ἂν δόξειε κατέχειν ποτὲ ἐσίας. *That therefore* TIME *exists not at all, or at least has but a faint and obscure existence, one may suspect from hence. A part of it has been, and is no more; a part of it is coming, and is not as yet; and out of these is made that infinite Time, which is ever to be assumed still farther and farther. Now that which is made up of nothing but Non-entities, it should seem was impossible ever to participate of Entity.* Natural. Ausc. L. IV. c. 14. See also Philop. M. S. Com. in Nicomach. p. 10.

tacle (such as a procession or a triumph) C. VII.
that abounds in every part with splendid
objects, some of which are still departing,
as fast as others make their appearance.
The Senses look on, while the sight passes,
perceiving as much as is *immediately present*,
which they report *with tolerable accuracy* to
the Soul's superior powers. Having done
this, they have done their duty, being con-
cerned with nothing, save what is present
and instantaneous. But to the *Memory*, to
the *Imagination*, and above all to the *Intellect*, the several *Nows* or *Instants* are not lost,
as to the *Senses*, but are preserved and made
objects of *steady* comprehension, however in
their own nature they may be *transitory* and
passing. "Now it is from contemplating two
"or more of these Instants under one view,
"together with that Interval of Continuity,
"which subsists between them, that we
"acquire insensibly the Idea of TIME (*e*)."
For

(*e*) Τότε φαμὲν γεγονέναι χρόνον, ὅταν τᾶ προτέρυ
ᾗ ὑςέρυ ἐν τῇ κινήσει αἴσθησιν λάβωμεν. Ὁρίζομεν
δὲ

C. VII. For example: *The Sun rises*; this I remember; *it rises again*; this too I remember. These Events are not together; there

is

δὲ τῇ ἄλλο κỳ ἄλλο ὑπολαβεῖν αὐτὰ, κỳ μεταξύ τι αὐτῶν ἕτερον· ὅταν γὰρ τὰ ἄκρα ἕτερα τῶ μέσω νοήσωμεν, κỳ δύο εἴπῃ ἡ ψυχὴ τὰ ΝΥΝ, τὸ μὲν πρότερον, τὸ δὲ ὕστερον, τότε κỳ τῶτο φαμὲν εἶναι ΧΡΟΝΟΝ. *It is then we say there has been* TIME, *when we can acquire a Sensation of prior and subsequent in Motion. But we distinguish and settle these two, by considering one first, then the other, together with an interval between them different from both. For as often as we conceive the Extremes to be different from the Mean, and the Soul talks of two* NOWS, *one prior and the other subsequent, then it is we say there is* TIME, *and this it is we call* TIME. Natural. Auscult. L. IV. c. 16. *Themistius*'s Comment upon this passage is to the same purpose. Ὅταν γὰρ ὁ νῶς ἀναμνησθεὶς τῶ ΝΥΝ, ὃ χθὲς εἶπεν, ἕτερον πάλιν εἴπῃ τὸ τήμερον, τότε κỳ χρόνου εὐθὺς ἐνενόησεν, ὑπὸ τῶν δύο ΝΥΝ ὁριζόμενον, οἷον ὑπὸ περάτων δυοῖν· κỳ ἥτω λέγειν ἔχει, ὅτι ποσόν ἐςι πεντεκαίδεκα ὡρῶν, ἢ ἑκκαίδεκα, οἷον ἐξ ἀπείρω γραμμῆς πηχυαίαν δύο σημείοις ἀποτεμνόμεν۞. *For when the Mind, remembering the* Now, *which it talked of yesterday, talks again of another* Now *to-day, then it is it immediately has an idea of* TIME, *terminated by these two Nows, as by two Boundaries; and thus is it enabled to say, that the Quantity is of fifteen, or of sixteen hours, as if it were to sever a Cubit's length from an infinite Line by two Points.* Themist. Op. edit. Aldi. p 45. b.

is an *Extenſion* between them—not however of *Space*, for we may ſuppoſe the place of riſing the ſame, or at leaſt to exhibit no ſenſible difference. Yet ſtill we recognize *ſome* Extenſion between them. Now what is this Extenſion, *but a natural Day?* And what is that, but pure *Time?* It is after the ſame manner, by recognizing two new Moons, and the Extenſion between theſe: two vernal Equinoxes, and the Extenſion between theſe; that we gain Ideas of other Times, ſuch as *Months* and *Years*, which are all ſo many Intervals, deſcribed as above; that is to ſay, *paſſing Intervals of Continuity between two Inſtants viewed together.*

C. VII.

AND thus it is THE MIND acquires the Idea of TIME. But this Time it muſt be remembered is PAST TIME ONLY, which is always the *firſt* Species, that occurs to the human intellect. How then do we acquire the Idea of TIME FUTURE? The anſwer is, we acquire it *by Anticipation.* Should it be demanded ſtill farther, *And what is Anticipation?* We anſwer, that in this

C. VII. this cafe it is a kind of reafoning by analogy from fimilar to fimilar; from fucceffions of events, that are paſt already, to fimilar fucceffions, that are prefumed hereafter. For example: I obferve as far back as my memory can carry me, how every day has been fucceeded by a night; that night, by another day; that day, by another night; and fo downwards in order to the Day that is now. Hence then I *anticipate a fimilar fucceffion* from the prefent Day, and thus gain the Idea of days and nights *in futurity*. After the fame manner, by attending to the periodical returns of New and Full Moons; of Springs, Summers, Autumns and Winters, all of which in Time paſt I find never to have failed, I *anticipate a like orderly and diverfified fucceffion*, which makes Months, and Seafons, and Years, *in Time future*.

WE go farther than this, and not only thus anticipate in thefe *natural* Periods, but even in matters of *human* and *civil* concern. For example: Having obferved in many

paſt

past instances how health had succeeded to exercise, and sickness to sloth; we anticipate *future* health to those, who, being *now* sickly, use exercise; and *future* sickness to those, who, being *now* healthy, are slothful. It is a variety of such observations, all respecting one subject, which when systematized by just reasoning, and made habitual by due practice, form the character of a Master-Artist, or Man of *practical* Wisdom. If they respect the human body (as above) they form the Physician; if matters military, the General; if matters national, the Statesman; if matters of private life, the Moralist; and the same in other subjects. All these several characters in their respective ways may be said to possess a kind of prophetic discernment, which not only presents them *the barren prospect* of futurity (a prospect not hid from the meanest of men) but shews withal those events, which are likely to attend it, and thus enables them to act with superior certainty and rectitude. And hence it is, that (if we except those, who have had diviner assistances)

C. VII.

C. VII. ances) we may juſtly ſay, as was ſaid of old, *He's the beſt Prophet, who conjectures well (f).*

FROM

(f) Μάντις δ' ἄριστος, ὅστις εἰκάζει καλῶς.
So *Milton.*
*Till old Experience do attain
To ſomething like Prophetic Strain.
Et facile exiſtimari poteſt, Prudentiam eſſe quodam-
modo Divinationem.*
Corn. Nep. in Vit. Attici.

There is nothing appears ſo clearly an object of the MIND or INTELLECT ONLY, as *the Future* does, ſince we can find no place for its exiſtence any where elſe. Not but the ſame, if we conſider, is equally true of *the Paſt.* For tho' it may have once had another kind of being, when (according to common Phraſe) *it actually was,* yet was it then ſomething *Preſent,* and not ſomething *Paſt.* As *Paſt,* it has no exiſtence but in THE MIND or MEMORY, ſince had it in fact any other, it could not properly be called Paſt. It was this intimate connection between TIME, and the SOUL, that made ſome Philoſophers doubt, *whether if there was no Soul, there could be any Time,* ſince Time appears to have its Being in no other region. Πότερον δὲ μὴ ἔσης ψυχῆς εἴη ἂν ὁ χρόνος, ἀπορήσειεν ἄν τις, κ. τ. λ. Natur. Auſcult. L. IV. c. 20. *Themiſtius,* who comments the above paſſage, expreſſes himſelf more poſitively. Εἰ τοίνυν διχῶς λέγεται τότε ἀριθμητὸν ᾗ τὸ ἀριθμούμενον, τὸ μὲν τὸ ἀριθμητὸν δηλαδὴ δυνάμει, τὸ δὲ ἐνεργείᾳ, ταῦτα δὲ ἐκ ἂν ὑποσαίη, μὴ ὄντος τῦ ἀριθμή

σοντος

Book the First.

C. VII.

From what has been reasoned it appears, that knowledge of *the Future* comes from knowledge of *the Past*; as does knowledge of *the Past* from knowledge of *the Present*, so that their *Order to us* is that of Present, Past, and Future.

Of these Species of knowledge, that of the *Present* is the lowest, not only as *first in perception,* but as far the more extensive, being necessarily common to all *animal* Beings, and reaching even to Zoophytes, as far as they possess *Sensation*. Knowledge of *the Past* comes next, which is superior to the *former*, as being confined to those animals, that have *Memory* as well as *Senses*. Knowledge of *the Future* comes last,

---

τουτος μήτε δυνάμει μήτε ἐνεργεία, φανερὸν ὡς οὐκ ἂν ὁ χρόνος εἴη, μὴ ἔσης ψυχῆς. Them. p. 48. Edit. Aldi. Vid. etiam ejusd. Comm. in Lib. de An. p. 94.

I

C. VII. laſt, as being derived from the other two, and which is for that reaſon *the moſt excellent* as well as *the moſt rare*, ſince Nature in her ſuperadditions riſes from worſe always to better, and is never found to ſink from better down to worſe *.

<small>Ariſt. de An. II. 3. p. 28.</small>

AND now having ſeen, how we acquire the knowledge of *Time paſt*, and *Time future*; which is firſt in perception, which firſt in dignity; which more common, which more rare; let us compare them both to the *preſent Now* or *Inſtant*, and examine what relations they maintain towards it.

IN the firſt place there may be *Times* both *paſt* and *future*, in which the *preſent Now* has no exiſtence, as for example in *Yeſterday*, and *To-morrow*.

AGAIN,

---

* See below, Note (r) of this Chapter.

AGAIN, the *present Now* may so far belong to *Time* of either sort, as to be *the End* of the past, and *the Beginning* of the future; but it cannot be included *within* the limits of either. For if it were possible, let us suppose C the *present Now* included

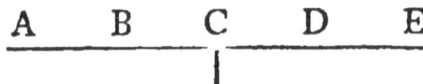

within the limits of the *past Time* A D. In such case C D, part of the past Time A D, will be subsequent to C the *present Now*, and so of course be *future*. But by the Hypothesis it is *past*, and so will be both Past and Future at once, which is absurd. In the same manner we prove that C cannot be included within the limits of a *future Time*, such as B E.

WHAT then shall we say of such *Times*, as *this* Day, *this* Month, *this* Year, *this*

C. VII. Century, all which include within them *the present Now?* They cannot be *past Times* or *future,* from what has been proved; and *present Time has no existence,* as has been proved likewise *. Or shall we allow them to be present, *from the present Now, which exists within them;* so that from the presence of *that* we call *these* also present, tho' the shortest among them has infinite parts always absent? If so, and in conformity to custom we allow such *Times present,* as present Days, Months, Years, and Centuries, each must of necessity be *a compound of the Past and the Future,* divided from each other by some present Now or Instant, and *jointly* called PRESENT, *while that Now remains within them.* Let us suppose for example the Time XY, which

$$f \ldots \overline{ X \quad A \quad B \quad C \quad D \quad E \quad Y } \ldots g$$

let

---

* Sup. p. 104.

BOOK THE FIRST. 117

let us call a Day, or a Century; and let C. VII.
the present *Now* or *Instant* exist at A.
I say, in as much as A exists within
X Y, that therefore X A is Time past,
and A Y Time future, and the whole
X A, A Y, *Time present*. The same
holds, if we suppose the present Now to
exist at B, or C, or D, or E, or any
where before Y. When the present Now
exists at Y, then is the whole X Y *Time
past*, and still more so, when the Now
gets to *g*, or onwards. In like manner
before the Present Now entered X, as
for example when it was at *f*, then was
the whole X Y *Time future*; it was the
same, when the present Now was at
X. When it had past that, then X Y
became *Time present*. And thus it is that
TIME is PRESENT, while passing, in its
PRESENT NOW or INSTANT. It is the
same indeed here, as it is in *Space*. A
Sphere passing over a Plane, and being
for that reason present to it, is only present to that Plane *in a single Point at once*,

I 3   while

HERMES.

C. VII. while during the whole progreſſion its parts abſent are *infinite* (g).

FROM what has been ſaid, we may perceive that ALL TIME, *of every denomination,*

(g) PLACE, according to the antients, was either mediate, or immediate. I am (for example) in *Europe*, becauſe I am in *England*; in *England*, becauſe in *Wiltſhire*; in *Wiltſhire*, becauſe in *Saliſbury*; in *Saliſbury*, becauſe in *my own houſe*; in *my own houſe*, becauſe in *my ſtudy*. Thus far MEDIATE PLACE. And what is my IMMEDIATE PLACE? *It is the internal Bound of that containing Body (whatever it be) which co-incides with the external Bound of my own Body.* Τᾶ περιέχοντος πέρας, καθ' ὃ περιέχει τὸ περιεχόμενον. Now as this *immediate* Place is included within the limits of all the former Places, it is from this relation that thoſe *mediate* Places alſo are called each of them *my Place*, tho' the leaſt among them ſo far exceed my magnitude. To apply this to TIME. The *Preſent Century* is preſent in *the preſent Year*; that, in *the preſent Month*; that, in *the preſent Day*; that, in *the preſent Hour*; that, in *the preſent Minute*. It is thus by circumſcription within circumſcription that we arrive at THAT REAL AND INDIVISIBLE INSTANT, which by being itſelf the *very Eſſence of the Preſent* diffuſes PRESENCE throughout

all

nomination, is divisible and extended But if so, then whenever we suppose *a definite Time,* even though it be a *Time present,* it must needs have a *Beginning,* a *Middle,* and *an End.* And so much for TIME.

C. VII.

Now from the above doctrine of TIME, we propose by way of Hypothesis the following Theorie of TENSES.

THE TENSES are used to mark Present, Past, and Future Time, either *indefinitely* with-

---

all even the largest of Times, which are found *to include it within their respective limits.* Nicephorus Blemmides speaks much to the same purpose. Ἐνεςῶς ἓν χρόνος ἐςὶν ὁ ἐφ' ἑκάτερα παρακείμενος τῷ κυρίως ΝΥΝ· χρόνος μερικὸς, ἐκ παρεληλυθότος κỳ μέλλοντος συνεςὼς, κỳ διὰ τὴν πρὸς τὸ κυρίως ΝΥΝ γειτνίασιν, ΝΥΝ λεγόμενος κỳ αὐτός. PRESENT TIME therefore is that which adjoins to the REAL NOW or INSTANT on either side, being a limited Time made up of Past and Future, and from its vicinity to that REAL NOW said to be Now also itself. Ἐπιτ. Φυσικῆς Κεφ. θ'. See also *Arist. Physic.* L. VI. c. 2, 3, &c.

C, VII. without reference to any Beginning, Middle, or End; or else *definitely*, in reference to such distinctions.

IF *indefinitely*, then have we THREE TENSES, an Aorist of the Present, an Aorist of the Past, and an Aorist of the Future. If *definitely*, then have we three Tenses to mark the *Beginnings* of these three Times; three, to denote their *Middles*; and three to denote their *Ends*; in all NINE.

THE three first of these Tenses we call the Inceptive Present, the Inceptive Past, and the Inceptive Future. The three next, the Middle Present, the Middle Past, and the Middle Future. And the three last, the Completive Present, the Completive Past, and the Completive Future.

AND thus it is, that the TENSES in their natural number appear to be TWELVE;

three

three to denote *Time absolute*, and *nine* to denote it *under its respective distinctions*.

Aorist of the Present.
Γράφω. *Scribo.* I write.

Aorist of the Past.
Ἔγραψα. *Scripsi.* I wrote.

Aorist of the Future.
Γράψω. *Scribam.* I shall write.

Inceptive Present.
Μέλλω γράφειν. *Scripturus sum,* I am going to write.

Middle or extended Present.
Τυγχάνω γράφων. *Scribo* or *Scribens sum.* I am writing.

Completive Present.
Γέγραφα. *Scripsi.* I have written.

Inceptive Past.
Ἔμελλον γράφειν. *Scripturus eram.* I was beginning to write.

Middle

C. VII.   Middle or extended Past.
"Εγραφον or ἐτύγχανον γράφων. *Scribebam.* I was writing.

Completive Past.
'Εγεγράφειν. *Scripseram.* I had done writing.

Inceptive Future.
Μελλήσω γράφειν. *Scripturus ero.* I shall be beginning to write.

Middle or extended Future.
"Εσομαι γράφων. *Scribens ero.* I shall be writing.

Completive Future.
"Εσομαι γεγραφώς. *Scripsero.* I shall have done writing.

It is not to be expected that the above Hypothesis should be justified through all instances in every language. It fares with

Tenses,

Tenſes, as with other affections of ſpeech; be the Language upon the whole ever ſo perfect, much muſt be left, in defiance of all analogy, to the harſh laws of mere authority and chance.

It may not however be improper to inquire, what traces may be diſcovered in favour of this ſyſtem, either in languages themſelves, or in thoſe authors who have written upon this part of Grammar, or laſtly in the nature and reaſon of things.

In the firſt place, as to Aorists. *Aoriſts* are uſually by Grammarians referred *to the Paſt*; ſuch are ἦλθον, *I went*; ἔπεσον, *I fell*, &c. We ſeldom hear of them in *the Future*, and more rarely ſtill in *the Preſent*. Yet it ſeems agreeable to reaſon, that *wherever Time is ſignified without any farther circumſcription, than that of Simple preſent, paſt, or future, the Tenſe is* an Aorist.

Thus

C. VII. THUS *Milton*,

Millions of spiritual creatures WALK *the earth
Unseen, both when we wake, and when we sleep.* P. L. IV. 277.

Here the verb (WALK) means not that they were walking *at that instant only, when Adam spoke, but* ἀορίϛως *indefinitely*, take any instant whatever. So when the same author calls *Hypocrisy*,

―――*the only Evil, that* WALKS *Invisible, except to God alone,*

the Verb (WALKS) hath the like *aoristical* or *indefinite application*. The same may be said in general of all Sentences of the *Gnomologic* kind, such as

Ad pœnitendum PROPERAT, *cito qui judicat.*
Avarus, nisi cum moritur, nil recte FACIT, &c.

ALL

C. VII.

ALL thefe Tenfes are fo many Aorists OF THE PRESENT.

Gnomologic Sentences after the fame manner make likewife Aorists of the Future.

Tu nihil ADMITTES *in te, formidine pœnæ.* Hor.

So too *Legiflative* Sentences, *Thou* SHALT *not kill, Thou* SHALT *not fteal,* &c. for this means no one *particular* future Time, but is a prohibition extended *indefinitely* to every part of Time future (*h*).

WE

(*h*) The *Latin* Tongue appears to be more than ordinarily deficient, as to the article of *Aorifts*. It has no peculiar Form even for *an Aorift of the Paft*, and therefore (as *Prifcian* tells us) the *Præteritum* is forced to do the double duty both of *that Aorift*, and of the *perfect Prefent,* its application in particular inftances being to
be

C. VII. We pass from *Aorists*, to THE INCEP-
TIVE TENSES.

These may be found in part supplied (like many other Tenses) by verbs auxiliar. ΜΕΛΛΩ γράφειν. *Scripturus* SUM. I AM GOING *to write*. But the *Latins* go farther, and have a species of Verbs, derived from others, which do the duty of these Tenses, and are themselves for that reason called *Inchoatives* or *Inceptives*. Thus from *Caleo, I am warm*, comes *Calesco, I begin to grow warm*; from *Tumeo, I swell*, comes *Tumesco, I begin to swell*. These *Inchoative* Verbs are so peculiarly appropriated to the *Beginnings* of Time, that they are defective as to all Tenses, which denote it in its *Completion*, and there-

---

be gathered from the Context. Thus it is that FECI means (as the same author informs us) both πεποίηκα and ἐποίησα, *I have done it*, and *I did it*; VIDI both ἑώρακα and εἶδον, *I have just seen it*, and *I saw it once*. *Prisc. Gram.* L. VIII. p. 814, 838. *Edit. Putsch.*

BOOK THE FIRST. 127

therefore have neither *Perfectum, Plus quam-perfectum,* or *Perfect Future.* There is likewife a fpecies of Verbs called in *Greek* Ἐφετικὰ, in *Latin Defiderativa,* the *Defideratives* or *Meditatives,* which if they are not ſtrictly *Inceptives,* yet both in *Greek* and *Latin* have a near affinity with them. Such are πολεμησείω, *Bellaturio, I have a defire to make war;* βρωσείω, *Efurio, I long to eat* (*i*). And fo much for THE INCEPTIVE TENSES.

C. VII.

THE two laſt orders of Tenfes which remain, are thofe we called (*k*) THE MIDDLE TENSES (which exprefs Time as *extended* and

---

(*i*) As all *Beginnings* have reference to what is *future,* hence we fee how properly thefe Verbs are formed, the *Greek* ones from a future Verb, the *Latin* from a future Participle. From πολεμήσω and βρώσω come πολεμησείω and βρωσείω; from *Bellaturus* and *Efurus* come *Bellaturio* and *Efurio.* See *Macrobius,* p. 691. Ed. Var. ἒ πάνυ γέ με νῦν δὴ ΓΕΛΑΣΕΙΟΝΤΑ ἐποίησας γελάσαι. Plato in Phædone.

(*k*) Care muſt be taken not to confound thefe *middle* Tenfes, with the Tenfes of thofe Verbs, which bear the fame name among Grammarians.

C. VII. and *paſſing*) and the PERFECT or COMPLE-
TIVE, which exprefs its *Completion* or *End*.

Now for thefe the authorities are many. They have been acknowledged already in the ingenious Accidence of Mr. *Hoadly*, and explained and confirmed by Dr. *Samuel Clarke*, in his rational edition of *Homer's Illiad*. Nay, long before either of thefe, we find the fame fcheme in *Scaliger*, and by him (*l*) afcribed to † *Grocinus*, as its author. The learned *Gaza*
(who

(*l*) *Ex his percipimus Grocinum acutè admodum Tempora diviſiſſe, ſed minus commodè. Tria enim conſtituit, ut nos, ſed quæ bifariam ſecat, Perfectum & Imperfectum: ſic, Præteritum imperfectum*, Amabam : *Præteritum perfectum*, Amaveram. *Rectè ſanè. Et Præſens imperfectum*, Amo. *Rectè hactenus ; continuat enim amorem, neque abſolvit. At Præſens perfectum*, Amavi : *quis hoc dicat ?—De Futuro autem ut non malè ſentit, ita controverſum eſt. Futurum, inquit, imperfectum*, Amabo : *Perfectum*, Amavero. *Non malè, inquam : ſignificat enim* Amavero, *amorem futurum & abſolutum iri :* Amabo *perfectionem nullam indicat.* De Cauſ. Ling. Lat. c. 113.

† His Name was *William Grocin*, an *Engliſhman*, contemporary with *Eraſmus*, and celebrated for his learning. He went to *Florence* to ſtudy under *Landin*, and was Profeſſor at *Oxford. Spec. Lit. Flor.* p. 205.

C. VII.

(who was himself a *Greek*, and one of the ablest restorers of that language in the western world) characterizes the Tenses in nearly the same manner (*m*). What *Apollonius* hints, is exactly consonant (*n*).

Priscian

(*m*) The PRESENT TENSE (as this Author informs us in his excellent Grammar) denotes τὸ ἐνιςάμενον χὶ ἀτελὲς, *that which is now inflant and incomplete*; THE PERFECTUM, τὸ παρεληλυθὸς ἄρτι, χὶ ἐυλελὲς τȣ ἐνεςῶτος, *that which is now immediately past, and is the Completion of the Present*; THE IMPERFECTUM, τὸ παραθ]ελαμένον χὶ ἀτελὲς τȣ παρῳχημένȣ, *the extended and incomplete part of the Past*; and THE PLUSQUAM-PERFECTUM, τὸ παρεληλυθὸς πάλαι, χὶ ευτελὲς τȣ παρακειμένȣ, *that which is past long ago, and is the completion of the præteritum.* Gram. L. IV.

(*n*) Ἐντεῦθεν δὲ πειθόμεθα, ὅτι ȣ παρῳχημένȣ συντέλειαν σημαίνει ὁ παρακείμενος, τήν γε μὴν ἐνεςῶσαν —*Hence we are persuaded that the Perfectum doth not signify the completion of the Past, but* PRESENT COMPLETION. *Apollon. L. III. c. 6.* The Reason, which persuaded him to this opinion, was the application and use of the Particle ἂν, of which he was then treating, and which, as it denoted *Potentiality* or *Contingence*, would assort (he says) with any of the passing, extended, and incomplete Tenses, but never with this PERFECTUM, because this implied such a *complete* and *indefeasible existence*, as never to be qualified into the nature of a *Contingent*.

K

C. VII. *Priscian* too advances the same doctrine from the *Stoics*, whose authority we esteem greater than all the rest, not only from the more early age when they lived, but from their superior skill in Philosophy, and their peculiar attachment to *Dialectic*, which naturally led them to great accuracy in these *Grammatical* Speculations (*o*).

BEFORE

(*o*) By these Philosophers the *vulgar present Tense* was called THE IMPERFECT PRESENT, and the *vulgar Præteritum*, THE PERFECT PRESENT, than which nothing can be more consonant to the system that we favour. But let us hear *Priscian*, from whom we learn these facts. PRÆSENS TEMPUS *proprie dicitur, cujus pars jam præteriit, pars futura est. Cum enim Tempus, fluvii more, instabili volvatur cursu, vix punctum habere potest in præsenti, hoc est, in instanti. Maxima igitur pars ejus (sicut dictum est) vel præteriit vel futura est.—Unde* STOICI *jure* HOC TEMPUS PRESENS *etiam* IMPERFECTUM *vocabant (ut dictum est) eo quod prior ejus pars, quæ præteriit, transacta est, deest autem sequens, id est, futura. Ut si in medio versu dicam,* scribo versum, *priore ejus parte scriptâ; cui adhuc deest extrema pars, præsenti utor verbo, dicendo,* scribo versum : *sed* IMPERFECTUM *est, quod deest adhuc versui, quod scribatur—Ex eodem igitur Præsenti nascitur etiam Perfectum. Si enim ad finem perveniat inceptum, statim utimur* PRÆTERITO PERFECTO ; *continuo enim, scripto ad finem versu, dico,* scripsi versum.—And soon after speaking of the *Latin*

Per-

BEFORE we conclude, we shall add a few miscellaneous observations, which will be more easily intelligible from the hypothesis here advanced, and serve withal to confirm its truth.

C. VII.

AND first the *Latins* used their *Præteritum Perfectum* in some instances after a very peculiar manner, so as to imply the very reverse of the verb in its natural signification. Thus, VIXIT, signified, IS DEAD; FUIT, signified, NOW IS NOT, IS NO MORE. It was in this sense that *Cicero* addressed the People of *Rome*, when he had put to death the leaders in the *Catalinarian* Conspiracy. He appeared in the Forum

---

Perfectum, he says——*sciendum tamen, quod Romani* PRÆTERITO PERFECTO *non solum in re modo completâ utuntur, (in quo vim habet ejus, qui apud Græcos* παρα- χείμενος *vocatur, quem* STOICI ΤΕΛΕΙΟΝ ΕΝΕΣ- ΤΩΤΑ *nominaverunt) sed etiam pro* Ἀορίϛυ *accipitur,* &c. Lib. VIII. p. 812, 813, 814.

C.VII. Forum, and cried out with a loud voice, * VIXERUNT. So *Virgil*,

—— || FUIMUS *Troes*, FUIT *Ilium &
ingens
Gloria Dardanidum*—— Æn. II.

And

---

* So among the *Romans*, when in a Caufe all the Pleaders had fpoken, the Cryer ufed to proclaim DIXERUNT, i. e. *they have done fpeaking*. Afcon. Pæd. in Verr. II.

|| So *Tibullus* fpeaking of certain Prodigies and evil Omens.

Hæc fuerint *olim. Sed tu, jam mitis, Apollo,
Prodigia indomitis merge fub æquoribus.*
Eleg. II. 5. ver. 19.

Let thefe Events HAVE BEEN *in days of old* ;—by Implication therefore—*But* HENCEFORTH *let them be no more*.

So *Eneas* in *Virgil* prays to *Phœbus*.

Hac Trojana tenus fuerit *fortuna fecuta*.

Let Trojan *Fortune* (that is, adverfe, like that of *Troy*, and its inhabitants,) HAVE *fo far* FOLLOWED *us*. By implication therefore, *but let it follow us no farther, Here let it end, Hic fit Finis*, as *Servius* well obferves in the place.

In which inftances, by the way, mark not only the force of the *Tenfe*, but of the *Mood*, the PRECATIVE or IMPERATIVE, not in the *Future* but in the PAST. See p. 154, 155, 156.

And again, C. VII.
———*Locus Ardea quondam*
Dictus avis, & nunc magnum manet
Ardea nomen,
* *Sed fortuna* FUIT— Æn. VII.

THE reason of these significations is derived from THE COMPLETIVE POWER of the Tense here mentioned. We see that the periods of Nature, and of human affairs are maintained by the reciprocal succession of *Contraries*. It is thus with Calm and Tempest; with Day and Night; with Prosperity and Adversity; with Glory and Ignominy; with Life and Death. Hence then, in the instances above, the *completion* of one contrary is put for the *commencement* of the other, and to say, HATH LIVED, or, HATH BEEN, has the same meaning with, IS DEAD, or, IS NO MORE.

K 3 IT

---

* *Certus in hospitibus non est amor; errat, ut ipsi:*
Cumque nihil speres firmius esse, FUIT.
Epist. Ovid. Helen. Paridi. ver. 190.
Sive erimus, seu nos Fata FUISSE *volent*.
Tibull. III. 5. 32.

C. VII. It is remarkable in * *Virgil*, that he frequently joins in the same sentence this *complete* and *perfect Present* with the *extended* and *passing Present*; which proves that he considered the two, as belonging to the same species of *Time*, and therefore naturally formed to co-incide with each other.

——*Tibi jam brachia* contrahit *ardens Scorpios, & cæli justâ plus parte* reliquit.
G. I.
Terra tremit; fugere *feræ*— G. I.
Præsertim si tempestas a vertice sylvis.
Incubuit, glomeratque *ferens incendia ventus.* G. II.
——*illa noto citius, volucrique sagittâ, Ad terram* fugit, *& portu se* condidit *alto.* Æn. V.

In

---

* See also *Spencer's Fairy Queen,* B. I. C. 3. St. 19. C. 3. St. 39. C. 8. St. 9.

He hath *his Shield* redeem'd, *and forth his Sword he* draws.

BOOK THE FIRST. 135

IN the fame manner he joins the fame C. VII.
two modifications of *Time in the Paſt*, that
is to ſay, the *complete* and *perfect* Paſt with
the *extended* and *paſſing*.

—— Inruerant *Danai, & tectum omne*
tenebant.   Æn. II.

Tris imbris torti radios, tris nubis aquoſæ
Addiderant, *rutuli tris ignis, & alitis*
auſtri.
Fulgores nunc terrificos, ſonitumque me-
tumque
Miſcebant *operi, flammiſque ſequacibus*
iras (p).   Æn. VIII.

As

(*p*) The Intention of *Virgil* may be better ſeen, in rendering one or two of the above paſſages into *Engliſh*.

—— *Tibi jam brachia* contrahit *ardens*
Scorpios, & cœli juſtâ plus parte reliquit.

For thee the ſcorpion IS NOW CONTRACTING *his claws,*
and HATH ALREADY LEFT *thee more than a juſt portion of Heaven.* The Poet, from a high ſtrain of poetic adulation, ſuppoſes the ſcorpion ſo deſirous of admitting *Auguſtus* among the heavenly ſigns, that though he *has already made* him more than room enough, yet he *ſtill*

K 4   *con-*

C. VII. It is remarkable in * *Virgil,* that he frequently joins in the same sentence this *complete* and *perfect Present* with the *extended* and *passing Present* ; which proves that he considered the two, as belonging to the same species of *Time,* and therefore naturally formed to co-incide with each other.

——*Tibi jam brachia* contrahit *ardens Scorpios, & cæli justâ plus parte* reliquit.
G. I.
Terra tremit ; fugere *feræ*— G. I.
Præsertim si tempestas a vertice sylvis.
Incubuit, glomeratque *ferens incendia ventus.* G. II.
——*illa noto citius, volucrique sagittâ, Ad terram* fugit, *& portu se* condidit *alto.* Æn. V.

In

---

* See also *Spencer's Fairy Queen,* B. I. C. 3. St. 19. C. 3. St. 39. C. 8. St. 9.

He hath *his Shield* redeem'd, *and forth his Sword he* draws.

BOOK THE FIRST. 135

IN the same manner he joins the same C. VII.
two modifications of *Time in the Past,* that
is to say, the *complete* and *perfect* Past with
the *extended* and *passing.*

———Inruerant *Danai, & tectum omne*
tenebant.   Æn. II.

Tris imbris torti radios, tris nubis aquosæ
Addiderant, *rutuli tris ignis, & alitis*
austri.
Fulgores nunc terrificos, sonitumque me-
tumque
Miscebant *operi, flammisque sequacibus*
iras (p).   Æn. VIII.

As

(*p*) The Intention of *Virgil* may be better seen, in rendering one or two of the above passages into *English.*

———*Tibi jam brachia* contrahit *ardens*
Scorpios, & cœli justâ plus parte reliquit.

For thee the scorpion IS NOW CONTRACTING *his claws,*
and HATH ALREADY LEFT *thee more than a just por-*
tion of Heaven. The Poet, from a high strain of poetic adulation, supposes the scorpion so desirous of admitting *Augustus* among the heavenly signs, that though he *has already made* him more than room enough, yet he *still*

K 4   *con-*

C. VII. As to the IMPERFECTUM, it is sometimes employed to denote what is *usual* and *customary*. Thus *surgebat* and *scribebat* signify not only, *he* WAS *rising, he* WAS *writing,* but upon occasion they signify, *he* USED *to rise, he* USED *to write.* The reason of this is, that whatever is *customary,* must be something which has been *frequently repeated.* But what has been *frequently repeated,* must needs require *an Extension of Time past,* and thus we fall insensibly into the TENSE here mentioned.

AGAIN,

---

continues to be making him more. Here then we have two acts, one *perfect,* the other *pending,* and hence the use of the two different Tenses. Some editions read *relinquit;* but *reliquit* has the authority of the celebrated *Medicean* manuscript.

———*Illa noto citius, volucrique sagittâ,*
Ad terram fugit, & portu se condidit alto.

The ship, quicker than the wind, or a swift arrow, CONTINUES FLYING *to land, and* IS HID *within the lofty harbour.* We may suppose this Harbour, (like many others) to have been surrounded with high Land. Hence the Vessel, immediately on entering it, was *completely hid* from those spectators, who had gone out to
see

AGAIN, we are told by *Pliny* (whofe C. VII. authority likewife is confirmed by many gems and marbles ftill extant) that the ancient painters and fculptors, when they fixed their names to their works, did it *pendenti titulo, in a fufpenfive kind of Infcription*, and employed for that purpofe the Tenfe here mentioned. It was Ἀπελλῆς ἐποίει, *Apelles faciebat*, Πολύκλειτ⸺ ἐποίει, *Polycletus faciebat*, and never ἐποίησε or *fecit*. By this they imagined that they avoided the fhew of arrogance, and had in cafe of cenfure an apology (as it were) prepared, fince it appeared from the work itfelf, that *it was once indeed in hand*, but no pretenfion that *it was ever finifhed* (*q*).

IT

---

fee the Ship-race, but yet might *ftill continue failing* towards the fhore within.

―――Inruerant *Danai, & tectum omne* tenebant.

The Greeks HAD ENTERED, *and* WERE THEN POSSESSING *the whole Houfe*; as much as to fay, *they had entered, and that was over*, but their Poffeffion *continued ftill*.

(*q*) *Plin. Nat. Hift. L. I.* The firft Printers (who were moft of them Scholars and Critics) in imitation of

the

C. VII. It is remarkable that the very manner, in which the *Latins* derive these tenses from one another, shews a plain reference to the system here advanced. From *the passing Present* come the passing Past, and Future. *Scribo, Scribebam, Scribam.* From *the perfect Present* come the perfect Past, and Future. *Scripsi, Scripseram, Scripsero.* And so in all instances, even where the verbs are irregular, as from *Fero* come *Ferebam* and *Feram*; from *Tuli* come *Tuleram* and *Tulero*.

We shall conclude by observing, that the ORDER of the Tenses, as they stand ranged by the old Grammarians, is not a fortuitous Order, but is consonant to our perceptions, in the recognition of Time, according to what we have explained already

---

the antient Artists used the same Tense. *Excudebat H. Stephanus. Excudebat Guil. Morelius. Absolvebat Joan. Benenatus*, which has been followed by Dr. *Taylor* in his late valuable edition of *Demosthenes*.

BOOK THE FIRST. 139

ready (r). Hence it is, that the *Present* C. VII.
Tense stands first; then *the Past Tenses*;
and lastly *the Future*.

AND now, having seen what authorities there are for Aorists, or those Tenses, which denote Time *indefinitely*; and what for those Tenses, opposed to Aorists, which mark it *definitely*, (such as the Inceptive, the Middle, and the Completive) we here finish the subject of TIME and TENSES, and proceed to consider THE VERB IN OTHER ATTRIBUTES, which it will be necessary to deduce from other principles.

(r) See before p. 109, 110, 111, 112, 113. Scaliger's observation upon this occasion is elegant.—*Ordo autem (Temporum scil.) aliter est, quam natura eorum. Quod enim præteriit, prius est, quam quod est, itaque primo loco debere poni videbatur. Verùm, quod primo quoque tempore offertur nobis, id creat primas species in animo: quamobrem Præsens Tempus primum locum occupavit; est enim commune omnibus animalibus. Præteritum autem iis tantum, quæ memoriâ prædita sunt. Futurum verò etiam paucioribus, quippe quibus datum est prudentiæ officium.* De Cauf. Ling. Lat. c. 113. See also *Senecæ Epist.* 124. *Mutum animal sensu comprehendit præsentia; præteritorum,* &c.

CHAP.

CHAP. VIII.

Concerning Modes.

C.VIII. WE have observed already (a) that the Soul's leading powers are those of *Perception* and those of *Volition*, which words we have taken in their most comprehensive acceptation. We have observed also, that *all Speech or Discourse* is a *publishing* or exhibiting some part of our soul, either a certain *Perception*, or a certain *Volition*. Hence then, according as we exhibit it either in *a different part*, or after *a different manner*, hence I say the variety of MODES or MOODS (b).

IF

(a) See Chapter II.

(b) *Gaza* defines a Mode exactly consonant to this doctrine. He says it is—βόλημα, ἤ᾽ ὃν πάθημα ψυχῆς, διὰ φωνῆς σημαινόμενον—*a Volition or Affection of the Soul, signified through some Voice, or Sound articulate.* Gram. L. IV. As therefore this is the nature of Modes, and Modes belong to Verbs, hence it is *Apollonius*

IF we simply *declare*, or *indicate* some- C. VIII.
thing to be, or not to be, (whether a Perception or Volition, it is equally the same)
this constitutes that Mode called the DE-
CLARATIVE or INDICATIVE.

A Perception.
—Nosco *crinis, incanaque menta
Regis Romani*——   Virg. Æn. VI.

A Volition.
In nova FERT ANIMUS *mutatas dicere
formas
Corpora*——   Ovid. Metam. I.

IF we do not strictly assert, as of something absolute and certain, but as of something *possible* only, and in the number of
Con-

---

nius observes—τοῖς ῥήμασιν ἐξαιρέτως παράκειται ἡ ψυ-
χικὴ διάθεσις—*the Soul's disposition is in an eminent degree attached to Verbs.* De Synt. L. III. c. 13. Thus
too *Priscian : Modi sunt diversæ* INCLINATIONES
ANIMI, *quas varia consequitur* DECLINATIO VERBI.
L. VIII. p. 821.

C.VIII. *Contingents,* this makes that Mode, which Grammarians call the POTENTIAL; and which becomes on such occasions the leading Mode of the sentence.

Sed tacitus pasci si posset Corvus, HA-
BERET
Plus dapis, &c. Hor.

YET sometimes it is not the leading Mode, but only *subjoined* to the Indicative. In such case, it is mostly used to denote the *End,* or *final Cause;* which End, as in human Life it is always a Contingent, and may never perhaps happen in despite of all our foresight, is therefore exprest most naturally by the Mode here mentioned. For example,

Ut JUGULENT *homines, surgunt de nocte latrones.* HOR.
Thieves rise by night, that they may cut mens throats.

HERE

HERE that they *rife*, is *pofitively afferted* C. VIII. in the *Declarative* or *Indicative* Mode; but as to their *cutting mens throats*, this is only delivered *potentially*, becaufe how truly foever it may be the *End* of their rifing, it is ftill but a *Contingent*, that may never perhaps happen. This Mode as even as it is in this manner fubjoined, is called by Grammarians not the Potential, but THE SUBJUNCTIVE.

BUT it fo happens, in the conftitution of human affairs, that it is not always fufficient merely *to declare* ourfelves to others. We find it often expedient, from a confcioufnefs of our inability, to addrefs them after a manner more interefting to ourfelves, whether to have *fome Perception informed*, or *fome Volition gratified*. Hence then new Modes of fpeaking; if we *interrogate*, it is the INTERROGATIVE MODE; if we *require*, it is the REQUISITIVE. Even the Requifitive itfelf hath its *fubordinate Species*: With refpect to inferiors, it is an IMPERATIVE MODE; with refpect to equals

C.VIII. equals and superiors, it is a PRECATIVE or OPTATIVE*.

AND thus have we established a variety of Modes; the INDICATIVE or DECLARATIVE, *to assert what we think certain*; the POTENTIAL, *for the Purposes of whatever we think Contingent*; THE INTERROGATIVE, *when we are doubtful, to procure us Information*; and THE REQUISITIVE, to *assist us in the gratification of our Volitions.* The Requisitive too appears under two distinct Species, either as it is IMPERATIVE to inferiors, or PRECATIVE to superiors (*c*).

As

---

* It was the confounding of this Distinction, that gave rise to a Sophism of *Protagoras*. *Homer* (says he) in beginning his Iliad with—*Sing, Muse, the Wrath,*—when he thinks to *pray*, in reality *commands*. εὔχεσθαι οἰόμενος, ἐπιτάτlει. Aristot. Poet. c. 19. The Solution is evident from the Division here established, the Grammatical Form being in both cases the same.

(*c*) The Species of *Modes* in great measure depend on the Species of *Sentences*. The *Stoics* increased the number of Sentences far beyond the *Peripatetics*. Besides those mentioned in Chapter II. Note (*b*) they had

many

As therefore all thefe feveral Modes C.VIII.
have their foundation in nature, fo have
certain

---

many more, as may be feen in *Ammonius de Interpret.*
p. 4. and *Diogenes Laertius*, L. VII. 66. The Peripatetics (and it feems too with reafon) confidered all
thefe additional Sentences as included within thofe,
which they themfelves acknowledged, and which they
made to be five in number, the Vocative, the Imperative, the Interrogative, the Precative, and the Affertive.
There is no mention of a *Potential* Sentence, which may
be fuppofed to co-incide with the Affertive, or Indicative. The Vocative (which the Peripatetics called the
εἶδος κλητικὸν, but the Stoics more properly προσαγο-
ρευτικὸν) was nothing more than the Form of addrefs
in point of names, titles, and epithets, with which we
apply ourfelves one to another. As therefore it feldom
included any Verb within it, it could hardly contribute
to form a verbal Mode. *Ammonius* and *Boethius*, the
one a *Greek* Peripatetic, the other a *Latin*, have illuftrated the Species of Sentences from *Homer* and *Virgil*,
after the following manner.

Ἀλλὰ τῶ λόγυ πέντε εἰδῶν, τῶ τε ΚΛΗΤΙΚΟΥ, ὡς τὸ,
   Ὦ μάκαρ Ἀτρείδη——
κỳ τῶ ΠΡΟΣΤΑΚΤΙΚΟΥ, ὡς τὸ,
   Βάσκ᾽ ἴθι, Ἴρι ταχεῖα——

L

C.VIII. certain marks or signs or them been introduced into languages, that we may be enabled

---

κ̓ τȣ̃ 'ΕΡΩΤΗΜΑΤΙΚΟΥ, ὡς τὸ,
 Τίς, πόθεν εἰς ἀνδρῶν;———
κ̓ τȣ̃ 'ΕΥΚΤΙΚΟΥ, ὡς τὸ,
 *Αἰ γὰρ Ζεῦ τε πάτερ———
κ̓ ἐπὶ τȣ́τοις, τȣ̃ 'ΑΠΟΦΑΝΤΙΚΟΥ, καθ' ὃν ἀπο-
φαινόμεθα περὶ ὁτȣȣ̃ν τῶν πραγμάτων, οἷον
———Θεοὶ δέ τε πάντα ἴσασιν———
ἃ περὶ παντὸς, &c. Εἰς τὸ περὶ Ἑρμ. p. 4.

Boethius's Account is as follows. *Perfectarum vero Orationum partes quinque sunt:* DEPRECATIVA, *ut*,
 Jupiter omnipotens, precibus si flecteris ullis,
 Da deinde auxilium, Pater, atque hæc omina firma.

IMPERATIVA, *ut,*
 Vade age, Nate, voca Zephyros, & labere pennis.

INTERROGATIVA, *ut.*
 Dic mihi, Damœta, cujum pecus?———

VOCATIVA, *ut,*
 O! Pater, O! hominum rerumque æterna potestas.

ENUNTIATIVA, *in quâ Veritas vel Falsitas invenitur, ut,*
 Principio arboribus varia est natura creandis.
  Boeth. in Lib. de Interp. p. 291.

enabled by our discourse to signify them, C.VIII.
one to another. And hence those various
MODES or MOODS, of which we find in
common Grammars so prolix a detail, and
which are in fact no more than "so many
"*literal* Forms, intended to express these
"*natural* Distinctions" (*d*).

ALL

In *Milton* the same Sentences may be found, as follows. THE PRECATIVE,
—*Universal Lord! be bounteous still
To give us only Good*——

THE IMPERATIVE,
Go then, Thou mightiest, in thy Father's might.

THE INTERROGATIVE,
Whence, and what art thou, execrable Shape?

THE VOCATIVE,
——Adam, *earth's hallow'd Mold,
Of God inspir'd*——

THE ASSERTIVE OR ENUNTIATIVE,
*The conquer'd also and enslav'd by war
Shall, with their freedom lost, all virtue lose.*

(*d*) The *Greek* Language, which is of all the most elegant and complete, expresses these several Modes,

and

C.VIII. ALL thefe MODES have this in common, that they exhibit fome way or other the

---

and all diftinctions of Time likewife, by an adequate number of Variations in each particular Verb. Thefe Variations may be found, fome at the beginning of the Verb, others at its ending, and confift for the moft part either in *multiplying* or *diminifhing* the number of Syllables, or elfe in *lengthening* or *fhortening* their refpective Quantities, which two methods are called by Grammarians the *Syllabic* and the *Temporal*. The *Latin*, which is but a Species of *Greek* fomewhat debafed, admits in like manner a large portion of thofe Variations, which are chiefly to be found at the Ending of its Verbs, and but rarely at their Beginning. Yet in its Deponents and Paffives it is fo far defective, as to be forced to have recourfe to the *Auxiliar*, *fum*. The modern Languages, which have ftill fewer of thofe Variations, have been neceffitated all of them to affume two Auxiliars at leaft, that is to fay, thofe which exprefs in each Language the Verbs, *Have*, and *Am*. As to the *Englifh* Tongue, it is fo poor in this refpect, as to admit no Variation for Modes, and only one for Time, which we apply to exprefs an Aorift of the Paft. Thus from *Write* cometh *Wrote*; from *Give*, *Gave*, from *Speak*, *Spake*, &c. Hence to exprefs Time, and Modes, we are compelled to employ no lefs than feven Auxiliars, viz. *Do*, *Am*, *Have*, *Shall*, *Will*, *May*, and *Can*; which we ufe fometimes fingly, as when we fay, I *am* writing,

BOOK THE FIRST. 149

the SOUL and its AFFECTIONS. Their C. VIII.
Peculiarities and Distinctions are in part,
as follows.

THE REQUISITIVE and INTERROGATIVE MODES are distinguished from *the Indicative* and *Potential*, that whereas these last seldom call for *a Return*, to the two former it is *always necessary*.

IF we compare THE REQUISITIVE MODE with THE INTERROGATIVE, we shall find these also distinguished, and that not only in the *Return*, but in other Peculiarities.

---

ing, I *have* written; sometimes two together, as, I *have been* writing, I *should have* written; sometimes no less than three, as I *might have been* lost, he *could have been* preserved. But for these, and all other speculations, relative to the *Genius* of the *English* Language, we refer the reader, who wishes for the most authentic information, to that excellent Treatise of the learned Dr. *Lowth*, intitled, *A short Introduction to English Grammar*.

C.VIII. *The Return to the Requisitive* is *sometimes* made in *Words*, *sometimes in Deeds*. To the Request of *Dido* to *Eneas*—

———*a primâ dic, hospes, origine nobis Insidias Danâum*———

the *proper* Return was in *Words*, that is, in an historical Narrative. To the Request of the unfortunate Chief———*date obolum Belisario*—the *proper* Return was in a Deed, that is, in a charitable Relief. But with respect to *the Interrogative, the Return is necessarily made in Words alone*, in Words, which are called a *Response* or *Answer*, and which are always actually or by implication some *definitive assertive Sentence*. Take Examples. *Whose Verses are these?*—the Return is a Sentence—*These are Verses of Homer*. *Was Brutus a worthy Man?*—the Return is a Sentence—*Brutus was a worthy Man*.

AND hence (if we may be permitted to digress) we may perceive the

BOOK THE FIRST. 151

the near affinity of this *Interrogative* Mode C.VIII.
with the *Indicative,* in which laft its Refponfe or Return is moftly made. So near
indeed is this Affinity, that in thefe two
Modes alone the Verb retains the fame
Form (*e*), nor are they otherwife diftinguifhed, than either by the Addition or
Abfence of fome fmall particle, or by fome
minute change in the collocation of the
words, or fometimes only by a change in
the Tone, or Accent *(f)*.

BUT

(*e*) Ἥγε ἐν προκειμένη ὁρισική ἔγκλισις, τὴν ἐγκει-
μένην κατάφασιν ἀποβάλλουσα, μεθίςαται τῦ καλεῖσθαι ὁρισική—ἀναπληρωθεῖσα δὲ τῆς καταφάσεως, ὑπο-
ςρέφει εἰς τὸ εἶναι ὁρισική. *The Indicative Mode, of
which we fpeak, by laying afide that Affertion, which by
its nature it implies, quits the name of Indicative—when it
reaffumes the Affertion, it returns again to its proper Character.* Apoll. de Synt. L. III. c. 21. *Theodore Gaza*
fays the fame, *Introd. Gram.* L. IV.

(*f*) It may be obferved of the INTERROGATIVE,
that as often as the *Interrogation* is *fimple* and *definite,*
the Refponfe may be made in almoft the *fame* Words,

L 4   by

C. VIII. But to return to our comparison between the *Interrogative* Mode and the *Requisitive*.

THE

by converting them into a sentence affirmative or negative, according as the Truth is either one or the other. For example—*Are these Verses of* Homer?—Response—*These Verses are of* Homer. *Are those Verses of* Virgil?—Response—*Those are not Verses of* Virgil. And here the Artists of Language, for the sake of brevity and dispatch, have provided two Particles, to represent all such Responses, YES, for all the affirmative ; NO, for all the negative.

But when the *Interrogation* is *complex*, as when we say—*Are these Verses of* Homer, *or of* Virgil?—much more, when it is *indefinite*, as when we say in general —*Whose are these Verses?*—we cannot then respond after the manner above mentioned. The Reason is, that no Interrogation can be answered by a simple *Yes*, or a simple *No*, except only those, which are themselves so simple, as of two possible answers to admit only one. Now the least complex Interrogation will admit of four Answers, two affirmative, two negative, if not perhaps of more. The reason is, a complex Interrogation cannot consist of less than two simple ones ; each of which may be separately affirmed and separately denied. For

instance

THE INTERROGATIVE (in the lan- C.VIII.
guage of Grammarians) has all *Perſons*
of

---

inſtance—*Are theſe Verſes* Homer's, *or* Virgil's? (1.)
They are Homer's—(2.) *They are not Homer's*—(3.)
They are Virgil's—(4.) *They are not Virgil's*—we may
add, (5.) *They are of neither.* The indefinite Interrogations go ſtill farther; for theſe may be anſwered by
infinite affirmatives, and infinite negatives. For inſtance—*Whoſe are theſe Verſes?* We may anſwer affirmatively—*They are* Virgil's, *They are* Horace's, *They
are* Ovid's, &c.—or negatively—*They are not* Virgil's,
They are not Horace's, *They are not* Ovid's, and ſo on,
either way to infinity. How then ſhould we learn from
a ſingle *Yes*, or a ſingle *No*, which particular is meant
among infinite Poſſibles? Theſe therefore are Interrogations which muſt be always anſwered by a *Sentence.*
Yet even here Cuſtom has conſulted for Brevity, by
returning for Anſwer only the *ſingle eſſential characteriſtic
Word*, and retrenching by an Ellipſis all the reſt, which
reſt the Interrogator is left to ſupply from himſelf.
Thus when we are aſked—*How many right angles equal
the angles of a triangle?*—we anſwer in the ſhort monoſyllable, Two; whereas, without the Ellipſis, the
anſwer would have been—*Two right angles equal the
angles of a triangle.*

The

C.VIII. of both *Numbers*. The REQUISITIVE or IMPERATIVE has no *firſt Perſon* of the *ſingular*, and that from this plain reaſon, that it is equally abſurd in *Modes* for a perſon to *requeſt* or *give commands to himſelf*, as it is in *Pronouns*, for the ſpeaker to become *the ſubject of his own addreſs* *.

AGAIN, we may *interrogate* as *to all Times*, both Preſent, Paſt, and Future. *Who* WAS *Founder of* Rome? *Who* IS *King of* China? *Who* WILL DISCOVER *the Longitude?*—But *Intreating* and *Commanding* (which are the eſſence of the Re-

---

The Antients diſtinguiſhed theſe two Species of Interrogation by different names. The ſimple they called Ἐρώτημα, *Interrogatio*; the complex, πύσμα, *Percontatio*. *Ammonius* calls the firſt of theſe Ἐρώτησις διαλεκτική; the other, Ἐρώτησις πυσματική. See *Am. in Lib. de Interpr.* p. 160. *Diog. Laert.* VII. 66. *Quintil. Inſt.* IX. 2.

* Sup. p. 74, 75.

Requifitive Mode) have a neceſſary re- C. VIII.
ſpect to the *Future* (g) only. For indeed
what

(g) *Apollonius*'s Account of the Future, implied in all Imperatives, is worth obſerving. Ἐπὶ γὰρ μὴ γινομένοις ἢ μὴ γεγονόσιν ἡ ΠΡΟΣΤΑΞΙΣ· τὰ δὲ μὴ γινόμενα ἢ μὴ γεγονότα, ἐπιτηδειότητα δὲ ἔχοντα εἰς τὸ ἔσεσθαι, ΜΕΛΛΟΝΤΟΣ ἐςι. A COMMAND *has reſpect to thoſe things which either are not doing, or have not yet been done. But thoſe things, which being not now doing, or having not yet been done, have a natural aptitude to exiſt hereafter, may be properly ſaid to appertain to* THE FUTURE. De Syntaxi, L. I. c. 35. Soon before this he ſays—Ἅπαντα τὰ προςακτικὰ εἰκειμένην ἔχει τὴν τῷ μέλλοντος διάθεσιν—σχηδὸν γὰρ ἐν ἴσῳ ἐςὶ τὸ, Ὁ ΤΥΡΑΝΝΟΚΤΟΝΗΣΑΣ ΤΙΜΑΣΘΩ, τῷ, ΤΙΜΗΘΗΣΕΤΑΙ, κατὰ τὴν χρόνε ἔννοιαν· τῇ ἐκκλίσει δι·ηλλαχὸς, καθὸ τὸ μὲν προςακτικὸν, τὸ δὲ ὁςιςικόν. *All* IMPERATIVES *have a diſpoſition within them, which rſpects* THE FUTURE—*with regard therefore to* TIME, *it is the ſame thing to ſay*, LET HIM, THAT KILLS A TYRANT, BE HONOURED, *or*, HE, THAT KILLS ONE, SHALL BE HONOURED ; *the difference being only in the Mode, in as much as one is* IMPERATIVE, *the other* INDICATIVE *or Declarative.* Apoll. de Syntaxi, L. I. c. 35. *Priſcian* ſeems to allow Imperatives a ſhare of *Preſent* Time, as well as *Future*. But if we attend, we ſhall find his *Preſent* to
be

C.VIII. what have they to do with the prefent or the paft, the natures of which are immutable and neceffary?

IT

be nothing elfe than *an immediate Future*, as oppofed to a more diftant one. *Imperativus vero Præfens & Futurum* [*Tempus*] *naturali quâdam neceffitate videtur poffe accipere. Ea etenim imperamus, quæ vel in præfenti ftatim volumus fieri fine aliquâ dilatione, vel in futuro.* Lib. VIII. p. 806.

It is true the *Greeks* in their Imperatives admit certain Tenfes of the Paft, fuch as thofe of the *Perfectum*, and of the two *Aorifts*. But then thefe Tenfes, when fo applied, either totally lofe their *temporary* Character, or elfe are ufed to infinuate fuch *a Speed of execution*, that the deed fhould be (as it were) *done*, in the very inftant when *commanded*. The fame difference feems to fubfift between our *Englifh* Imperative, BE GONE, and thofe others of, Go, or BE GOING. The firft (if we pleafe) may be ftiled *the Imperative of the Perfectum*, as calling in the very inftant for the completion of our Commands; the others may be ftiled *Imperatives of the Future*, as allowing a reafonable time to begin firft, and finifh afterward.

It is thus *Apollonius*, in the Chapter firft cited, diftinguifhes between σκαπτέτω τὰς ὀμπέλας, *Go to digging the Vines*, and σκαψάτω τὰς ἀμπέλας, *Get the Vines dug*.

C. VIII.

It is from this connection of *Futurity* with *Commands*, that the *Future Indicative* is sometimes used for the *Imperative*, and that to say to any one, YOU SHALL DO THIS, has often the same force with the Imperative, DO THIS. So in the Decalogue—THOU SHALT NOT KILL —THOU SHALT NOT BEAR FALSE WITNESS

---

dug. The first is spoken (as he calls it) εἰς παράτασιν, *by way of Extenſion, or allowance of Time for the work;* the second, εἰς συντελείωσιν, *with a view to immediate Completion.* And in another place, explaining the difference between the same Tenses, Σκάπτε and Σκάψον, he says of the last, ὰ μόνον τὸ μὴ γινόμενον προςάσσει, ἀλλὰ ᴋ̓ τὸ γινόμενον ἐν παρατάσει ἀπαγορεύει, *that it not only commands something, which has not been yet done, but forbids also that, which is now doing in an Extenſion, that is to say, in a flow and lengthened progreſs.* Hence, if a man has been a long while writing, and we are willing to hasten him, it would be wrong to say in *Greek,* ΓΡΑΦΕ, WRITE (for that he is *now,* and has been *long* doing) but ΓΡΑΨΟΝ, GET YOUR WRITING DONE; MAKE NO DELAYS. See *Apoll.* L. III. c. 24. See also *Macrobius de Diff. Verb. Græc. & Lat.* p. 680. *Edit. Varior. Latini non æstimaverunt,* &c.

C.VIII. WITNESS—which denote (we know) the strictest and most authoritative Commands.

As to the POTENTIAL MODE, it is distinguished from all the rest, by its *subordinate* or *subjunctive* Nature. It is also farther distinguished from the *Requisitive* and *Interrogative*, by implying a kind of feeble and weak *Assertion*, and so becoming in some degree susceptible of Truth and Falshood. Thus, if it be said potentially, *This may be*, or, *This might have been*, we may remark without absurdity, *It is true*, or *It is false*. But if it be said, *Do this*, meaning, *Fly to Heaven*, or, *Can this be done?* meaning, *to square the Circle*, we cannot say in either case, *it is true* or *it is false*, though the Command and the Question are about things impossible. Yet still the *Potential* does not aspire to the Indicative, because it implies but a *dubious* and *conjectural* Assertion,

Affertion, whereas that of the Indicative C. VIII. is abfolute, and without referve.

THIS therefore (the INDICATIVE I mean) is the Mode, which, as in all Grammars it is the firſt in order, fo is truly firſt both in dignity and ufe. It is this, which publiſhes our fublimeſt perceptions; which exhibits the Soul in her pureſt Energies, fuperior to the Imperfection of defires and wants; which includes the whole of *Time*, and its minuteſt diſtinctions; which, in its various *Paſt* Tenfes, is employed by Hiſtory, to preferve to us the Remembrance of former Events; in its *Futures* is ufed by Prophecy, or (in default of this) by wife Forefight, to inſtruct and forewarn us, as to that which is coming; but above all in its *Preſent* Tenfe ferves Philofophy and the Sciences, by juſt Demonſtrations to eſtabliſh *neceſſary Truth*; THAT TRUTH, which from its nature *only exiſts*

C.VIII. *ists in the Present;* which knows no distinctions either of Past or of Future, but is every where and always invariably one (*h*).

THROUGH

(*h*) See the quotation, Note (*c*), Chapter the Sixth. *Cum enim dicimus,* DEUS EST, *non eum dicimus nunc esse, sed,* &c.

Boethius, author of the sentiment there quoted, was by birth a *Roman* of the first quality; by religion, a Christian; and by philosophy, a Platonic and Peripatetic; which two Sects, as they sprang from the same Source, were in the latter ages of antiquity commonly adopted by the same Persons, such as *Themistius, Porphyry, Iamblichus, Ammonius,* and others. There were no Sects of Philosophy, that lay greater Stress on the distinction between things existing *in Time* and *not in Time,* than the two above-mentioned. The Doctrine of the Peripatetics on this Subject (since it is these that *Boethius* here follows) may be partly understood from the following Sketch.

" THE THINGS, THAT EXIST IN TIME. are
" *those whose Existence Time can measure.* But if their
" Existence may be measured by Time, then there
" may be assumed a Time greater than the Existence
" of any one of them, as there may be assumed a
" number greater than the greatest multitude, that is
" capable

THROUGH all the above Modes, with C.VIII.
their refpective Tenfes, the Verb being
con-

"capable of being numbered. And hence it is that
"*things temporary* have their Exiftence, as it were li-
"*mited* by Time ; that they are confined within it, as
"within fome bound ; and that in fome degree or other
"they *all fubmit to its power*, according to thofe com-
"mon Phrafes, that *Time is a deftroyer* ; that *things*
"*decay through Time* ; that *men forget in Time, and lofe*
"*their abilities*, and feldom that they improve, or grow
"young, or beautiful. The truth indeed is, *Time al-*
"*ways attends Motion*. Now the natural effect of Mo-
"tion is *to put fomething, which now is, out of that*
"*ftate, in which it now is,* and fo far therefore to de-
"ftroy that ftate.

"The reverfe of all this holds with THINGS THAT
"EXIST ETERNALLY. Thefe exift *not in Time*, be-
"caufe Time is fo far from being able to meafure their
"Exiftence, that *no Time can be affumed, which their*
"*Exiftence doth not furpafs*. To which we may add,
"that they *feel none of its effects*, being no way ob-
"noxious either to damage or diffolution.

"To inftance in examples of either kind of Being.
"There are fuch things at this inftant, as *Stonehenge*
"and the *Pyramids*. It is likewife true at this inftant,
"that the *Diameter of the fquare is commenfurable*
"*with its fide*. What then fhall we fay ? Was there
M   "ever

C. VIII. considered as denoting an ATTRIBUTE, has always reference to some Person, or SUBSTANCE. Thus if we say, *Went*, or, *Go*, or *Whither goeth*, or, *Might have gone*, we must add a Person or Substance, to make the Sentence complete. Cicero *went*; Cæsar *might have gone*; *whither goeth the Wind? Go! Thou Traitor!* But there is a Mode or Form, under which Verbs sometimes appear, where they have no reference at all to Persons or Substances. For example—*To eat is pleasant;* but

---

" ever a Time, when it was *not incommensurable*, as
" it is certain there was a Time, when there was no
" Stonehenge, or Pyramids? or is it *daily* growing *less*
" *incommensurable*, as we are assured of Decays in both
" those mass'y Structures?" From these unchangeable Truths, we may pass to their Place, or Region; to the unceasing Intellection of the universal Mind, ever perfect, ever full, knowing no remissions, languors, &c. See *Nat. Ausc.* L. IV. c. 19. Metaph. L. XIV. c. 6, 7, 8, 9, 10. Edit. Du Val. and Vol. I. p. 262. Note VII. The following Passage may deserve Attention.

Τοῦ γὰρ Νοῦ ὁ μὲν ἀεὶν πέφυκεν, ἢ μὴ νοῶν· ὁ δὲ ἢ πέφυκε, ἢ νοεῖ. ἀλλὰ ἢ ἴωτις ἴοπω τέλεος, ἂν μὴ προσθῆς αὐτῷ τὸ ἢ νοεῖν ἀεὶ, ἢ πάντα νοεῖν, ἢ μὴ ἄλλοτε ἄλλα. ὥςε εἴη ἂν ἐντελέςατος ὁ νοῶν ἀεὶ ἢ πάντα, ἢ ἅμα. Max. Tyr. D.ff. XVII p. 201. Ed. Lond.

but to faft is wholefome. Here the Verbs, *To* C. VIII. *eat,* and, *To faft,* ftand alone by themfelves, nor is it requifite or even practicable to prefix a Perfon or Subftance. Hence the *Latin* and modern Grammarians have called Verbs under this Mode, from this their indefinite nature, INFINITIVES. *Sanctius* has given them the name of *Imperfonals*; and the *Greeks* that of Ἀπαρέμφατα, from the fame reafon of their *not difcovering* either Perfon or Number.

THESE INFINITIVES go farther. They not only lay afide the character of *Attributives,* but they alfo affume that of *Subftantives,* and as fuch themfelves become diftinguifhed with their feveral *Attributes.* Thus in the inftance above, *Pleafant* is the Attribute, attending the Infinitive, *To Eat*; *Wholefome* the attribute attending the Infinitive, *To Faft.* Examples in *Greek* and *Latin* of like kind are innumerable.

Dulce & decorum eft pro patria MORI.
SCIRE *tuum nihil eft—*

C.VIII. Ὀυ κατθανεῖν γὰρ δεινὸν, ἀλλ' αἰσχρῶς θανεῖν (i).

THE *Stoics* in their grammatical inquiries had this Infinitive in such esteem, that they

---

(i) It is from the INFINITIVE thus participating the nature of a Noun or Substantive, that the best Grammarians have called it sometimes Ὄνομα ῥηματικὸν, A VERBAL NOUN; sometimes Ὄνομα ῥήματος, THE VERB'S NOUN. The Reason of this Appellation is in *Greek* more evident, from its taking the prepositive Article before it in all cases; τὸ γράφειν, τȣ̃ γράφειν, τῷ γράφειν. The same construction is not unknown in *English.*
Thus *Spencer,*

For not to have been dipt in Lethe *lake,*
Could save the Son of Thetis FROM TO DIE—

ἀπὸ τȣ̃ θανεῖν. In like manner we say, *He did it, to be rich,* where we must supply by an Ellipsis the Preposition, FOR. *He did it, for to be rich,* the same as if we had said, *He did it for gain*——ἕνεκα τȣ̃ πλȣτεῖν, ἕνεκα τȣ̃ κέρδȣς——in *French, pour s'enricher.* Even when we speak such Sentences, as the following, *I choose* TO PHILOSOPHIZE, *rather than* TO BE RICH, τὸ φιλοσοφεῖν βȣ́λομαι, ἤπερ τὸ πλȣτεῖν, the Infinitives are in nature as much Accusatives, as if we were to say, *I choose* PHILOSOPHY *rather than* RICHES, τὴν φιλο-

they held this alone to be the genuine
PHMA or VERB, a name, which they
denied to all the other Modes. Their reafoning was, they confidered the true verbal character to be contained *simple* and
unmixed in the *Infinitive only*. Thus the
Infinitives, Περιπαῖεῖν, *Ambulare*, *To walk*,
mean *simply* that energy, and *nothing more*.
The other Modes, befides expreffing this
energy, *fuperadd certain Affections*, which
refpect perfons and circumftances. Thus
Ambulo and *Ambula* mean not fimply *To
walk*, but mean, *I walk*, and, *Walk Thou*.
And

C. VIII.

Φιλοσοφίαν βάλομαι, ἥπερ τὸν πλᾶτον. Thus too
Prifcian, fpeaking of *Infinitives*—CURRERE *enim eft*
CURSUS; & SCRIBERE, SCRIPTURA; & LEGERE,
LECTIO. *Itaque frequentur & Nominibus adjunguntur,
& aliis cafualibus, more Nominum*; *ut Perfius*,

Sed pulcrum eft digito monftrari, & dicier, hic eft.

And foon after—*Cum enim dico*, BONUM EST LE-
GERE, *nihil aliud fignifico, nifi*, BONA EST LECTIO.
L. XVIII. p. 1130. See alfo *Apoll*. L. I. c. 8. *Gaza*
Gram. L. IV. Τὸ δὲ ἀπαρέμφατον, ὄνομά ἐςι ῥήμα-
τος κ. τ. λ.

C.VIII. And hence they are all of them resolvable into *the Infinitive, as their Prototype,* together with *some sentence or word, expressive of their proper Character. Ambulo, I walk;* that is, *Indico me ambulare, I declare myself to walk. Ambula, Walk Thou;* that is, *Impero te ambulare, I command thee to walk;* and so with the Modes of every other species. Take away therefore the *Assertion,* the *Command,* or whatever else gives *a Character* to any one of these Modes, and there remains nothing more than THE MERE INFINITIVE, which (as *Priscian* says) *significat ipsam rem, quam continet Verbum* (*k*).

THE

(*k*) See *Apollon.* L. III. 13. Καθόλυ παν παρηγμένου ἀπό τινος κ. τ. λ. See also *Gaza,* in the note before. *Igitur a Constructione quoque* Vim rei Verborum (*id est, Nominis, quod significat ipsam rem*) *habere* INFINITIVUM *possumus dignoscere;* res autem in Personas distributa *facit* alios verbi motus.—*Itaque omnes modi in hunc, id est,* Infinitivum, *transumuntur sive* resolvuntur. *Prisc.* L. XVIII. p. 1131. From these Principles *Apollonius* calls the Infinitive Ῥῆμα γενικώτατον, and *Priscian,* Verbum generale.

THE application of this Infinitive is C.VIII. somewhat singular. It *naturally coalesces* with all those Verbs, that denote any *Tendence, Desire,* or *Volition of the Soul,* but not readily with others. Thus it is sense as well as syntax, to say βέλομαι ζῆν, *Cupio vivere, I desire to live;* but not to say Ἐσθίω ζῆν, *Edo vivere,* or even in *English, I eat to live,* unless by an Ellipsis, instead of *I eat for to live;* as we say ἕνεκα τȣ̃ ζῆν, or *pour vivre.* The reason is, that though *different Actions* may unite in the *same Subject,* and therefore be coupled together (as when we say, *He walked and discoursed)* yet the Actions notwithstanding remain separate and distinct. But it is not so with respect to *Volitions,* and *Actions.* Here the coalescence is often so intimate, that *the Volition* is unintelligible, till *the Action* be exprest. *Cupio, Volo, Desidero—I desire, I am willing, I want—*What?—The sentences, we see, are defective and imperfect.

We

We must help them then by *Infinitives*, C.VIII. which express the proper Actions to which they tend. *Cupio legere, Volo discere, Desidero videre, I desire to read, I am willing to live, I want to see.* Thus is the whole rendered complete, as well in sentiment, as in syntax *(l)*.

AND so much for MODES, and their several SPECIES. We are to attempt to denominate them according to their most eminent characters, it may be done in the following manner. As every necessary truth, and every demonstrative syllogism (which last is no more than a combination of such truths) must always be exprest under positive assertions, and as positive

---

(l) Priscian calls these Verbs, which naturally precede Infinitives, *Verba Voluntativa*; they are called in Greek Προαιρετικά. See L. XVIII. 1129. but more particularly see *Apolonius*, L. III. c. 13. where this whole doctrine is explained with great Accuracy. See also *Macrobius de Diff. Verb. Gr. & Lat. p.* 685. *Ed. Var.*

—*Nec omne* ἀπαρέμφατον *cuicunque Verbo,* &c,

BOOK THE FIRST.

fitive affertions only belong to the *Indi-* C.VIII, *cative,* we may denominate it for that reafon the MODE OF SCIENCE (*m*). Again, as the *Potential* is only converfant about *Contingents,* of which we cannot fay with certainty that they will happen or not, we may call this Mode, THE MODE OF CONJECTURE. Again, as thofe that are ignorant and would be informed, muft afk of thofe that already know, this being the natural way of becoming *Proficients;* hence we may call the *Interrogative,* THE MODE OF PROFICIENCY.

> *Inter cuncta leges, &* PERCONTABERE
> *doctos,*
> *Quâ ratione queas traducere leniter ævum,*
> *Quid purè tranquillet,* &c.   Hor.

Farther ftill, as the higheft and moft excellent ufe of the *Requifitive* Mode is legiflative

---

(*m*) *Ob nobilitatem præivit* INDICATIVUS, *folus Modus aptus Scientiis, folus Pater Veritatis.* Scal. de Cauf. L. Lat. c. 116.   2

C.VIII. giflative command, we may ftile it for this reafon THE MODE OF LEGISLATURE. *Ad Divos adeunto cafle*, fays *Cicero* in the character of a *Roman* law-giver; *Be it therefore enacted*, fay the laws of *England*; and in the fame *Mode* fpeak the *laws* of every other nation. It is alfo in this *Mode* that the geometrician, with the authority of a legiflator, orders lines to be bifected, and circles defcribed, as preparatives to that fcience, which he is about to eftablifh.

THERE are other *fuppofed* affections of Verbs, fuch as *Number* and *Perfon*. But thefe furely cannot be called a part of their effence, nor indeed are they the effence of any other Attribute, being in fact the properties, not of Attributes, but of Subftances. The moft that can be faid, is, that Verbs in the more elegant languages are provided with certain terminations, which refpect the *Number* and *Perfon* of every *Subftantive*, that we may know

know with more precision, in a complex C.VIII. sentence, each particular substance, with its attendant verbal Attributes. The same may be said of *Sex*, with respect to Adjectives. They have terminations which vary, as they respect Beings male or female, tho' *Substances* past dispute are alone susceptible of sex (*n*). We therefore pass over these matters, and all of like kind,

as

(*n*) It is somewhat extraordinary, that so acute and rational a Grammarian as *Sanctius*, should justly deny *Genders*, or the distinction of Sex to *Adjectives*, and yet make *Persons* appertain, not to *Substantives*, but to *Verbs*. His commentator *Perizonius* is much more consistent, who says—*At vero si rem recte consideres, ipsis Nominibus & Pronominibus vel maxime, imò unicè inest ipsa Persona; & Verba se habent in Personarum ratione ad Nomina planè sicuti Adjectiva in ratione Generum ad Substantiva, quibus solis autor* (Sanctius scil. L. I. c. 7.) *& rectè Genus adscribit, exclusis Adjectivis.* Sanct. Minerv. L. I. c. 12. There is indeed an exact Analogy between the Accidents of *Sex* and *Person*. There are but two *Sexes*, that is to say, the Male and the Female; and but two *Persons* (or Characters essential to discourse) that is to say, the Speaker, and the Party addressed. The third Sex and third Person are improperly so called, being in fact but Negations of the other two.

C. VIII. as being rather among the elegancies, than the essentials (*o*) of language, which essentials are the subject of our present inquiry. The principal of these now remaining is THE DIEFERENCE OF VERBS, AS TO THEIR SEVERAL SPECIES, which we endeavour to explain in the following manner.

(*o*) Whoever would see more upon a subject of importance, referred to in many parts of this treatise, and particularly in note (*h*) of this chapter, may consult *Letters concerning Mind*, an Octavo Volume published 1750, the Author Mr. *John Petvin Vicar of Ilsington in Devon*, a person who, though from his retired situation little known, was deeply skilled in the Philosophy both of the Antients and Moderns, and, more than this, was valued by all that knew him for his virtue and worth.

CHAP. IX.

Concerning the Species of Verbs, and their other remaining Properties.

ALL Verbs, that are strictly so called, denote (a) Energies. Now as all Energies are *Attributes*, they have reference of course to certain *energizing Substances.* Thus it is impossible there should be such Energies, as *To love, to fly, to wound,* &c. if there were not such beings as *Men, Birds, Swords,* &c. Farther, every Energy doth not only require an Energizer, but is necessarily conversant about some *Subject.* For example, if we say, *Brutus loves*—we must needs supply—loves *Cato, Cassius,*

(a) We use this word ENERGY, rather than *Motion*, from its more comprehensive meaning; it being a sort of Genus, which includes within it both *Motion* and its *Privation.* See before, p. 94, 95.

Ch. IX. *Caſſius, Portia,* or ſome one. *The Sword wounds*—i. e. wounds *Hector, Sarpedon, Priam,* or ſome one. And thus is it, that every Energy is neceſſarily ſituate between two Subſtantives, an Energizer which is *active,* and a Subject which is *paſſive.* Hence then, if the Energizer lead the ſentence, the Energy follows its character, and becomes what we call A VERB ACTIVE.—Thus we ſay *Brutus amat, Brutus loves.* On the contrary, if the paſſive Subject be principal, it follows the character of this too, and then becomes what we call A VERB PASSIVE.—Thus we ſay, *Portia amatur, Portia is loved.* It is in like manner that the *ſame Road* between the ſummit and foot of the ſame mountain, with reſpect to the ſummit is *Aſcent,* with reſpect to the foot is *Deſcent.* Since then every Energy reſpects an Energizer or a paſſive Subject; hence the Reaſon why every Verb, whether active or paſſive, has in language a neceſſary reference

ference to some *Noun* for its *Nominative* Ch.IX.
Case (*b*).

But to proceed still farther from what has been already observed. *Brutus loved Portia.*—Here *Brutus* is the Energizer; *loved,* the *Energy,* and *Portia,* the *Subject.* But it might have been, *Brutus loved Cato,* or *Cassius,* or the *Roman Republic*; for the Energy is referable to Subjects infinite. Now among these infinite Subjects, when that happens to occur, which is the Energizer also, as when we say *Brutus* loved *himself,* slew *himself,* &c. in such Case *the Energy* hath to the *same* being *a double Relation,* both active and passive. And this it is which gave rise
among

(*b*) The doctrine of Imperfonal Verbs has been justly rejected by the best Grammarians, both antient and modern. See *Sanct. Min.* L. I. c. 12 L. III c. 1. L. IV. c. 3. *Priscian.* L. XVIII. p. 1134. *Apoll* L. III. sub fin. In which places the reader will see a proper Nominative supplied to all Verbs of this supposed Character.

Ch. IX. among the *Greeks* to that species of Verbs, called VERBS MIDDLE (*c*), and such was their true and original use, however in many instances they may have since happened to deviate. In other languages the Verb still retains its active Form, and the passive Subject *(se* or *himself)* is expressed like other accusatives.

AGAIN, in some Verbs it happens that the Energy *always keeps within* the Energizer, and *never passes out* to any foreign extraneous Subject. Thus when we say, *Cæsar walketh, Cæsar sitteth,* it is impossible

---

(*c*) Τὰ γὰρ καλέμενα μεσότητος σχήματα συνέμπλω-σιν ἀνεδέξατο ἐνεργετικῆς κὴ παθητικῆς διαθέσεως. *The Verbs, called Verbs middle, admit a Coincidence of the active and passive Character.* Apollon. L. III. c. 7. He that would see this whole Doctrine concerning the power of THE MIDDLE VERB explained and confirmed with great Ingenuity and Learning, may consult a small Treatise of that able Critic *Kuster*, entitled, *De vero Usu Verborum Mediorum.* A neat edition of this scarce piece has been lately published.

BOOK THE FIRST. 177

ble *the Energy should pass out* (as in the case of those Verbs called by the Grammarians VERBS TRANSITIVE) because both the *Energizer* and the *Passive Subject* are united in *the same Person*. For what is the cause of this walking or sitting?—It is the *Will* and *Vital Powers* belonging to *Cæsar*. And what is the Subject, made so to move or to sit?—— It is the *Body* and *Limbs* belonging also to the same *Cæsar*. It is this then forms that species of Verbs, which grammarians have thought fit to call VERBS NEUTER, as if indeed they were void both of *Action* and *Passion*, when perhaps (like Verbs middle) they may be rather said *to imply both*. Not however to dispute about names, as these Neuters *in their Energizer* always discover *their passive Subject* (c), which other

Ch. IX.

(c) This Character of Neuters the *Greeks* very happily express by the Terms, 'Αυτοπάθεια and 'Ιδιοπάθεια, which *Priscian* renders, *quæ ex se in scipsâ sit intrinsecus Passio*. L. VIII. 790. *Consentii Ars apud Putsch.* p. 2051.

N   It

Ch. IX. other Verbs cannot, their paſſive Subjects being infinite; hence the reaſon why it is as ſuperfluous in theſe Neuters to have the Subject expreſſed, as in other Verbs it is neceſſary, and cannot be omitted. And thus it is that we are taught in common grammars

---

It may be here obſerved, that even thoſe Verbs, called *Actives*, can upon occaſion lay aſide their tranſitive character; that is to ſay, can drop their ſubſequent Accuſative, and *aſſume the Form of Neuters*, ſo as to ſtand by themſelves. This happens, when the Diſcourſe reſpects the mere *Energy* or *Affection* only, and has no regard to the Subject, be it this thing or that. Thus we ſay, ἐκ οἶδεν ἀναγινώσκειν ὗτος, *This Man knows not how to read*, ſpeaking only of the Energy, in which we ſuppoſe him deficient. Had the Diſcourſe been upon the Subjects of reading, we muſt have added them. ἐκ οἶδεν ἀναγινώσκειν τὰ Ὁμήρε, *He knows not how to read Homer*, or *Virgil*, or *Cicero*, &c.

Thus *Horace*,

Qui CUPIT *aut* METUIT, *juvat illum ſic domus aut res,*
Ut lippum pictæ tabulæ——

He that DESIRES *or* FEARS (not this thing in particular nor that, but in general he within whoſe breaſt theſe

mars that *Verbs Active require an Accu-* Ch. IX. *sative,* while *Neuters require none.*

OF the above species of Verbs, the *Middle* cannot be called necessary, because most languages have done without it. THE SPECIES OF VERBS therefore remaining are the ACTIVE, the PASSIVE and the NEUTER, and those seem essential to all languages whatever (*d*).

---

these affections prevail) *has the same joy in a House or Estate, as the Man with bad Eyes has in fine Pictures.* So *Cæsar* in his celebrated *Laconic* Epistle of, VENI, VIDI, VICI, where two Actives we see follow one Neuter in the same detached Form, as that Neuter itself. The Glory it seems was *in the rapid Sequel of the Events.* Conquest came as quick, as he could come himself, and look about him. *Whom* he saw, and *whom* he conquered, was not the thing, of which he boasted. See *Apoll.* L. III. c. 31. p. 279.

(*d*) The STOICS, in their logical view of Verbs, as making part in Propositions, considered them under the four following Sorts.

When

Ch. IX. THERE remains a remark or two farther, and then we quit the Subject of Verbs. It is true in general that the greater part of them denote Attributes of *Energy*

When a *Verb*, co-inciding with the *Nominative of some Noun*, made *without farther help* a perfect assertive Sentence, as Σωκράτης περιπατεῖ, *Socrates walketh*; then as the Verb in such case implied the Power of a perfect Predicate, they called it for that reason Κατηγόρημα, a *Predicable*; or else, from its readiness συμ-Εαίνειν, *to co-incide with its Noun in completing the Sentence*, they called it Σύμβαμα, a *Co-incider*.

When a *Verb* was able with a *Noun* to form a perfect assertive Sentence, yet could not associate with such Noun, but under some *oblique Case*, as Σωκράτει μεταμέλει, *Socratem pœnitet*: Such a Verb, from its *near approach to just Co-incidence, and Predication,* they called Παρασύμβαμα or Παρακατηγόρημα.

When a Verb, though regularly co-inciding with a Noun in its Nominative, *still required*, to complete the Sentiment, *some other Noun under an oblique Case*, as Πλάτων φιλεῖ Δίωνα, *Plato loveth Dio*, (where without *Dio* or some other, the Verb *loveth* would rest indefinite:)

Energy and *Motion*. But there are some **Ch.IX.** which appear to denote nothing more, than a *mere simple Adjective*, joined to an Assertion, Thus ἰσάζει in *Greek*, and *Equalleth* in *English*, mean nothing more than

---

nite:) Such Verb, from this Defect they called ἧττον ἢ σύμβαμα, or ἢ κατηγόρημα, *something less than a Co-incider, or less than a Predicable*.

Lastly, when a Verb required *two Nouns in oblique Cases*, to render the Sentiment complete; as when we say Σωκράτει Ἀλκιβιάδης μέλει, *Tædet me Vitæ*, or the like: Such Verb they called ἧττον, or ἔλαττον ἢ παρασύμβαμα, or ἢ παρακατηγόρημα. *something less than an imperfect Co-incider, or an imperfect Predicable*.

These were the *Appellations* which they gave to Verbs, when employed along with Nouns to the forming of Propositions. As to the Name of ῬΗΜΑ, or VERB, they denied it to them all, giving it only to the *Infinitive*, as we have shewn already. See page 164. See also *Ammon. in Lib. de Interpret.* p. 37. *Apollon. de Syntaxi* L. I. c. 8. L. III. c. 31. p. 279. c. 32. p. 295. *Theod. Gaz. Gram.* L. IV.

From the above Doctrine it appears, that all *Verbs Neuter* are Συμβάματα; *Verbs Active*, ἥττονα ἢ συμβάματα.

Ch. IX. than ἴσός ἐςι, *is equal.* So *Albeo* in *Latin* is no more than *albus sum.*

—*Campique ingentes ossibus albent.* Virg.

THE same may be said of *Tumeo. Mons tumet,* i. e. *tumidus est, is tumid.* To express the Energy in these instances, we must have recourse to the Inceptives.

Fluctus uti primo cœpit cum ALBESCERE *Vento.* Virg.

—— —— *Freta ponti Incipiunt agitata* TUMESCERE. ' Virg.

THERE are Verbs also to be found, which are formed out of Nouns. So that as in *Abstract Nouns* (such as *Whiteness* from *White, Goodness* from *Good)* as also in the *Infinitive Modes* of Verbs, *the Attributive is converted into a Substantive;* here *the Substantive on the contrary is converted into an Attributive.* Such are Κυνίζειν from κύων, *to act the part of a Dog,* or *be a Cynic;*

nic; Φιλιππίζειν from Φίλιππ⊙-, *to Philip-pize*, or *favour Philip*; *Syllaturire* from *Sylla*, to *meditate acting the same part as Sylla did.* Thus too the wife and virtuous Emperour, by way of counsel to himself—ὅρα μὴ ἀποκαισαρωθῇς, *beware thou beest not* BECÆSAR'D; as though he said, *Beware, that by being Emperor thou dost not dwindle into* A MERE CÆSAR (*e*). In like manner one of our own witty Poets,

STERNHOLD *himself he* OUT-STERN-HOLDED.

And long before him the facetious *Fuller*, speaking of one *Morgan*, a sanguinary Bishop in the Reign of Queen *Mary*, says of him, *that he* OUT-BONNER'D *even* BONNER *himself**.

AND so much for that Species of ATTRIBUTES, called VERBS IN THE STRICTEST SENSE.

(*e*) *Marc. Antonin.* L. VI. § 30.
* *Church Hist.* B. VIII. p. 21.

CHAP. X.

Concerning thofe other Attributives, Participles and Adjectives.

Ch. X. THE nature of Verbs being underſtood, that of PARTICIPLES is no way difficult. Every complete Verb is expreſſive of an *Attribute*; *of Time*; and of *an Aſſertion*. Now if we take away the *Aſſertion*, and thus deſtroy the *Verb*, there will remain the *Attribute* and the *Time*, which make the eſſence of a PARTICIPLE. Thus take away the Aſſertion from the Verb, Γράφει, *Writeth*, and there remains the Participle, Γράφων, *Writing*, which (without the *Aſſertion*) denotes the *ſame Attribute*, and *the ſame Time*. After the ſame manner, *by withdrawing the Aſſertion*, we diſcover Γράψας in Ἔγραψε, Γράψων in Γράψει, for we chuſe to refer to the *Greek*, as being of all languages

the

the moſt complete, as well in this reſpect, Ch. X.
as in others.

AND ſo much for PARTICIPLES (*a*).

THE

(*a*) The *Latins* are defective in this Article of Par‑
ticiples. Their Active Verbs, ending in *or*, (com‑
monly called Deponents) have Active Participles of all
Times (ſuch as *Loquens*, *Locutus*, *Locuturus*) but none
of the Paſſive. Their Actives ending in *O*, have Par‑
ticiples of the Preſent and Future (ſuch as *Scribens*, and
Scripturus) but none of the Paſt. On the contrary,
their Paſſives have Participles of the Paſt (ſuch as *Scrip‑
tus*) but none of the Preſent or Future, unleſs we ad‑
mit ſuch as *Scribendus* and *Docendus* for Futures, which
Grammarians controvert. The want of theſe Partici‑
ples they ſupply by a Periphraſis—for γράψας they ſay,
cum ſcripſiſſet—for γραφόμενος, *dum ſcribitur*, &c. In
Engliſh we have ſometimes recourſe to the ſame Peri‑
phraſis ; and ſometimes we avail ourſelves of the ſame
Auxiliars, which form our Modes and Tenſes.

The *Engliſh* Grammar lays down a good rule with
reſpect to its Participles of the Paſt, that they all ter‑
minate in D, T, or N. This Analogy is perhaps lia‑
ble to as few Exceptions, as any. Conſidering there‑
fore how little Analogy of any kind we have in our
Lan‑

Ch. X. THE nature of *Verbs* and *Participles* being underſtood, that of ADJECTIVES becomes eaſy. A *Verb* implies (as we have ſaid) both an *Attribute*, and *Time*, and an *Aſſertion*; a *Participle* only implies an *Attribute*, and *Time*; and an ADJECTIVE only implies an *Attribute*; that is to ſay, in other Words, an ADJECTIVE *has no Aſſertion, and only denotes ſuch an Attribute, as has not its eſſence either in Motion or its Privation.* Thus in general the Attributes of quantity, quality, and relation (ſuch as *many* and *few*, *great* and *little*,

---

Language, it ſeems wrong to annihilate the few Traces, that may be found. It would be well therefore, if all writers, who endeavour to be accurate, would be careful to avoid a corruption, at preſent ſo prevalent, of ſaying, *it was wrote*, for, *it was written*; *he was drove*, for, *he was driven*; *I have went*, for, *I have gone*, &c. in all which inſtances a Verb is abſurdly uſed to ſupply the proper Participle, without any neceſſity from the want of ſuch Word.

Ch. X.

little, black and *white, good* and *bad, dou-ble, treble, quadruple,* &c.) are all denoted by ADJECTIVES.

IT muſt indeed be confeſſed, that ſometimes even thoſe Attributes, which are wholly foreign to the idea of *Motion*, aſſume an aſſertion, and appear as Verbs. Of ſuch we gave inſtances before, in *albeo, tumeo,* ἰσάζω, and others. Theſe however, compared to the reſt of Verbs, are but few in number, and may be called, if thought proper, *Verbal Adjectives.* It is in like manner, that Participles inſenſibly paſs too into Adjectives. Thus *doctus* in *Latin*, and *learned* in *Engliſh* loſe their power, as *Participles*, and mean a Perſon poſſeſſed of an habitual Quality. Thus *Vir eloquens* means not *a man now ſpeaking*, but a man, *who poſſeſſes the habit of ſpeaking*, whether he ſpeak or no. So when we ſay in *Engliſh*, he is a *thinking* Man, an *underſtanding* Man, we mean not a perſon, whoſe mind is *in actual Energy,*

Ch. X. *Energy,* but whofe *mind is enriched with a larger portion of thofe powers.* It is indeed no wonder, as all Attributives are homogeneous, that at times the feveral fpecies fhould appear to interfere, and the difference between them be fcarcely perceptible. Even in *natural* fpecies, which are congenial and of kin, the fpecific difference is not always to be difcerned, and in appearance at leaft they feem to run into each other.

WE have fhewn already (b) in the Inftances of Φιλιππίζειν, *Syllaturire,* Ἀποκαισαρωθῆναι, and others, how *Subftantives* may be transformed into *Verbal Attributives.* We fhall now fhew, how they may be converted into *Adjectives.* When we fay the party of *Pompey,* the ftile of *Cicero,* the philofophy of *Socrates,*
in

(b) Sup. p. 182, 183.

in thefe cafes the party, the ftile, and the philofophy fpoken of, receive a ftamp and character from the perfons, whom they refpect. Thofe perfons therefore perform the part of Attributes, that is, ftamp and characterize their refpective Subjects. Hence then *they actually pafs into Attributes*, and affume, as fuch, the form of *Adjectives*. And thus it is we fay, the *Pompeian* party, the *Ciceronian* ftile, and the *Socratic* philofophy. It is in like manner for a trumpet *of Brafs*, we fay a *brazen* Trumpet; for a Crown *of Gold*, a *golden* Crown, &c. Even *Pronominal* Subftantives admit the like mutation. Thus inftead of faying, the Book *of Me*, *of Thee*, and *of Him*, we fay *My* Book, *Thy* Book, and *His* Book; inftead of faying the Country *of Us*, *of You*, and *of Them*, we fay, *Our* Country, *Your* Country, and *Their* Country, which Words may be called fo many *Pronominal Adjectives*.

I T

Ch. X. It has been obferved already, and muft needs be obvious to all, that Adjectives, as marking Attributes, can have no fex (c). And yet their having terminations conformable to the fex, number, and cafe of their Subftantive, feems to have led grammarians into that ftrange abfurdity of ranging them with Nouns, and feparating them from Verbs, tho' with refpect to thefe they are perfectly homogeneous; with refpect to the others, quite contrary. They are homogeneous with refpect to Verbs, as both forts denote *Attributes*; they are heterogeneous with refpect to Nouns, as *never properly denoting Subftances*. But of this we have fpoken before (d).

(c) Sup. p. 171.
(d) Sup. C. VI. Note (a). See alfo C. III. p. 28, &c.

The Attributives hitherto treated, that Ch. X.
is to fay, VERBS, PARTICIPLES, and
ADJECTIVES, may be called ATTRIBU-
TIVES OF THE FIRST ORDER. The
reafon of this name will be better underftood, when we have more fully dif-
cuffed ATTRIBUTIVES OF THE SECOND
ORDER, to which we now proceed in the
following chapter.

CHAP. XI.

Concerning Attributives of the second Order.

Ch.XI. AS the Attributives hitherto mentioned denote *the Attributes of Substances,* so there is an inferior class of them, which denote *the Attributes only of Attributes.*

To explain by examples in either kind —when we say, *Cicero and Pliny were both of them eloquent; Statius and Virgil both of them wrote;* in these instances the Attributives, *eloquent,* and *wrote,* are immediately referable to the substantives, *Cicero, Virgil,* &c. As therefore denoting THE ATTRIBUTES OF SUBSTANCES, we call them ATTRIBUTIVES OF THE FIRST ORDER. But when we say *Pliny was moderately eloquent, but Cicero exceedingly eloquent; Statius wrote indifferently, but Virgil wrote admirably;*

in

BOOK THE FIRST.

in thefe inftances, the Attributives, *Mo-* Ch. XI. *derately, Exceedingly, Indifferently, Admirably,* are not referable to *Subflantives,* but to *other Attributives,* that is, to the words, *Eloquent,* and *Wrote.* As therefore denoting *Attributes of Attributes,* we call them ATTRIBUTIVES OF THE SECOND ORDER.

GRAMMARIANS have given them the Name of 'Επιρρήματα, ADVERBIA, ADVERBS. And indeed if we take the word Ῥῆμα, or, *Verb,* in its moſt *comprehenſive Signification,* as including not only *Verbs properly ſo called,* but alſo *Participles* and *Adjectives* [an uſage, which may be juſtified by the beſt authorities (*a*)] we ſhall find

---

(*a*) Thus *Ariſtotle* in his Treatiſe *de Interpretatione,* inſtances Ἄνθρωπος as *a Noun,* and Λεῦκος as *a Verb.* So *Ammonius*—κατὰ τᾶτο τὸ σημαινόμενον, τὸ μὲν ΚΑΛΟΣ κὰ ΔΙΚΑΙΟΣ κὰ ὅσα τοιαῦτα—ῬΗΜΑΤΑ λέγεσθαι κὰ ἐκ ΟΝΟΜΑΤΑ. *According to this Signification* (that is of denoting the Attributes of Subſtance

O and

Ch. XI. find the name, Επίῤῥημα, or ADVERB, to be a very juſt appellation, as denoting A PART OF SPEECH, THE NATURAL APPENDAGE OF VERBS. So great is this dependence in Grammatical Syntax, that an *Adverb* can no more ſubſiſt without its *Verb*, than a *Verb* can ſubſiſt without its *Subſtantive*. It is the ſame here, as in certain natural Subjects. Every Colour for its exiſtence as much requires a Superficies, as the Superficies for its exiſtence requires a ſolid Body (*b*).

AMONG

---

and the Predicate in Propoſitions) *the words*, FAIR, JUST, *and the like*, *are called* VERBS, *and not* NOUNS. *Am. in libr. de Interp.* p. 37. b. *Ariſt. de Interp.* L. I. c. 1. See alſo of this Treatiſe, c. 6. Note (*a*) p. 87.

In the ſame manner the *Stoics* talked of the Participle. *Nam* PARTICIPIUM *connumerantes Verbis*, PARTICIPIALE VERBUM *vocabant vel* CASUALE. *Priſcian.* L. I. p. 574.

(*b*) This notion *of ranging the Adverb under the ſame Genus with the Verb* (by calling them both Attributives) and *of explaining it to be the Verb's Epithet or Adjective*
(by

Ch. XI. AMONG the Attributes of Substance are reckoned Quantities, and Qualities. Thus we say, *a white Garment, a high Mountain.* Now some of these Quantities and Qualities are capable of Intension, and Remission. Thus we say, *a Garment* EXCEEDINGLY *white; a Mountain* TOLERABLY *high,*

(by calling it the Attributive of an Attributive) is conformable to the best authorities. *Theodore Gaza* defines an ADVERB, as follows—μέρος λόγε ἄπίωτον, κατὰ ῥήματος λεγόμενον, ἢ ἐπιλεγόμενον ῥήματι, ἢ οἷον ἐπίθετον ῥήματος. *A Part of Speech devoid of Cases, predicated of a Verb, or subjoined to it, and being as it were the Verb's Adjective.* L. IV. (where by the way we may observe, how properly the Adverb is made an *Aptote*, since its principal sometimes *has* cases, as in *Valdè Sapiens*; sometimes *has none*, as in *Valdè amat.*) *Priscian*'s definition of an Adverb is as follows—ADVERBIUM *est pars orationis indeclinabilis, cujus significatio Verbis adjicitur. Hæc enim perficit Adverbium Verbis additum, quod adjectiva nomina appellativis nominibus adjuncta*; *ut* prudens *homo*; prudenter *egit*; felix *Vir*; feliciter *vivit.* L. XV. p. 1003. And before, speaking of the *Stoics*, he says—*Etiam* ADVERBIA *Nominibus vel* VERBIS CONNUMERABANT, *&* quasi ADJECTIVA VERBORUM *nominabant.* L. I. p. 574. See also *Apoll. de Synt.* L. I. c. 3. *sub fin.*

Ch. XI. *high*, or MODERATELY *high*. It is plain therefore that Intenſion and Remiſſion are among the Attributes of ſuch Attributes. Hence then one copious Source of ſecondary Attributives, or Adverbs, to denote theſe two, that is, *Intenſion*, and *Remiſſion*. The *Greeks* have their θαυμαϛῶς, μάλιϛα, πάνυ, ἥκιϛα; the *Latins* their *valdè, vehementer, maximè, ſatis, mediocriter*; the *Engliſh* their *greatly, vaſtly, extremely, ſufficiently, moderately, tolerably, indifferently*, &c.

FARTHER than this, where there are different Intenſions of the ſame Attribute, they may be *compared* together. Thus if the Garment A be EXCEEDINGLY *White*, and the Garment B be MODERATELY *White*, we may ſay, *the Garment A is* MORE *white than the Garment B*.

IN theſe inſtances the Adverb MORE not only denotes Intenſion, but *relative Intenſion*. Nay we ſtop not here. We not

not only denote Intenſion *merely relative* Ch.XI.
but *relative Intenſion, than which there is*
none greater. Thus we not only ſay *the*
Mountain A is MORE *high than the Moun-*
tain B, but that *it is the* MOST *high of all*
Mountains. Even *Verbs, properly ſo called,*
as they admit *ſimple* Intenſions, ſo they
admit alſo theſe *comparatives* ones. Thus
in the following Example———*Fame he*
LOVETH MORE *than Riches, but Virtue of*
all things he LOVETH MOST—the Words
MORE and MOST denote the different *com-*
parative Intenſions of the Verbal Attributive, *Loveth.*

AND hence the riſe of COMPARISON,
and of its different *Degrees;* which cannot well be more, than the two Species
above mentioned, one to denote *Simple*
Exceſs, and one to *denote Superlative.*
Were we indeed to introduce *more* degrees
than theſe, we ought perhaps to introduce
infinite, which is abſurd. For why ſtop
at a limited Number, when in all ſubjects,

Ch. XI. fufceptible of Intenfion, the intermediate Exceffes are in a manner infinite? There are infinite Degrees of *more* White, between the *firſt Simple White*, and the *Superlative, Whiteſt*; the fame may be faid of *more* Great, *more* Strong, *more* Minute, &c. The Doctrine of Grammarians about *three* fuch Degrees, which they call the Pofitive, the Comparative and the Superlative, muſt needs be abfurd; both becauſe in their Pofitive there is † no Comparifon at all, and becauſe their *Superlative* is a Comparative, as much as their *Comparative* itſelf. Examples to evince this may be found every where. *Socrates was the* MOST WISE *of all the Athenians*—*Homer was the* MOST SUBLIME *of all Poets*.—

—*Cadit et Ripheus,* JUSTISSIMUS UNUS
Qui fuit in Teucris— Virg.

IT

---

† *Qui (ſcil. Gradus Poſitivis) quoniam perfectus eſt, a quibuſdam in numero Graduum non computatur.* Confentii Ars apud Putſch. p. 2022.

It must be confessed these Comparatives, Ch. XI. as well the *simple*, as the *superlative*, seem sometimes to part with their *relative* Nature, and only retain their *intensive*. Thus in the Degree, denoting *simple* Excess,

Tristior, *et lacrumis oculos suffusa nitentes.*   Virg.
Rusticior *paulo est—*   Hor.

In the *Superlative* this is more usual. *Vir doctissimus, Vir fortissimus, a most learned Man, a most brave Man,*—that is to say, not the *bravest* and *most learned* Man, that ever existed, but a Man possessing those Qualities *in an eminent Degree.*

The Authors of Language have contrived a method to retrench these Comparative Adverbs, by expressing their force in the Primary Attributive. Thus instead of *More fair,* they say Fairer; instead of *Most fair,* Fairest, and the same holds

Ch. XI. true both in the *Greek* and *Latin*. This Practice however has reached no farther than to *Adjectives*, or at least to *Participles*, sharing the nature of *Adjectives*. Verbs perhaps were thought too much diversified already, to admit more Variations without perplexity.

As there are some Attributives, which admit of Comparison, so there are others, which admit of none. Such for example are those, which denote *that Quality of Bodies arising from their Figure*; as when we say, a *Circular* Table, a *Quadrangular* Court, a *Conical* Piece of Metal, &c. The reason is, that a million of things, participating the same Figure, participate it *equally*, if they participate it at all. To say therefore that while A and B are both quadrangular, A is *more* or *less* quadrangular than B, is absurd. The same holds true in all Attributives, denoting *definite Quantities*, whether *continuous* or *discrete*, whether *absolute* or *relative*. Thus the *two-foot* Rule

A

A cannot be *more a two-foot* Rule, than any other of the same length. *Twenty* Lions cannot be *more twenty*, than *twenty* Flies. If A and B be both *triple,* or *quadruple* to C, they cannot be *more triple,* or *more quadruple,* one than the other. The reason of all this is, there can be *no Comparison* without *Intension and Remission;* there can be no Intension and Remission in things *always definite;* and such are the Attributives, which we have last mentioned.

In the same reasoning we see the cause, why *no Substantive is susceptible of these Comparative Degrees.* A *Mountain* cannot be said MORE TO BE, or TO EXIST, than a *Mole-hill,* but the *More* and *Less* must be sought for in their Quantities. In like manner, when we refer many Individuals to one Species, the Lion A cannot be called *more a Lion,* than the Lion B, but if more any thing, he is *more fierce, more speedy,* or exceeding in some such Attribute. So again, in referring many Species to one

Genus,

Ch. XI. Genus, a Crocodile is not more an Animal, than a Lizard; nor a Tiger, more than a Cat, but if any thing, they are *more bulky, more strong*, &c. the Excefs, as before, being derived from their Attributes. So true is that faying of the acute *Stagirite—that* SUBSTANCE *is not fufceptible of* MORE *and* LESS (*c*). But this by way of digreffion, to return to the fubject of Adverbs.

OF the Adverbs, or fecondary Attributives already mentioned, thefe denoting Intenfion or Remiffion may be called Adverbs of *Quantity continuous*; *Once, Twice, Thrice*, are Adverbs of *Quantity difcrete*; *More* and *Moft, Lefs* and *Leaft*, to which may be added *Equally, Proportionally, &c.* are

---

(*c*) ἐκ ἂν ἐπιδέχοιτο ἡ ὐσία τὸ μᾶλλον κ᾽ τὸ ἧττον, *Categor.* c. 5. See alfo *Sanctius*, L. I. c. 11. L. II. c. 10, 11. where the fubject of Comparatives is treated in a very mafterly and philofophical manner. See alfo *Prifcian*, p. 598. *Derivantur igitur Comparativa a Nominibus Adjectivis*, &c.

BOOK THE FIRST. 203

are Adverbs of *Relation.* There are others Ch.XI.
of *Quality,* as when we fay, HONESTLY
induſtrious, PRUDENTLY *brave, they fought*
BRAVELY, *he painted* FINELY, a *Portico
formed* CIRCULARLY, *a Plain cut* TRI-
ANGULARLY, *&c.*

AND here it is worth while to obſerve, how the fame thing, participating the fame Eſſence, aſſumes different grammatical Forms from its different relations. For example, ſuppoſe it ſhould be aſked, how differ *Honeſt, Honeſtly,* and *Honeſty.* The Anſwer is, they are *in Eſſence* the fame, but they differ, in as much as *Honeſt* is the *Attributive of a Subſtantive; Honeſtly, of a Verb*; and *Honeſty,* being diveſted of theſe its attributive Relations, aſſumes *the Power of a Subſtantive,* ſo as to ſtand by itſelf.

THE Adverbs, hitherto mentioned, are common to *Verbs of every Species*; but there

Ch. XI. there are some, which are peculiar to *Verbs properly so called*, that is to say, to such as denote *Motion* or *Energy*, with their *Privations*. All MOTION and REST imply TIME and PLACE, as a kind of necessary *Coincidents*. Hence then, if we would express the *Place* or *Time* of either, we must needs have recourse to the proper Adverbs; *of Place*, as when we say, *he stood* THERE; *he went* HENCE; *he travelled* FAR, &c. of *Time*, as when we say, *he stood* THEN; *he went* AFTERWARD; *he travelled* FORMERLY, &c. Should it be asked——why *Adverbs of Time*, when Verbs have *Tenses?* The Answer is, tho' Tenses may be sufficient to denote the greater Distinctions of Time, yet to denote them all by Tenses would be a perplexity without end. What a variety of Forms, to denote *Yesterday, To-day, To-morrow, Formerly, Lately, Just now, Now, Immediately, Presently, Soon, Hereafter*, &c.? It was this then that made the

the *Temporal* Adverbs neceſſary, over and above the *Tenſes*.

To the Adverbs juſt mentioned may be added thoſe, which denote the *Intenſions and Remiſſions peculiar to Motion*, ſuch as *ſpeedily, haſtily, ſwiftly, ſlowly*, &c. as alſo *Adverbs of Place, made out of Prepoſitions*, ſuch as ἄνω and κάτω from ἀνὰ and κατὰ, in *Engliſh upward* and *downward*, from *up* and *down*. In ſome inſtances the Prepoſition ſuffers no change, but becomes an Adverb by nothing more than its Application, as when we ſay, CIRCA *equitat, he rides* ABOUT ; PROPE *cecidit, he was* NEAR *falling* ; *Verum ne* POST *conferas culpam in me, But do not* AFTER *lay the blame on me* (*d*).

THERE

(*d*) Soſip. Chariſii Inſt. Gram. p. 170. Terent. Eun. Act. II. Sc. 3.

Ch. XI. THERE are likewise *Adverbs of Interrogation*, such as *Where, Whence, Whither, How*; of which there is this remarkable, that when they lose their *Interrogative* power, they assume that of a *Relative*, so as even to represent the *Relative* or *Subjunctive Pronoun.* Thus *Ovid*

Et Seges est, UBI *Troja fuit—*

translated in our old *English* Ballad,

And Corn doth grow, WHERE *Troy town stood.*

That is to say, *Seges est in eo loco,* IN QUO *&c. Corn groweth in that place,* IN WHICH, *&c.* the power of the *Relative*, being implied in the *Adverb.* Thus *Terence*,

Hujusmodi mihi res semper comminiscere,
UBI *me excarnufices—* Heaut. IV. 6.

where UBI relates to *res,* and stands for *quibus rebus.*

IT

It is in like manner that the *Relative* Ch. XI.
Pronoun upon occasion becomes an *Interrogative*, at least in *Latin* and *English*.
Thus *Horace*,

Quem *Virum aut Heroa lyrâ, vel acri Tibiâ sumes celebrare, Clio?*

So *Milton*,

Who *first seduc'd them to that foul revolt?*

The reason of all this is as follows. *The Pronoun* and *Adverbs* here mentioned are all alike, in their original character, Relatives. Even when they become Interrogatives, they lose not this character, but are still Relatives, as much as ever. The difference is, that *without* an Interrogation, they have reference to a Subject, which is *antecedent, definite* and *known*; *with* an *Interrogation*, to a Subject which is *subsequent, indefinite,* and *unknown*, and
which

Ch. XI. which it is expected that *the Answer* should express and ascertain,

Who first seduc'd them?———

The very Question itself supposes a Seducer, to which, tho' *unknown*, the Pronoun, Who, has a *reference*.

Th' infernal Serpent———

Here in the *Answer* we have *the Subject, which was indefinite, ascertained*; so that the Who in the *Interrogation* is (we see) as much a *Relative*, as if it had been said originally, without any interrogation at all, *It was the Infernal* Serpent, who *first seduced them*.

And thus is it that *Interrogatives* and *Relatives* mutually pass into each other.

And so much for Adverbs, peculiar to Verbs properly so called. We have already spoken of those, which are common to all Attributives. We have likewise attempted

BOOK THE FIRST. 209

tempted to explain *their general Nature*, Ch. XI.
which we have found to confift in being
the Attributes of Attributes. There remains only to add, that ADVERBS *may be
derived from almoſt every Part of Speech*:
from PREPOSITIONS, as when from *After*
we derive *Afterwards*—from PARTICIPLES, and through thefe from *Verbs*, as
when from *Know* we derive *Knowing*, and
thence *Knowingly*; from *Scio*, *Sciens*, and
thence *Scienter*—from ADJECTIVES, as
when from Virtuous and Vicious, we derive
Virtuouſly and *Viciouſly*—from SUBSTANTIVES, as when from Πίθηκ☉, *an Ape*, we
derive Πιθήκειον βλέπειν, *to look* APISHLY;
from Λέων, *a Lion*, Λεον]ωδῶς, *Leoninely*—
nay even from PROPER NAMES, as when
from *Socrates* and *Demoſthenes*, we derive
Socratically and *Demoſthenically*. *It was
Socratically reaſoned*, we fay; *it was Demoſthenically ſpoken* *. Of the fame fort
P   are

---

* *Ariſtotle* has Κυκλοπικῶς *Cyclopically*, from Κύκλωψ
a Cyclops. Eth. Nic. X. 9.

Ch. XI. are many others, cited by the old Grammarians, such as *Catiliniter* from *Catilina*, *Sisenniter* from *Sisenna*, *Tullianè* from *Tullius*, &c. (*e*).

NOR are they thus extensive only in *Derivation*, but in *Signification* also. *Theodore Gaza* in his Grammar informs us (*f*), that ADVERBS may be found in every one of the Predicaments, and that the readiest way to reduce their Infinitude, was to refer them by classes to those ten universal Genera. The *Stoics* too called the ADVERB by the name of Πανδέκ]ης, and that from a view to the same *multiform Nature*. *Omnia in se capit quasi collata per satiram, concessâ sibi rerum variâ potestate.* It is thus that *Sosipater* explains the

---

(*e*) See *Prisc.* L. XV. p. 1022. *Sos. Charis.* 161. Edit. *Putschii.*

(*f*) —διὸ δὴ ϰ) ἄμεινον ἴσως δίϰα ϰ) τῶν ἐπιρρημάτων γένη θέσθαι ἐϰεῖνα, ἐσίαν, ποιὸν, ποσὸν, πρός τι, ϰ. τ. λ. Gram. Introd. L. II.

the Word (*g*), from whose authority we know it to be *Stoical*. But of this enough.

Ch.XI.

And now having finished those PRINCIPAL PARTS of Speech, the SUBSTANTIVE and the ATTRIBUTIVE, which are SIGNIFICANT WHEN ALONE, we proceed to those AUXILIARY PARTS, which are ONLY SIGNIFICANT, WHEN ASSOCIATED. But as these make the Subject of a Book by themselves, we here conclude the first Book of this Treatise.

(*g*) *Sosip. Char.* p. 175. Edit. *Putschii.*

HERMES

OR A PHILOSOPHICAL INQUIRY
CONCERNING UNIVERSAL GRAMMAR.

BOOK II.

CHAP. I.

Concerning Definitives.

WHAT remains of our Work, is a matter of lefs difficulty, it being the fame here, as in fome Hiftorical Picture; when the principal Figures are once formed, it is an eafy labour to defign the reft.

De-

Ch. I. DEFINITIVES, the Subject of the present Chapter, are commonly called by Grammarians, ARTICLES, ARTICULI, Ἄρθρα. They are of two kinds, either those *properly and strictly so called*, or else the *Pronominal Articles*, such as *This*, *That*, *Any*, &c.

WE shall first treat of those *Articles more strictly so denominated*, the reason and use of which may be explained, as follows.

THE visible and individual Substances of Nature are infinitely more numerous, than for each to admit of a particular Name. To supply this defect, when any Individual occurs, which either wants a proper Name, or whose proper Name is not known, we ascertain it, as well as we can, by referring it to its Species; or, if the Species be unknown, then at least

least to some Genus. For example—a certain Object occurs, with a head and limbs, and appearing to possess the powers of Self-motion and Sensation. If we know it not as an Individual, we refer it to its proper Species, and call it *Dog*, or *Horse*, or *Lion*, or the like. If none of these Names fit, we go to the Genus, and call it, *Animal*.

Ch. I.

BUT this is not enough. The Thing, at which we are looking, is neither a Species, nor a Genus. What is it then? An Individual.—Of what kind? *Known*, or *unknown*? Seen now *for the first time*, or *seen before*, and now remembered?—It is here we shall discover the use of the two Articles (A) and (THE). (A) respects our *primary* Perception, and denotes Individuals as *unknown*; (THE) respects our *secondary* Perception, and denotes Individuals as *known*. To explain by an example—I see an object pass by

Ch. I. by, which I never faw till now. What do I fay?—*There goes* A *Beggar with* A *long Beard.* The Man departs, and returns a week after. What do I fay then?—*There goes* THE *Beggar with* THE *long Beard.* The Article only is changed, the reft remains un-altered.

YET mark the force of this apparently minute Change. The Individual, *once vague,* is now recognized *as fomething known,* and that merely by the efficacy of this latter Article, which tacitly infinuates a kind of *previous* acquaintance, by referring the prefent Perception to a like Perception already paft (*a*).

THE Truth is, the Articles (A) and (THE) are both of them *definitives,* as they circumfcribe the latitude of Genera and Species, by reducing them for the moft

---

(*a*) See B. I. c. 5. p. 63, 64.

most part to denote Individuals. The difference however between them is this; the Article (A) leaves the Individual itself *unascertained,* whereas the Article (THE) *ascertains the Individual also,* and is for that reason the more accurate Definitive of the two.

IT is perhaps owing to the imperfect manner, in which the Article (A) defines, that the *Greeks* have no Article correspondent to it, but supply its place, by a negation of their Article, Ὁ. Ὁ ἄνθρωπ۞ ἔπεσεν, THE *man fell*—ἄνθρωπ۞ ἔπεσεν, A *Man fell,* without any thing prefixed, but only the Article withdrawn (*b*). Even in *English,* where the Article

---

(*b*) Τὰ γὰρ ἀορίζωδῶς ποτὲ νοούμενα, ἢ τῦ ἄρθρε παράθεσις ὑπὸ ὁρισμὸν τῦ προσώπε ἄγει. *Those things, which are at times understood indefinitely, the addition of the Article makes to be definite as to their Person.* Apoll. L. IV. c. 1. See of the same author, L. I. c. 6, 36.

ποιεῖ

Ch. I. Article (A) cannot be used, as in plurals, its force is exprest by the same Negation. *Those are* THE *Men,* means those are Individuals, of which we possess some *previous* Knowledge. *Those are Men,* the Article apart, means no more than that they are so many *vague* and *uncertain* Individuals, just as the Phrase, *A Man,* in the singular, implies one of the same number.

BUT

ποιεῖ (τὸ Ἄρθρον sc.) δ᾽ ἀναπόλησιν προεγνωσμένε τᾶ ἐν τῇ συντάξει· οἷον εἰ μὲν λέγοι τις, ΑΝΘΡΩΠΟΣ ΗΚΕ, ἄδηλον τίνα ἄνθρωπον λέγει. εἰ δὲ Ο ΑΝΘΡΩΠΟΣ, δῆλον, προεγνωσμένον γάρ τινα ἄνθρωπον λέγει. Τῦτο δὲ αὐτὸ βέλονται κ᾽ οἱ φάσκοντες τ᾽ ἄρθρον σημαντικὸν πρώτης γνώσεως κ᾽ δευτέρας. *The Article causes a Review within the Mind of something known before the texture of the Discourse. Thus if any one* says Ἄνθρωπος ἧκε, MAN CAME *(which is the same, as when we say in English* A *man came) it is not evident, of whom he speaks. But if he says* ὁ ἄνθρωπος ἧκε, THE MAN CAME, *then it is evident; for he speaks of some Person known before. And this is what those mean, who say that the Article is expressive of the First and Second Knowledge together.* Theod. Gazæ. L. IV.

Book the Second.

Ch. I.

BUT tho' the *Greeks* have no Article correspondent to the Article (A,) yet nothing can be more nearly related, than their Ὁ, to the Article, THE. Ὁ βασιλεῦς, THE *King*; ΤΟ δῶρον, THE *Gift*, &c. Nor is this only to be proved by parallel examples, but by the Attributes of the *Greek* Article, as they are described by *Apollonius*, one of the earliest and most acute of the old Grammarians, now remaining.

Ἔϛιν ἒν καθὸ κỳ ἐν ἄλλοις ἀπεφηνάμεθα, ἴδιον ἄρθρων ἡ ἀναφορὰ, ἥ ἐϛι προκατειλεγμένε προσώπε παραϛατική.—*Now the peculiar Attribute of the Article, as we have shewn elsewhere, is that Reference, which implies some certain Person already mentioned.* Again—Οὐ γὰρ δήγε τὰ ὀνόματα ἐξ αὐτῶν ἀναφορὰν παρίϛησιν, εἰ μὴ συμπαραλάβοιεν τὸ ἄρθρον, ὃ ἐξαίρετός ἐϛιν ἡ ἀναφορά. *For Nouns of themselves imply not*

Re-

Ch. I. *Reference, unless they take to them the Article, whose peculiar Character is Reference.* Again—Τὸ ἄρθρον προϋφεςῶσαν γνῶσιν δηλοῖ —*The Article indicates a pre-established acquaintance* (c).

His reasoning upon *Proper Names* is worth remarking. Proper Names (he tells us) often fall into *Homonymie*, that is, different Persons often go by the same Name. To solve this ambiguity, we have recourse to *Adjectives* or *Epithets*. For example—there were two *Grecian* chiefs, who bore the name of *Ajax*. It was not therefore without reason, that *Menestheus* uses Epithets, when this intent was to distinguish the one of them from the other.

Ἀλλὰ

(c) *Apoll.* de Synt. L. I. c. 6, 7. His account of REFERENCE is as follows—Ἰδίωμα ἀναφορᾶς προκατειλεγμένῳ προσώπῳ δευτέρα γνῶσις. *The peculiar character of Reference is the second or repeated Knowledge of some Person already mentioned.* L. II. c. 3.

Ἀλλὰ περ οἶὸς ἴτω Τελαμώνιὸς ἄλκιμὸς Ch. I.
Αἴας.   Hom.

If both Ajaxes (fays he) *cannot be fpared,*
———*at leaft alone*
Let mighty Telamonian Ajax come.

Apollonius proceeds———Even Epithets themfelves are diffufed thro' various Subjects, in as much as the fame Adjective may be referred to many Subftantives.

IN order therefore to render both Parts of Speech equally definite, that is to fay the Adjective as well as the Subftantive, the Adjective itfelf affumes *an Article* before it, that it may indicate *a Reference to fome fingle Perfon only,* μοναδικὴ ἀναφορὰ, according to the Author's own Phrafe. And thus it is we fay, Τρύφων ὁ Γραμματικὸς, *Trypho* THE *Grammarian;* Ἀπολλόδωρὸς ὁ Κυρηναῖὸς, *Apollodorus* THE *Cyrenean,* &c. The Author's Conclufion of
this

Ch. I. this Section is worth remarking. Δεόν-τως ἄρα κὴ κατὰ τὸ τοιἕτον ἡ πρόσθεσίς ἐςι τἕ ἄρθρἕ, συνιδιάζἕσα τὸ ἐπιθετικὸν τῷ κυρίῳ ὀνόματι—*It is with reason therefore that the Article is here also added, as it brings the Adjective to an Individuality, as precise, as the proper Name (d).*

WE may carry this reasoning farther, and shew, how by help of the *Article* even *common Appellatives* come to have the force of *proper Names*, and that unassisted by epithets of any kind. Among the *Athenians* Πλοῖον meant *Ship*; Ἕνδεκα, *Eleven*; and Ἄνθρωπ☉, *Man*. Yet add but the Article, and Τὸ Πλοῖον, THE SHIP, meant *that particular Ship, which they sent annually to Delos*; Οἱ Ἕνδεκα, THE ELEVEN, meant, *certain Officers of Justice*; and Ὁ Ἄνθρωπ☉, THE MAN, meant *their public Executioner*. So in *English*, City, is a Name

---

(d) See *Apoll.* L. I. c. 12. where by mistake *Menelaus* is put for *Menestheus*.

Ch. I.

Name common to many places; and Speaker, a Name common to many Men. Yet if we prefix the Article, THE CITY means our Metropolis; and THE SPEAKER, *a high Officer* in the *British* Parliament.

AND thus it is by an easy transition, that the Article, from denoting *Reference*, comes to denote *Eminence* also; that is to say, from implying an *ordinary* pre-acquaintance, to presume a kind of *general and universal Notoriety*. Thus among the Greeks Ὁ Ποιητής, THE POET, meant *Homer* (e); and Ὁ Σταγειρίτης, THE STAGIRITE, meant *Aristotle*; not that there were not

---

(e) There are so few exceptions to this Observation, that we may fairly admit it to be generally true. Yet *Aristotle* twice denotes *Euripides* by the Phrase ὁ ποιητής, once at the end of the seventh Book of his *Nicomachian Ethics*, and again in his *Physics*, L. II. 2. *Plato* also in his tenth Book of Laws (p. 901. *Edit. Serr.*) denotes *Hesiod* after the same manner.

Ch. I. not many Poets, beside *Homer*; and many Stagirites, beside *Aristotle*; but none equally illustrious for their Poetry and Philosophy.

It is on a like principle that *Aristotle* tells us, it is by no means the same thing to assert—εἶναι τὴν ἡδονὴν ἀγαθὸν, or, TO ἀγαθόν—that, *Pleasure is* A Good, or, The Good. The first only makes it a *common Object of Desire*, upon a level with many others, which daily raise our wishes; the last supposes it *that supreme and sovereign Good*, the ultimate Scope of all our Actions and Endeavours *(f)*.

But to pursue our Subject. It has been said already that the Article has no meaning, but when associated to some other word.—To what words then may it be associated?—To such as require *defining*, for

---

(f) Analyt. Prior. L I. c. 40.

BOOK THE SECOND.

for it is by nature a *Definitive.*—And what *Words* are thefe?—Not thofe which already are *as definite, as may be.* Nor yet thofe, which, *being indefinite, cannot properly be made otherwife.* It remains then they muſt be *thoſe, which though indefinite, are yet capable, through the Article, of becoming definite.*

UPON theſe Principles we ſee the reafon, why it is abfurd to fay, O ΕΓΩ, THE I, or O ΣΥ, THE THOU, becauſe nothing can make thofe Pronouns more *definite,* than they are (g). The fame may be aſſerted of

---

(g) *Apollonius* makes it part of the Pronoun's Definition, to refuſe co-aleſcence with the Article. Ἐκεῖνο ἐν Ἀντωνυμία, τὸ μετὰ δείξεως ἢ ἀναφορᾶς αὐτονομα-ζόμενον, ᾧ ἒ σύνεςι τὸ ἄρθρον. *That therefore is a Pronoun, which with Indication or Reference is put for a Noun, and* WITH WHICH THE ARTICLE DOTH NOT ASSOCIATE. L. II. c. 5. So *Gaza,* ſpeaking of Pronouns—Πάνΐη δὲ—ἐκ ἐπιδέχονΐαι ἄρθρον. L. IV. *Priſcian* ſays the ſame. *Jure igitur apud Græcos prima*

Ch. I. of Proper Names, and though the *Greeks* say ὁ Σωκράτης, ἡ Ξάνθιππη, and the like, yet the Article is a mere Pleonaſm, unleſs perhaps it ſerve to diſtinguiſh Sexes. By the ſame rule we cannot ſay in *Greek* ΟΙ ΑΜΦΟΤΕΡΟΙ, or in *Engliſh*, THE BOTH, becauſe theſe Words *in their own nature* are each of them perfectly *defined,* ſo that to define them farther would be quite ſuperfluous. Thus if it be ſaid, *I have read* BOTH *Poets*, this plainly indicates *a definite pair,* of whom ſome mention has been made already; Δυὰς ἐγνωσμένη, a *known Duad,* as *Appollonius* expreſſes him-ſelf, (*h*) when he ſpeaks of this Subject. On the contrary, if it be ſaid, *I have read* Two *Poets*, this may mean *any Pair* out of

---

et ſecunda perſona pronominum, quæ ſine dubio demonſtra-tivæ ſunt, articulis adjungi non poſſunt; nec tertia, quando demonſtrativa eſt. L. XII. p. 938.—In the beginning of the ſame Book, he gives the true reaſon of this. *Supra omnes alias partes orationis* FINIT PERSONAS PRONO-MEN.

(*h*) *Apollon.* L. I. c. 16.

BOOK THE SECOND. 227

of all that ever exifted. And hence this Ch. I.
Numeral, being in this Senfe *indefinite* (as
indeed are all others, as well as itfelf) is
forced *to affume the Article,* whenever it
would become *definite*.* And thus it is,
THE Two in *Englifh,* and ΟΙ ΔΥΟ in
Greek, mean nearly the fame thing, as
BOTH or ΑΜΦΟΤΕΡΟΙ. Hence alfo it
is, that as Two, when taken alone, has
reference to fome *primary* and *indefinite*
Perception, while the Article, THE, has
reference to fome *fecondary* and *definite* †;
hence I fay the Reafon, why it is bad *Greek*
to fay ΔΥΟ ΟΙ ΑΝΘΡΩΠΟΙ, and bad
Englifh, to fay Two THE MEN. Such
Syntax is in fact a *Blending of Incompati-*
Q 2   *bles,*

---

* This explains *Servius* on the XIIth Æneid. v. 511.
where he tells us that *Duorum* is put for *Amborum*. In
Englifh or *Greek* the Article would have done the bufinefs, for *the Two,* or τοῖν δυοῖν are equivalent to *Both*
or ἀμφοτέρων, but not fo *Duorum,* becaufe the *Latins*
have no Articles to prefix.

† Sup. p. 215, 216.

Ch. I. *bles*, that is to say of a *defined Substantive* with an *undefined Attributive*. On the contrary to say in *Greek* ΑΜΦΟΤΕΡΟΙ ΟΙ ΑΝΘΡΩΠΟΙ, or in *English*, BOTH THE MEN, is good and allowable, because the Substantive cannot possibly be less apt, by being defined, to coalesce with an Attributive, which is defined as well as itself. So likewise, it is correct to say, ΟΙ ΔΥΟ ΑΝΘΡΩΠΟΙ, THE TWO MEN, because here the Article, being placed in the beginning, *extends its Power* as well through Substantive as Attributive, and equally contributes to *define* them both.

As some of the words above admit of no Article, *because they are by Nature as definite as may be*, so there are others, which admit it not, *because they are not to be defined at all.* Of this sort are all INTERROGATIVES. If we question about *Substances*, we cannot say Ο ΤΙΣ ΟΥΤΟΣ, THE WHO IS THIS; but ΤΙΣ ΟΥ-

ΟΥΤΟΣ, Who is this? (*i*). The same as to *Qualities* and both kinds of *Quantity*. We say without an Article ΠΟΙΟΣ, ΠΟ-ΣΟΙ, ΠΗΛΙΚΟΣ, in *English*, WHAT SORT OF, HOW MANY, HOW GREAT. The Reason is, that the Articles Ὁ, and THE respect Beings, *already known*; Interrogatives respect Beings, *about which we are ignorant*; for as to what we know, Interrogation is superfluous.

IN a word *the natural Associators with Articles* are all those *common Appellatives*, which denote the several Genera and Species of Beings. It is these, which, by assuming a different *Article*, serve either to explain an Individual upon its first being perceived, or else to indicate, upon its return, a Recognition, or repeated Knowledge (*k*).

(*i*) *Apollonius* calls ΤΙΣ, ἐναντιώτατον τῶν ἄρθρων, a Part of Speech, *most contrary, most averse to Articles*. L. IV. c. I.

(*k*) What is here said respects *the two* Articles, which we have in *English*. In *Greek*, the Article does no more, than imply *a Recognition*. See before p. 216, 217, 218.

Ch. I. WE shall here subjoin a few Instances of the Peculiar Power of ARTICLES.

EVERY Proposition consists of a *Subject*, and a *Predicate*. In *English* these are distinguished by their Position, the Subject standing *first*, the Predicate *last*. *Happiness is Pleasure*—Here, *Happiness* is the Subject; *Pleasure*, the *Predicate*. If we change their order, and say, *Pleasure is Happiness*; then *Pleasure* becomes *the Subject*, and *Happiness* the *Predicate*. In *Greek* these are distinguished not by any Order or Position, but by help of the *Article*, which the Subject always assumes, and the Predicate in most instances (some few excepted) rejects. *Happiness is Pleasure*—ἡδονὴ ἡ εὐδαιμονία—*Pleasure is Happiness*—ἡ ἡδονὴ εὐδαιμονία—*Fine things are difficult*—χαλεπὰ τὰ καλά—*Difficult things are fine*—τὰ χαλεπά καλά.

IN

IN *Greek* it is worth attending, how in Ch. I. the fame Sentence, the fame *Article*, by being prefixed to a different Word, quite changes the whole meaning. For example—'Ο Πτολεμαῖος γυμνασιαρχήσας ἐτιμήθη —*Ptolemy, having prefided over the Games, was publickly honoured.* The Participle γυμνασιαρχήσας has here no other force, then to denote to us *the Time, when* Ptolemy was honoured, *viz.* after having prefided over the Games. But if, inſtead of the Subſtantive, we join the Participle to the *Article*, and fay, 'Ο γυμνασιαρχήσας Πτολεμαῖος ἐτιμήθη, our meaning is then— *The Ptolemy, who prefided over the Games, was honoured.* The Participle in this cafe, *being joined to the Article,* tends tacitly to indicate not one *Ptolemy* but many, of which number a particular one participated of honour (*l*).

(*l*) *Apollon.* L. I. c. 33, 34.

Ch. I. In *English* likewife it deferves remarking, how the Senfe is changed by changing of the *Articles*, tho' we leave every other Word of the Sentence untouched.—*And Nathan faid unto David*, THOU ART THE MAN *. In that fingle, THE, that diminutive Particle, all the force and efficacy of the Reafon is contained. By that alone are the Premifes applied, and fo firmly fixed, as never to be fhaken. It is poffible this Affertion may appear at firft fomewhat ftrange; but let him, who doubts it, only change the *Article*, and then fee what will become of the Prophet and his reafoning.—*And Nathan faid unto David*, THOU ART A MAN. Might not the King well have demanded upon fo impertinent a pofition,

Non dices hodie, quorfum hæc tam putida tendant?

BUT

---

* ΣΥ ΕΙ 'Ο ΑΝΗΡ. Βασιλ. Β'. κεφ. ιϛ'.

BOOK THE SECOND. 233

BUT enough of such Speculations. The only remark, which we shall make on them, is this; that " minute Change in " PRINCIPLES leads to mighty Change in " EFFECTS; so that well are PRINCIPLES " intitled to our regard, however *in ap-* " *pearance* they may be trivial and low."

Ch. I.

THE ARTICLES already mentioned are those *strictly* so called; but besides these there are the PRONOMINAL ARTICLES; such as *This, That, Any, Other, Some, All, No,* or *None,* &c. Of these we have spoken already in our Chapter of Pronouns (*m*),

where

(*m*) See B. I. c. 5. p. 72, 73. It seems to have been some view of words, like that here given, which induced *Quintilian* to say of the *Latin* Tongue—*Noster sermo Articulos non desiderat ; ideoque in alias partes orationis sparguntur.* Inst. Orat. L. I. c. 4. So *Scaliger. His declaratis, satis constat Græcorum Articulos non neglectos a nobis, sed eorum usum superfluum. Nam ubi aliquid præscribendum est, quod Græci per articulum efficiunt* (ἔλεξεν ὁ δεῖλος;) *expletur a Latinis per* Is *aut* ILLE ; Is,
aut

Ch. I. where we have shewn, when they may be taken as Pronouns, and when as Articles. Yet in truth it must be confessed, if the Essence of an Article be *to define* and *ascertain*, they are much more properly Articles, than any thing else, and as such should be considered in Universal Grammar. Thus when we say, THIS *Picture I approve, but* THAT *I dislike*, what do we perform by the help of these Definitives, but bring down the common Appellative to denote two Individuals, the one as *the more near*, the other as *the more distant?* So when we say, SOME *men* are *virtuous, but* ALL *men are mortal* what is the natural Effect of this ALL and SOME, but to define that *Universality*, and *Particularity*, which would remain indefinite, were we to take them

---

aut, Ille servus dixit, *de quo servo antea facta mentio sit, aut qui alio quo pacto notus sit. Additur enim Articulus ad rei memoriam renovandam, cujus antea non nescii sumus, aut ad praescribendam intellectionem, quæ latius patere queat ; veluti cum dicimus,* C. Cæsar, Is qui postea dictator fuit. *Nam alii fuere* C. Cæsares. *Sic Græcè* Καῖσαρ ὁ αὐτοκράτωρ. De Cauf. Ling. Lat. c. 131.

4

BOOK THE SECOND. 235

them away? The same is evident in such Ch. I.
Sentences, as—SOME *substances have sensa-*
tion; OTHERS *want it—Chuse* ANY *way of*
acting, and SOME *men will find fault,* &c.
For here SOME, OTHER, and ANY, serve
all of them to *define* different Parts of a
given Whole; SOME, to denote a *definite*
Part; ANY, to denote an *indefinite;* and
OTHER, to denote the *remaining* Part,
when a Part has been assumed already.
Sometimes this last Word denotes *a large*
indefinite Portion, set in opposition to some
single, definite, and *remaining Part*, which
receives from such Opposition no small degree of heightening. Thus *Virgil,*

Excudent ALII *spirantia molliùs æra;*
(Credo equidem) vivos ducent de marmore
  vultus;
Orabunt causas meliùs, cælique meatus
Describent radio, et surgentia sidera
  dicent:
Tu regere imperio populos, ROMANE,
  memento, &c.   Æn. VI.

NOTHING

Ch. I. Nothing can be ſtronger or more ſublime, than this Antitheſis; *one Act* ſet as equal to *many other Acts taken together*, and the Roman *ſingly* (for it is *Tu Romane*, not *Vos Romani*) to *all other* Men; and yet this performed by ſo trivial a cauſe, as the juſt oppoſition of Alii to Tu.

But here we conclude, and proceed to treat of Connectives.

CHAP. II.

Concerning Connectives, and first those called Conjunctions.

CONNECTIVES are the subject of what follows; which, according as they connect either *Sentences* or *Words*, are called by the different Names of CONJUNCTIONS, or PREPOSITIONS. Of these Names, that of the *Preposition* is taken from a *mere accident*, as it commonly stands in connection before the Part, which it connects. The name of the *Conjunction*, as is evident, has reference to its *essential character*.

Ch. II.

OF these two we shall consider the CONJUNCTION first, because it connects, not Words, but *Sentences*. This is conformable to the Analysis, with which we began this inquiry*, and which led us, by

parity

---

* Sup. p. 11, 12.

Ch. II. parity of reason, to consider *Sentences themselves* before *Words*. Now the Definition of a CONJUNCTION is as follows—*a Part of Speech, void of Signification itself, but so formed as to help Signification, by making* TWO *or more significant Sentences to be* ONE *significant Sentence* (*a*).

THIS

(*a*) Grammarians have usually considered the Conjunction as connecting rather *single Parts of Speech*, than *whole Sentences*, and that too with the addition of like with like, Tense with Tense, Number with Number, Case with Case, &c. This *Sanctius* justly explodes. *Conjunctio neque casus, neque alias partes orationis (ut imperiti docent) conjungit, ipsæ enim partes inter se conjunguntur—sed conjunctio Orationes inter se conjungit.* Miner. L. III. c. 14. He then establishes his doctrine by a variety of examples. He had already said as much, L. I. c. 18. and in this he appears to have followed *Scaliger*, who had asserted the same before him. *Conjunctionis autem nctionem veteres paullo inconsultiùs prodidere ; neque enim, quod aiunt, partes alias conjungit (ipsæ enim partes per se inter se conjunguntur)—sed Conjunctio est, quæ conjungit Orationes plures.* De Cauf. Ling. Lat. c. 165.

This

Ch. II.

THIS therefore being the general Idea of Conjunctions, we deduce their Species in

---

This Doctrine of theirs is confirmed by *Apollonius*, who in the several places, where he mentions the Conjunction, always considers it in Syntax as connecting *Sentences*, and *not* Words, though in his works now extant he has not given us its Definition. See L. I. c. 2. p. 14. L. II. c. 12. p. 124. L. III. c. 15. p. 234.

But we have stronger authority than this to support *Scaliger* and *Sanctius*, and that is *Aristotle*'s Definition, as the Passage has been corrected by the best Critics and Manuscripts. A Conjunction, according to him, is φωνὴ ἄσημος, ἐκ πλειόνων μὲν φωνῶν μιᾶς, σημαντικῶν δὲ, ποιεῖν πεφυκυῖα μίαν φωνὴν σημαντικήν. *An articulate Sound, devoid of Signification, which is so formed as to make* ONE *significant articulate Sound out of several articulate Sounds, which are each of them significant.* Poet. c. 20. In this view of things, the *one significant articulate Sound, formed by the Conjunction*, is not the Union of two or more Syllables in one simple Word, nor even of two or more Words in one simple Sentence, but of two or more *simple Sentences* in *one complex Sentence*, which is considered as ONE, from that Concatenation of Meaning effected by the *Conjunctions*. For example, let us take the Sentence, which follows. *If Men are by nature social, it is their Interest to be just, though it were*

Ch. II. in the following manner. CONJUNCTIONS, while they *connect sentences*, either *connect also*

---

were not so ordained by the Laws of their Country. Here are three Sentences. (1.) *Men are by nature social.* (2.) *It is Man's Interest to be just.* (3.) *It is not ordained by the Laws of every Country that Man should be just.* The first two of these Sentences are made *One* by the Conjunction, IF; these, *One* with the third Sentence, by the Conjunction, THO'; and the three, thus united, make that φωνὴ μία σημαντικὴ, *that one significant articulate Sound*, of which *Aristotle* speaks, and which is the result of the conjunctive Power.

This explains a passage in his Rhetoric, where he mentions the same Subject. Ὁ γὰρ σύνδεσμος ἓν ποιεῖ τὰ πολλά· ὥςτε ἐὰν ἐξαιρεθῇ, δῆλον ὅτι τοὐναντίον ἔςαι τὸ ἓν πολλά. *The Conjunction makes many,* ONE; *so that if it be taken away, it is then evident on the contrary that one will be* MANY. Rhet. III. c. 12. His instance of a Sentence, divested of its Conjunctions, and thus made *many* out of *one*, is, ἦλθον, ἀπήντησα, ἐδεόμην, *veni, occurri, rogavi*, where by the way the three Sentences, resulting from this Dissolution, (for ἦλθον, ἀπήντησα, and ἐδεόμην, are each of them, when unconnected, so many perfect Sentences) prove that these are the proper Subjects of the *Conjunction's* connective faculty.

Ammonius's

Book the Second.

Ch. II.

alſo their meanings, or not. For example: let us take theſe two Sentences—*Rome was enſlaved—Cæſar was ambitious*—and connect them together by the Conjunction, BECAUSE. *Rome was enſlaved,* BECAUSE *Cæſar was ambitious.* Here the *Meanings,* as well as the *Sentences,* appear to be connected. But if I ſay,—*Manners muſt be reformed,* OR *Liberty will be loſt*—here the Conjunction, OR, though *it join the*

Ammonius's account of the uſe of this Part of Speech is elegant. Διὸ κỳ τῶν λόγων ὁ μὲν ὕπαρξιν μίαν σημαίνων, ὁ κυρίως εἷς, ἀνάλογῶν ἂν εἴη τῇ μηδέπω τετμημένῳ ξύλῳ, κỳ διὰ τᾶτο ἑνὶ λεγομένῳ· ὁ δὲ πλείονας ὑπάρξεις δηλῶν, ἕνα (lege διὰ) τινὰ δὲ σύνδεσμον ἡνῶσθαί πως δοκῶν, ἀναλογεῖ τῇ νηὶ τῇ ἐκ πολλῶν συγκειμένῃ ξύλων, ὑπὸ δὲ τῶν γόμφων φαινομένην ἐχέσῃ τὴν ἕνωσιν. *Of Sentences that, which denotes one Exiſtence ſimply, and which is ſtrictly* ONE, *may be conſidered as analogous to a piece of Timber not yet ſevered, and called on this account One. That, which denotes ſeveral Exiſtences, and which appears to be made* ONE *by ſome Conjunctive Particle, is analogous to a Ship made up of many pieces of Timber, and which by means of the nails has an apparent Unity.* Am. in Lib. de Interpret. p. 54; 6.

R

Ch. II. *the Sentences*, yet as to their respective *Meanings*, is a perfect *Disjunctive*. And thus it appears, that though all Conjunctions *conjoin Sentences*, yet with respect to the *Sense*, some are CONJUNCTIVE, and some DISJUNCTIVE; and hence (*b*) it is that we derive their different Species.

The Conjunctions, which conjoin both Sentences and their Meanings, are either COPULATIVES, or CONTINUATIVES. The principal Copulative in *English* is, AND. The Continuatives are, IF, BECAUSE, THEREFORE, THAT, *&c.* The *Difference between these is this—The Copulative* does no more than barely *couple* Sentences, and is therefore applicable to all Subjects, whose Natures *are not incompatible. Continuatives,* on the contrary, by a more intimate connection, consolidate Sen-

---

(*b*) Thus *Scaliger. Aut ergo Sensum conjungunt, ac Verba; aut Verba tantum conjungunt, Sensum vero disjungunt.* De C. L. Lat. c. 167.

Sentences into *one continuous Whole*, and Ch. II. are therefore applicable only to Subjects, which have an *essential Co-incidence*.

To explain by examples—It is no way improper to say, *Lysippus was a Statuary*, AND *Priscian was a Grammarian—The Sun shineth*, AND *the Sky is clear*—because these are things that may co-exist, and yet imply no absurdity. But it would be absurd to say, *Lysippus was a Statuary*, BECAUSE *Priscian was a Grammarian*; tho' not to say, *the Sun shineth*, BECAUSE *the Sky is clear*. The Reason is, with respect to the first, *the Co-incidence* is merely *accidental*; with respect to the last, it is *essential*, and founded in nature. And so much for the Distinction between *Copulatives* and *Continuatives* (*c*).

As

(*c*) *Copulativa est, quæ copulat tam Verba, quam Sensum.* Thus *Priscian*, p. 1026. But *Scaliger* is more explicit—*si Sensum conjungunt (conjunctiones sc.) aut necessario,*

Ch. II. As to *Continuatives*, they are either Suppositive, such as, If; or Positive, such as, Because, Therefore, As, &c. Take Examples of each—*you will live happily*, if *you live honestly*—*you live happily*, because *you live honestly*. The Difference between these Continuatives is this—The *Suppositives* denote *Connection*, but assert not actual *Existence*; the *Positives* imply *both the one and the other* (*d*).

Farther

---

cessariò, aut non necessariò : & si non necessario, tum fiunt Copulativæ, &c. De C. Ling. Lat. c. 167. *Priscian's* own account of Continuatives is as follows. *Continuativæ sunt, quæ continuationem & consequentiam rerum significant*—ibid. *Scaliger's* account is—*caussam aut præstituunt, aut subdunt.* Ibid. c. 168. The *Greek* name for the Copulative was Σύνδεσμος συμπλεκτικός ; for the Continuative, συναπτικός ; the Etymologies of which words justly distinguish their respective characters.

(*d*) The old *Greek* Grammarians confined the name Συναπτικοὶ, and the *Latins* that of *Continuativæ* to those Con-

FARTHER than this, the Positives above Ch. II. mentioned are either CAUSAL, such as, BECAUSE, SINCE, AS, &c. or COLLECTIVE, such as, THEREFORE, WHEREFORE, THEN, &c. The Difference between these is this—the *Causals* subjoin *Causes to Effects—The Sun is in Eclipse,*

BE-

Conjunctions, which we have called *Suppositive* or *Conditional*, while the Positive they called παρασυναπτικοὶ, or *Subcontinuativæ*. They agree however in describing their proper Characters. The first according to *Gaza* are, οἱ ὕπαρξιν μὲν ὄ, ἀκολοθίαν δέ τινα κỳ τάξιν δη-λῶντες—L. IV. *Priscian* says, they signify to us, *qualis est ordinatio & natura rerum, cum dubitatione aliquâ essentiæ rerum*—p. 1027. And *Scaliger* says, they conjoin *sine subsistentiâ necessariâ; potest enim subsistere & non subsistere; utrumque enim admittunt.* Ibid. c. 168. On the contrary of the Positive, or παρασυναπτικοὶ (to use his own name) *Gaza* tells us, ὅτι κỳ ὕπαρξιν μετὰ τάξεως σημαίνουσιν ἔτοιγε—And *Priscian* says, *causam continuationis ostendunt consequentem cum essentia rerum*—And *Scaliger*, *non ex hypothesi, sed ex eo, quod subsistit, conjungunt.* Ibid.

Ch. II. BECAUSE *the Moon intervenes—The Collectives* subjoin *Effects to Causes—The Moon intervenes,* THEREFORE *the Sun is in Eclipse.* Now we use *Causals* in those instances, where, the Effect being conspicuous, we seek its Cause; and *Collectives,* in *Demonstrations,* and *Science properly so called,* where the Cause being known

---

It may seem at first somewhat strange, why the *Positive* Conjunctions should have been considered as Subordinate to the *Suppositive,* which by their antient Names appears to have been the fact. Is it, that the Positive are confined to what *actually is*; the Suppositive extend to *Possibles,* nay even as far as to *Impossibles?* Thus it is false to affirm, *As it is Day, it is Light,* unless it actually be Day. But we may at midnight affirm, *If it be Day, it is Light,* because the, IF, extends to Possibles also. Nay we may affirm, by its help (if we please) even Impossibles. We may say, *If the Sun be cubical, then is the Sun angular;* If *the Sky fall, then shall we catch Larks.* Thus too *Scaliger* upon the same occasion—*amplitudinem Continuativæ percipi ex eo, quod etiam impossibile aliquando præsupponit.* De C. L. Lat C. 168. In this sense then the Continuative, Suppositive or Conditional Conjunction is (as it were) superior to the Positive, as being of greater latitude in its application.

known firſt, by its help we diſcern conſe- Ch. II.
quences (*e*).

ALL theſe *Continuatives* are reſolvable into *Copulatives*. Inſtead of, BECAUSE *it is Day, it is light*, we may ſay, *It is Day,* AND *it is Light*. Inſtead of, IF *it be Day, it is Light*, we may ſay, *It is at the ſame time neceſſary to be Day,* AND *to be Light*. and ſo in other Inſtances. The Reaſon is, that the Power of the *Copulative* extends to all Connections, as well to the *eſſential*, as to the *caſual* or *fortuitous*. Hence therefore the Continuative may be reſolved into *a Copulative and ſomething more*, that is to ſay, into a Copulative implying an *eſſential* Co-incidence *(f)* in the Subjects conjoined.

R 4 As

(*e*) The *Latins* called the Cauſals, *Cauſales* or *Cauſativæ*; the Collectives, *Collectivæ* or *Illativæ*: The *Greeks* called the former 'Αιτιολογικοὶ, and the latter Συλλογιϛικοί.

(*f*) *Reſolvuntur autem in Copulativas omnes hæ, propterea quod Cauſa cum Effectu Suâpte naturâ conjuncta eſt.* Scal. de C. L. Lat. c. 169.

Ch. II. As to *Caufal* Conjunctions (of which we have spoken already) there is no one of the four Species of Caufes, which they are not capable of denoting: for example, THE MATERIAL CAUSE—*The Trumpet founds*, BECAUSE *it is made of Metal*—THE FORMAL—*The Trumpet founds*, BECAUSE *it is long and hollow*—THE EFFICIENT—*The Trumpet founds*, BECAUSE *an Artift blows it*—THE FINAL—*The Trumpet founds*, THAT *it may raife our courage.* Where it is worth obferving, that the three firft Caufes are expreft by the ftrong affirmation of the *Indicative Mode*, becaufe if the Effect actually be, thefe muft of neceffity be alfo. But the laft Caufe has a different Mode, namely, the *Contingent* or *Potential.* The Reafon is, that the Final Caufe, tho' it may be *firft in Specuation*, is always *laft in Event.* That is to fay, however it may be the End, which fet the Artift firft to work, it may ftill be an End beyond his Power to obtain, and which

BOOK THE SECOND. 249

which like other Contingents, may either Ch. II.
happen, or not (*g*). Hence alſo it is connected by Conjunctions of a peculiar kind,
ſuch as, THAT, ἵνα, UT, &c.

The Sum is, that ALL CONJUNCTIONS, *which connect both Sentences and their Meanings,* are either COPULATIVE, or CONTINUATIVE; the Continuatives are either *Conditional,* or *Poſitive;* and the Poſitives are either *Cauſal* or *Collective.*

AND now we come to the DISJUNCTIVE CONJUNCTIONS, a Species of Words which bear this contradictory Name, becauſe, while they *disjoin the Senſe,* they *conjoin the Sentences* (*h*).

WITH

(*g*) See B. I. c. 8. p. 142. See alſo Vol. I. Note VIII. p. 271. For the four Cauſes ſee Vol. I. Note XVII. p. 280.

(*h*) Ὁι δὲ διαζευκτικοὶ τὰ διαζευγμένα συντιθέασι, ᾗ ἢ πρᾶγμα ἀπὸ πράγματⒼ, ἢ πρόσωπον ἀπὸ προσώπȣ διαζευγνῦντες, τὴν φράσιν ἐπισυνδȣ̈σιν. *Gazæ*
Gram.

Ch. II. WITH respect to these we may observe, that as there is a Principle of UNION diffused throughout all things, by which THIS WHOLE is kept together, and preserved from Dissipation; so there is a Principle of DIVERSITY diffused in like manner, the Source of Distinction, of Number, and of Order (*i*).

Now

Gram. L. IV. *Disjunctivæ sunt, quæ, quamvis dictiones conjungant, sensum tamen disjunctum habent.* Prisc. L. XVI. p. 1029. And hence it is, that a Sentence, connected by Disjunctives, has a near resemblance to a *simple negative Truth.* For though this as to its Intellection be *disjunctive* (its end being to disjoin the Subject from the Predicate) yet as it combines Terms together into one Proposition, it is as truly *synthetical*, as any Truth, that is *affirmative.* See Chap. I. Note (*b*). p. 3.

(*i*) The DIVERSITY, which adorns Nature, may be said to heighten by degrees, and as it passes to different Subjects, to become more and more intense. Some things only differ, when considered as *Individuals*, but if we recur to their *Species*, immediately lose all Distinction: such for instance are *Socrates* and *Plato.* Others differ as to *Species*, but as to *Genus* are the same: such are

Now it is *to exprefs in fome degree the* Ch. II.
Modifications of this Diverfity, that Dis-
JUNCTIVE CONJUNCTIONS feem firſt to
have been invented.

OF thefe DISJUNCTIVES, fome are
SIMPLE, fome ADVERSATIVE—*Simple*,
as when we fay, EITHER *it is Day*, OR *it
is*

are *Man* and *Lion*. There are others again, which *differ as to Genus*, and co-incide only in thofe *tranfcendental Comprehenfions* of Ens, Being, Exiſtence, and the like : fuch are *Quantities* and *Qualities*, as for example an *Ounce*, and the Colour, *White*. Laſtly ALL BEING whatever differs, as *Being*, from *Non-being*.

Farther, in all things different, however moderate their Diverfity, there is an appearance of OPPOSITION with refpect to each other, in as much as each thing *is it felf*, and *not any* of the reſt. But yet in all Subjects this Oppofition is not *the fame*. In RELATIVES, fuch as Greater and Lefs, Double and Half, Father and Son, Caufe and Effect, in *thefe* it is *more ſtriking*, than in or‐ dinary Subjects, becaufe *thefe* always fhew it, *by necef- farily inferring each other*. In CONTRARIES, fuch as Black and White, Even and Odd, Good and Bad, Virtuous

Ch. II. *is Night—Adversative*, as when we say, *It is not Day*, BUT *it is Night*. The Difference between these is, that the simple do no more, than *merely disjoin*; the *Adversative* disjoin, with an *Opposition concomitant*. Add to this, that the Adversative are *definite*; the Simple, *indefinite*. Thus when we say, *The Number Three is not an*

Virtuous and Vitious, in these the Opposition goes still farther, because these not only *differ*, but are even *destructive of each other*. But *the most potent Opposition* is that of 'Αντίφασις, or CONTRADICTION, when we oppose *Proposition* to *Proposition*, *Truth* to *Falshood*, asserting of any Subject, *either it is, or is not*. This indeed is an *Opposition*, which extends itself to all things, for every thing conceivable must needs have its *Negative*, though multitudes by nature have neither *Relatives*, nor *Contraries*.

Besides these Modes of DIVERSITY, there are others that deserve notice; such for instance, as the Diversity between the *Name* of a thing, and *its Definition*; between the *various Names*, which belong to the *same thing*, and the *various things*, which are denoted by the *same Name*; all which *Diversities* upon occasion become a Part of our Discourse. And so much, in short, for the Subject of DIVERSITY.

2

BOOK THE SECOND.

an even Number, BUT *an odd,* we not only Ch. II. disjoin two oppofite Attributes, but we definitely affirm one, and deny the other. But when we fay, *The Number of the Stars is* EITHER *even* OR *odd,* though we affert one Attribute *to be,* and the other *not to be,* yet the Alternative notwithftanding is left indefinite. And fo much for *fimple Disjunctives* (*k*).

As

(*k*) The fimple Disjunctive ἤ, or *Vel,* is moftly ufed *indefinitely,* fo as to leave an Alternative. But when it is ufed *definitely,* fo as to leave no Alternative it is then a perfect Disjunctive of the Subfequent from the Previous, and has the fame force with ϗ ἐ, or, *Et non.* It is thus *Gaza* explains that Verfe of *Homer.*

Βέλομ' ἐγὼ λαὸν σόον ἔμμεναι, ἤ ἀπολέσθαι.

Ιλ. Α.

That is to fay, *I defire the people fhould be faved,* AND NOT *be deftroyed,* the Conjunction ἤ being ἀναιρετικὸς, or *fublative.* It muft however be confeft, that this Verfe is otherwife explained by an Ellipfis, either of μᾶλλον, or αὐτίς, concerning which fee the Commentators.

Ch. II. As to *Adverfative Disjunctives*, it has been said already that they imply OPPOSITION. Now there can be no Oppofition of the *same Attribute,* in the *same Subject,* as when we say, *Nireus was beautiful;* but the Oppofition muft be either of the *same Attribute* in *different Subjects,* as when we say, *Brutus was a Patriot,* BUT *Cæsar was not*—or of *different Attributes* in the *same Subject,* as when we say, *Gorgias was a Sophift,* BUT *not a Philofopher*—or of *different Attributes* in *different Subjects,* as when we say, *Plato was a Philofopher,* BUT *Hippias was a Sophift.*

THE *Conjunctions* used for all these purposes may be called ABSOLUTE ADVERSATIVES.

BUT there are *other Adverfatives,* befides thefe; as when we say, *Nireus was more beautiful,* THAN *Achilles*—*Virgil was*

AS *great a Poet*, AS *Cicero was an Orator.* Ch. II. The Character of thefe latter is, that they go farther than the former, by marking not only *Oppofition*, but that *Equality* or *Excefs*, which arifes among Subjects from their being *compared*. And hence it is they may be called ADVERSATIVES OF COM-PARISON.

BESIDES the Adverfatives here mentioned, there are two other Species, of which the moft eminent are UNLESS and ALTHO'. For example—*Troy will be taken*, UNLESS *the Palladium be preferved*—*Troy will be taken*, ALTHO' *Hector defend it*. The Nature of thefe *Adverfatives* may be thus explained. As every *Event* is naturally *allied* to its *Caufe*, fo by parity of reafon it is *oppofed* to its *Preventive*. And as every Caufe is either *adequate (l)* or *in-adequate* (in-adequate,

---

(l) This Diftinction has reference to *common Opinion*, and the *form of Language*, *confonant thereto*. In ftrict metaphyfical truth, *No Caufe, that is not adequate, is any Caufe at all*.

quate, when it endeavours, without being effectual) so in like manner is every *Preventive*. Now *adequate Preventives* are exprest by such Adversatives, as UNLESS—*Troy will be taken,* UNLESS *the Palladium be preserved*; that is, *This alone is sufficient to prevent it.* The *In-adequate* are exprest by such Adversatives, as ALTHO'—*Troy will be taken,* ALTHO' *Hector defend it* ; that is, *Hector's Defence will prove in-effectual.*

THE Names given by the old Grammarians to denote these last Adversatives, appear not sufficiently to express their Natures (*m*). They may be better perhaps called ADVERSATIVES ADEQUATE, and IN-ADEQUATE.

AND thus it is that all DISJUNCTIVES, that is CONJUNCTIONS, *which conjoin Sentences,*

(*m*) They called them for the most part, without sufficient Distinction of their Species, *Adversativæ,* or ’Εναντιωματικοί.

tences, but not their Meanings, are either
SIMPLE or ADVERSATIVE; and that all
ADVERSATIVES are either *Abſolute* or *Comparative*; or elſe *Adequate* or *In-adequate*.

WE ſhall finiſh this Chapter with a few
miſcellany Obſervations.

IN the firſt place it may be obſerved,
through all the Species of Disjunctives,
that the *ſame* Disjunctive appears to have
greater or *leſs* force, according as the Subjects, which it disjoins, are more or leſs
disjoined by Nature. For example, if
we ſay, *Every Number is even*, OR *odd—
Every Propoſition is true*, OR *falſe*—nothing
ſeems to disjoin *more ſtrongly* than the
Disjunctive, becauſe no things are in Nature more *incompatible* than the Subjectſ.
But if we ſay, *That Object is a Triangle*,
OR *Figure contained under three right lines*
—the (OR) in this caſe hardly ſeems to
disjoin, or indeed to do more, than *diſtinctly* to expreſs the Thing, firſt by its
S   *Name,*

Ch. II. AND so much for CONJUNCTIONS, their Genus, and their Species.

---

the rest, should have their works filled with Particles of all kinds, and with Conjunctions in particular; while in the modern polite works, as well of ourselves as of our neighbours, scarce such a Word as a Particle, or Conjunction is to be found. Is it, that where there is *Connection in the Meaning*, there must be *Words had to connect*; but that where the Connection is little or none, such Connectives are of little use? That Houses of Cards, without cement, may well answer their end, but not those Houses, where one would chuse to dwell? Is this the Cause? or have we attained an Elegance, to the Antients unknown?

Venimus ad summam fortunæ, &c.

CHAP. III.

Concerning those Connectives, called Prepositions.

PREPOSITIONS by their name express their *Place*, but not their *Character*. Their Definition will distinguish them from the former Connectives. A PREPOSITION *is a Part of Speech, devoid itself of Signification, but so formed as to unite two Words that are significant, and that refuse to co-alesce or unite of themselves* (*a*).

This

(*a*) The Stoic Name for a Preposition was Προθετικὸς Σύνδεσμος, *Præpositiva Conjunctio*, a *Prepositive Conjunction*. Ὡς μὲν ἓν ᾗ κατὰ τὰς ἄλλας παραθέσεις αἱ προθέσεις συνδεσμικῆς συντάξεως γίνονῙαι παρεμφατικαὶ, λέλεκῙαι ἡμῖν· ἐξ ὧν ᾗ ἀφορμὴ εὕρηται παρὰ τοῖς Στωικοῖς τῶ καλεῖσθαι αὐτὰς Προθετικὰς Συνδέσμως. *Now in what manner even in other applications* (besides the present) *Prepositions give proof of their Conjunctive Syntax, we have mentioned already; whence too the Stoics took*

Ch. III. This connective Power, (which relates to *Words* only, and not *Sentences*) will be better understood from the following Speculations.

SOME things co-alesce and unite *of themselves*; others refuse to do so *without help*, and as it were compulsion. Thus in Works of Art, the Morter and the Stone co-alesce of themselves; but the Wainscot and the Wall not without Nails and Pins. In nature this is more conspicuous. For example; all Quantities, and Qualities co-alesce immediately with their Substances. Thus it is we say, *a fierce Lion, a vast Mountain*; and from *this Natural Concord of Subject and Accident*, arises *the Grammatical Concord of Substantive and Adjective*. In like

---

took occasion to call them PREPOSITIVE CONJUNCTIONS. *Apollon.* L. IV. c. 5. p. 313. Yet is this in fact rather a descriptive *Sketch*, than a complete *Definition*, since there are other Conjunctions, which are Prepositive as well as these. See *Gaz.* L. IV. de Præposit. *Prisc.* L. XIV. p. 983.

like manner Actions co-alesce with their Ch. III.
Agents, and Passions with their Patients.
Thus it is we say, *Alexander conquers; Darius is conquered.* Nay, as every Energy is a kind of Medium between its Agent and Patient, the whole three, *Agent, Energy,* and *Patient,* co-alesce with the same facility; as when we say, *Alexander conquers Darius.* And hence, that is from *these Modes of natural Co-alescence,* arises *the Grammatical Regimen of the Verb by its Nominative, and of the Accusative by its Verb.* Farther than this, Attributives themselves may be most of them characterized; as when we say of such Attributives as *ran, beautiful, learned,* he *ran swiftly,* she was *very beautiful,* he was *moderately learned,* &c. And hence the *Co-alescence of the Adverb* with *Verbs, Participles,* and *Adjectives.*

THE general Conclusion appears to be this. "THOSE PARTS OF SPEECH UNITE
" OF THEMSELVES IN GRAMMAR, WHOSE
" ORIGINAL ARCHETYPES UNITE OF
" THEM-

Ch. III. *"* THEMSELVES IN NATURE." To which we may add, as following from what has been said, that *the great Objects of Natural Union are* SUBSTANCE *and* ATTRIBUTE. Now tho' *Substances* naturally co-incide with their *Attributes,* yet they abfolutely refufe doing fo, *one with another* (*b*). And hence thofe known Maxims in Phyfics, that *Body is impenetrable;* that *two Bodies cannot poſſeſs the ſame place;* that *the ſame Attribute cannot belong to different Subſtances,* &c.

FROM thefe Principles it follows, that when we form a Sentence, the *Subſtantive* without difficulty co-incides with the *Verb,* from the natural Co-incidence of *Subſtance* and *Energy*—THE SUN WARMETH. So likewife the *Energy* with the *Subject,* on

which

(*b*) *Cauſa, propter quam duo Subſtantiva non ponuntur ſine copulâ, e Philoſophiâ petenda eſt: neque enim duo ſubſtantialiter unum eſſe poteſt, ſicut Subſtantia et Accidens; itaque non dicas,* CÆSAR, CATO PUGNAT. *Scal. de Cauſ. Ling. Lat. c.* 177.

which it operates——WARMETH THE Ch.III.
EARTH. So likewise both *Subſtance* and
Energy with their proper *Attributes*.—
THE SPLENDID SUN,—GENIALLY WARM-
ETH—THE FERTILE EARTH. But ſuppoſe we were deſirous to add other Subſtantives, as for inſtance, AIR, or BEAMS.
How would theſe co-incide, or under what
Character could they be introduced? Not
as *Nominatives* or *Accuſatives*, for both
thoſe places are already filled; the Nominative by the Subſtance, SUN; the Accuſative by the Subſtance, EARTH. Not as
Attributes to theſe laſt, or to any other
thing; for *Attributes by nature they neither are, nor can be made.* Here then we
perceive the Riſe and Uſe of PREPOSI-
TIONS. By theſe we connect thoſe Subſtantives to Sentences, which at the time
are unable to co-aleſce *of themſelves.* Let
us aſſume for inſtance a pair of theſe Connectives, THRO', and WITH, and mark
their Effect upon the Subſtances here mentioned. *The ſplendid Sun* WITH *his Beams
genially*

Ch. III. *genially warmeth* THRO' *the Air the fertile Earth.* The Sentence, as before, remains *intire and one;* the *Substantives* required are both *introduced;* and not a Word, which was there before, is detruded from its proper place.

IT must here be observed that most, if not all Prepositions seem originally formed to denote the *Relations of* PLACE (*c*). The reason is, this is that grand *Relation,* which *Bodies* or *natural Substances* maintain at all times one to another, whether they are contiguous or remote, whether in motion, or at rest.

IT may be said indeed that *in the Continuity of Place* they form this UNIVERSE

or

(*c*) *Omne corpus aut movetur aut quiescit: quare opus fuit aliquâ notâ, quæ* TO ΠΟΥ *significaret, sive esset inter duo extrema, inter quæ motus fit, sive esset in altero extremorum, in quibus fit quies. Hinc eliciemus Præpositionis essentialem definitionem.* Scal. de Cauf. Ling. Lat. c. 152.

or VISIBLE WHOLE, and are made as much ONE by that general Comprehenfion, as is confiftent with their feveral Natures, and fpecific Diftinctions. Thus it is we have Prepofitions to denote the *contiguous Relation* of Body, as when we fay, *Caius walked* WITH *a Staff*; *the Statue ftood* UPON *a Pedeftal*; *the River ran* OVER *a Sand*; others for *the detached* Relation, as when we fay, *He is going* TO *Italy*; *the Sun is rifen* ABOVE *the Hills*; *thefe Figs came* FROM *Turky*. So as to *Motion* and *Reft*, only with this difference, that *here* the Prepofition varies its character with the Verb. Thus if we fay, *that Lamp hangs* FROM *the Ceiling*, the Prepofition, FROM, affumes a Character of *Quiefcence*. But if we fay, *that Lamp is falling* FROM *the Ceiling*, the Prepofition in fuch cafe affumes a Character of *Motion*. So in *Milton*,

—*To fupport uneafie Steps*
OVER *the burning Marle*—Par. L. I.

Here OVER denotes *Motion*.

Ch. III.

Again

Ch. III. Again—

—*He—with looks of cordial Love Hung* OVER *her enamour'd*—Par. L. IV.

Here OVER denotes *Rest*.

BUT though the original use of Prepositions was to denote *the Relations of Place*, they could not be confined to this Office only. They by degrees extended themselves to Subjects *incorporeal*, and came to denote Relations, as well *intellectual* as *local*. Thus, because in Place he, who is *above*, has commonly the advantage over him, who is *below*, hence we transfer OVER and UNDER to *Dominion* and *Obedience*; of a King we say, *he ruled* OVER *his People*; of a common Soldier, *he served* UNDER *such a General*. So too we say, *with* Thought; *without* Attention; thinking *over* a Subject; *under* Anxiety; *from* Fear; *out of* Love; *through* Jealousy, &c. All which instances, with many others of like kind,

BOOK THE SECOND. Ch. III.

kind, shew that the *first Words* of Men, like their *first Ideas*, had an immediate reference to *sensible Objects*, and that in afterdays, when they began to discern with their *Intellect*, they took those Words, which they found *already* made, and transferred them by metaphor to *intellectual* Conceptions. There is indeed no Method to express new Ideas, but either this of *Metaphor*, or that of *Coining new Words*, both which have been practised by Philosophers and wise Men, according to the nature, and exigence of the occasion (*d*).

IN

(*d*) Among the Words new coined we may ascribe to *Anaxagoras*, Ὁμοιομέρεια; to *Plato*, Ποιότης; to *Cicero*, *Qualitas*; to *Aristotle*, Ἐντελέχεια; to the *Stoics*, Ὄυτις, κεράτις, and many others.—Among the Words transferred by Metaphor from *common* to *special* Meanings, to the *Platonics* we may ascribe Ἰδέα; to the *Pythagoreans* and *Peripatetics*, Κατηγορία, and Κατηγορεῖν; to the *Stoics*, Κατάληψις, ὑπόληψις, καθῆκον; to the *Pyrrhonists*, Ἕξεσι, ἐνδέχεται, ἐπέχω, &c.

And

Ch. III. IN the foregoing use of Prepositions, we have seen how they are applied κατὰ παράθεσιν, *by way of Juxta-position*, that is to say, where they are prefixt to a Word, with-

---

And here I cannot but observe, that he who pretends to discuss the Sentiments of any one of these Philosophers, or even to cite and translate him (except in trite and obvious Sentences) without accurately knowing the *Greek* Tongue in general; the nice differences of many Words apparently synonymous; the peculiar Stile of the Author whom he presumes to handle; the new coined Words, and new Significations given to old Words, used by such Author, and his Sect; the whole Philosophy of such Sect, together with the Connections and Dependencies of its several Parts, whether Logical, Ethical, or Physical;—He I say, that, without this previous preparation, attempts what I have said, will shoot in the dark; will be liable to perpetual blunders; will explain, and praise, and censure merely by chance; and though he may possibly to Fools appear as a wise Man, will certainly among the wise ever pass for a Fool. Such a Man's Intellect comprehends antient Philosophy, as his Eye comprehends a distant Prospect. He may see perhaps enough, to know Mountains from Plains, and Seas from Woods; but for an accurate discernment of particulars, and their character, this without farther helps, it is impossible he should attain.

BOOK THE SECOND. 271

without becoming a Part of it. But they Ch. III. may be used also κατὰ σύνθεσιν, by way of *Composition*, that is, they may be prefixt to a Word, so as to become a real Part of it (*e*). Thus in *Greek* we have Ἐπίϛασθαι, in *Latin*, *Intelligere*, in *English*, to *Understand*. So also, to *foretel*, to *overact*, to *undervalue*, to *outgo*, &c. and in *Greek* and *Latin*, other Instances innumerable. In this case the Prepositions commonly transfuse something of their own Meaning into the Word, with which they are compounded; and this imparted Meaning in most instances will be found ultimately resolvable into some of the Relations of PLACE, (*f*) as used either in its *proper* or *metaphorical* acceptation.

LASTLY,

―――――――――――――

(*e*) See *Gaz.* Gram. L. IV. Cap. de Præpositione.

(*f*) For example, let us suppose some given Space. E & Ex signify *out of* that Space; PER, *through it*, from beginning to end; IN, *within it*; SUB, *under it*.

Hence

Ch. III. LASTLY, there are times, when Prepositions totally lose their connective Nature,
being

Hence then E and PER in composition augment; *Enormis*, something not simply big, but big in excess; something got *out of the rule*, and *beyond the measure*; *Dico*, to *speak*; *Edico*, to *speak out*; whence *Edictum*, an *Edict*, something so effectually spoken, as all are supposed to hear, and all to obey. So *Terence*,

Dico, Edico vobis—Eun. V. 5. 20.

which (as *Donatus* tells us in his Comment) is an Αὔξησις. *Fari, to speak*; *Effari, to speak out*—hence *Effatum*, an *Axiom*, or self-evident Proposition, something addressed as it were to all men, and calling for universal Assent. *Cic.* Acad. II. 29. *Permagnus, Perutilis*, great *throughout*, useful *through every part*.

On the contrary, IN and SUB diminish and lessen. *Injustus, Iniquus, unjust, inequitable*, that lies *within* Justice and Equity, that reaches not so far, that falls *short of them*; *Subniger, blackish*; *Subrubicundus, reddish*; tending to black, and tending to red, but yet *under* the standard, and *below* perfection.

Emo originally signified *to take away*; hence it came to signify *to buy*, because he, who buys, *takes away* his purchase. INTER, *Between*, implies *Discontinuance*,

being converted into Adverbs, and used in Ch. III. Syntax accordingly. Thus *Homer*,

—Γέλασσε δὲ πᾶσα περὶ χθών.
—*And Earth smil'd all around.*

Ιλ. T. 362.

But of this we have spoken in a preceding Chapter (*g*). One thing we must however observe, before we finish this Chapter, which is, that whatever we may be told of CASES in modern Languages, there are in fact no such things; but their force and power is exprest by two Methods,

---

ance, for in things continuous there can nothing lie between. From these two comes, *Interimo, to kill,* that is to say, *to take a Man away in the midst of Life,* by making a *Discontinuance of his vital Energy.* So also *Perimo, to kill* a Man, that is to say, *to take him away thoroughly*; for indeed what more thorough taking away can well be supposed? The *Greek* Verb, Ἀναιρεῖν, and the *English* Verb, *To take off,* seem b th to carry the same allusion. And thus it is that Prepositions become Parts of other Words.

(*g*) See before p. 205.

T

thods, either by *Situation*, or by *Prepofi-tions*; *the Nominative and Accufative Cafes* by Situation; *the reft*, by Prepofitions. But this we fhall make the Subject of a Chapter by itfelf, concluding here our Inquiry concerning Prepofitions.

CHAP. IV.

Concerning Cases.

AS CASES, or at least their various Powers, depend on the knowledge partly of *Nouns*, partly of *Verbs*, and partly of *Prepositions*; they have been reserved, till those Parts of Speech had been examined and discussed, and are for that reason made the Subject of so late a Chapter, as the present.

THERE are no CASES in the modern Languages, except a few among the *primitive Pronouns*, such as I, and ME; JE, and MOY; and the *English Genitive*, formed by the addition of s, as when from *Lion*, we form *Lion's*; from *Ship*, *Ship's*. From this defect however we may be enabled to discover in some instances *what a Case is*, the *Periphrasis*, which supplies

Ch. IV. plies its place, being *the Cafe* (as it were) unfolded. Thus *Equi* is analized into *Du Cheval, Of the Horfe*; *Equo* into *Au Cheval, To the Horfe*. And hence we fee that the GENITIVE and DATIVE CASES imply the joint Power of a *Noun* and a *Prepofition*, the Genitive's Prepofition being *A*, *De*, or *Ex*, the Dative's Prepofition being *Ad*, or *Verfus*.

WE have not this affiftance as to the ACCUSATIVE, which in modern Languages (a few inftances excepted) is only known from its pofition, that is to fay, by being fubfequent to its Verb, in the collocation of the words.

THE VOCATIVE we pafs over from its little ufe, being not only unknown to the modern Languages, but often in the antient being fupplied by the *Nominative*.

THE ABLATIVE likewife was ufed by the *Romans* only; a Cafe they feem to have adopted

BOOK THE SECOND. 277

adopted *to affociate with their Prepofitions*, Ch.IV; as they had deprived their *Genitive* and *Dative* of that privilege; a Cafe certainly not neceffary, becaufe the *Greeks* do as well without it, and becaufe with the *Romans* themfelves it is frequently undiftinguifhed.

THERE remains the NOMINATIVE; which whether it were a Cafe or no, was much difputed by the Antients. The *Peripatetics* held it to be no *Cafe*, and likened the Noun, in this its *primary* and *original Form*, to a perpendicular Line, fuch for example, as the line AB.

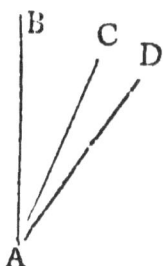

The Variations from the Nominative, they confidered as if A B were to fall from its perpendicular, as for example, to A C, or A D. Hence then they only called thefe Variations, ΠΤΩΣΕΙΣ, CASUS, CASES, or

T 3   FAL-

Ch. IV. FALLINGS. The *Stoics* on the contrary, and the Grammarians with them, made the *Nominative* a CASE alfo. Words they confidered (as it were) *to fall from the Mind*, or *difcurfive Faculty*. Now when a Noun fell thence *in its primary Form*, they then called it ΠΤΩΣΙΣ ΟΡΘΗ, CASUS RECTUS, AN ERECT, or UPRIGHT CASE or FALLING, fuch as A B, and by this name they diftinguifhed the *Nominative*. When *it fell from the Mind under any of its variations*, as for example in the form of a *Genitive*, a *Dative*, or the like, fuch variations they called ΠΤΩΣΕΙΣ ΠΛΑΓΙΑΙ, CASUS OBLIQUI, OBLIQUE CASES, or SIDELONG FALLINGS (fuch as A C, or A D) in oppofition to the other (that is A B) which was erect and perpendicular (*a*). Hence too Grammarians called the Method of enumerating the various Cafes of a Noun, ΚΛΙΣΙΣ, DECLINATIO, a DECLENSION,

it

(*a*) See *Ammon.* in Libr. de Interpr. p. 35.

it being a fort of *progreſſive Deſcent from* Ch.IV; *the Noun's upright Form thro' its various declining Forms*, that is, a Deſcent from A B, to A C, A D, *&c.*

OF theſe CASES we ſhall treat but of four, that is to ſay, the NOMINATIVE, the ACCUSATIVE, the GENITIVE, and the DATIVE.

IT has been ſaid already in the preceding Chapter, that the great Objects of natural Union are SUBSTANCE and ATTRIBUTE. Now from this *Natural Concord* ariſes the *Logical Concord* of SUBJECT and PREDICATE, and the *Grammatical Concord of* SUBSTANTIVE and ATTRIBUTIVE (*b*). Theſe CONCORDS in SPEECH produce PROPOSITIONS and SENTENCES, as that previous CONCORD in NATURE produces NATURAL BEINGS. This being admitted,

(*b*) See before, p. 264.

Ch.IV. admitted, we proceed by obferving, that when a Sentence is regular and orderly, *Nature's Subſtance*, the *Logician's Subject*, and the *Grammarian's Subſtantive* are all denoted by that Cafe, which we call the NOMINATIVE. For example, CÆSAR *pugnat*, ÆS *fingitur*, DOMUS *ædificatur*. We may remark too by the way, that *the Character of this Nominative* may be learnt from its *Attributive*. The Action implied in *pugnat*, fhews its Nominative CÆSAR to be an Active efficient Caufe; the Paffion implied in *fingitur*, fhews its Nominative Æs to be a Paffive Subject, as does the Paffion in *ædificatur* prove DOMUS to be an Effect.

As therefore every Attributive would as far as poffible conform itfelf to its Subftantive, fo for this reafon, when it has Cafes, it imitates its Subftantive, and appears as a *Nominative* alfo. So we find it in fuch inftances as—CICERO *eſt* ELOQUENS; VITIUM *eſt* TURPE; HOMO *eſt* ANIMAL,

ANIMAL, &c. When it has no Cafes, Ch.IV. (as happens with Verbs) it is forced to content itfelf with fuch affimilations as it has, thofe of Number and Perfon*; as when we fay, CICERO LOQUITUR; NOS LOQUIMUR; HOMINES LOQUUNTUR.

FROM what has been faid, we may make the following obfervations—that as there can be *no Sentence without a Subflantive*, fo that Subftantive, if the Sentence be *regular*, is always denoted by a *Nominative*—that on this occafion *all the Attributives, that have Cafes*, appear as *Nominatives* alfo—that there may be a regular and perfect Sentence *without any of the other Cafes*, but that *without one Nominative at leaft*, this is utterly impoffible. Hence therefore we form its Character and Defcription—THE NOMINATIVE *is that Cafe, without which there can be no regular*

---

* What fort of Number and Perfon Verbs have, fee before, p. 170, 171.

Ch. IV. *lar (c) and perfect Sentence.* We are now to search after another Case.

WHEN the *Attributive* in any Sentence is some *Verb denoting Action,* we may be assured *the principal Substantive* is some *active efficient* Cause. So we may call *Achilles* and *Lysippus* in such Sentences as *Achilles vulneravit, Lysippus fecit.* But though this be evident and clearly understood, the Mind is still *in suspence,* and finds its conception *imcomplete.* ACTION, it well knows, not only requires some *Agent,* but it must have a *Subject* also to work on, and it must produce some *Effect.* It is then to denote one of these (that is, the *Subject* or the *Effect)* that the Authors of Language

---

(c) We have added *regular* as well as *perfect,* because there may be *irregular* Sentences, which may be *perfect without a Nominative.* Of this kind are all Sentences, made out of those Verbs, called by the *Stoics* Παρασυμβάματα or Παρακατηγορήματα, such as Σωκράτει μεταμέλει, *Socratem pœnitet,* &c. See before, p. 180.

guage have deftined THE ACCUSATIVE. Ch.IV. *Achilles vulneravit* HECTOREM—here the Accufative denotes the Subject. *Lyfippus fecit* STATUAS——here the Accufative denotes the Effect. By thefe additional Explanations the Mind becomes fatisfied, and the Sentences acquire a Perfection, which before they wanted. In whatever other manner, whether figuratively, or with Prepofitions, this Cafe may have been ufed, its firft deftination feems to have been that here mentioned, and hence therefore we fhall form its Character and Defcription—THE ACCUSATIVE *is that Cafe, which to an efficient Nominative and a Verb of Action fubjoins either the Effect or the paffive Subject.* We have ftill left the Genitive and the Dative, which we inveftigate, as follows.

IT has been faid in the preceding Chapther (*d*), that when the Places of the *No-*
minative

(*d*) See before, p. 265.

Ch. IV. *minative* and the *Accufative* are filled by proper Subftantives, other Subftantives are annexed by the help of *Prepofitions*. Now, though this be fo far true in the modern Languages, that (a very few inftances excepted) they know no other method; yet is not the rule of equal latitude with refpect to the *Latin* or *Greek*, and that from reafons which we are about to offer.

AMONG the various Relations of Subftantives denoted by Prepofitions, there appear to be two principal ones; and thefe are, the *Term* or *Point*, which fomething commences FROM, and the *Term* or *Point*, which fomething tends TO. Thefe Relations the *Greeks* and *Latins* thought of fo great importance, as to diftinguifh them, when they occurred, *by peculiar Terminations of their own*, which expreft their force, *without the help of a Prepofition*. Now it is here we behold the Rife of the antient Genitive, and Dative, the GENITIVE *being formed to exprefs all Relations com-*

commencing FROM *itself*; THE DATIVE, Ch.IV.
all Relations tending TO *itself*. Of this
there can be no stronger proof, than the
Analysis of these Cases in the modern
Languages, which we have mentioned
already (*e*).

IT is on these Principles that they say in
Greek—Δεομαί ΣΟΥ, δίδωμί ΣΟΙ, OF
thee I ask, To *thee I give*. The reason
is, in requests the person requested is one
whom something is expected *from*; in
donations, the person presented, is one
whom something passes *to*. So again—
(*f*) Πεποίηται λίθȣ, *it is made of Stone*. Stone
was the passive Subject, and thus it appears
in the *Genitive*, as being the *Term from*,
or *out of which*. Even in *Latin*, where
the Syntax is more formal and strict, we
read—

Implentur

(*e*) See before, p. 275. 276.

(*f*) Χρυσȣ̃ πεποιημένος, χ̀ ἐλέφανΊος, *made of Gold
and Ivory*. So says *Pausanias* of the *Olympian Jupiter*,
L. V. p. 400. See also *Hom. Iliad*. Σ. 574.

Ch. IV. *Implentur veteris Bacchi, pinguisque ferinæ.*   Virg.

The old Wine and Venison were the funds or stores, *of* or *from* which they were filled. Upon the same principles, Πίνω τȣ̃ ὕδατος, is a Phrase in *Greek*; and, *Je bois de l'eau,* a Phrase in *French,* as much as to say, *I take some or a certain part,* FROM or OUT OF *a certain whole.*

WHEN we meet in Language such Genitives as *the Son of a Father; the Father of a Son; the Picture of a Painter; the Painter of a Picture,* &c. these are all RELATIVES, and therefore each of them reciprocally a *Term or Point* to the other, FROM or OUT OF which it derives its *Essence,* or at least its *Intellection* (*g*).

THE

(*g*) All Relatives are said to reciprocate, or mutually infer each other, and therefore they are often exprest by this Case, that is to say, the Genitive. Thus *Aristotle,* Πάντα δὲ τὰ πρός τι πρός ἀντιστρέφοντα λέγεται, οἷον

THE *Dative*, as it implies *Tendency to*, Ch.IV.
is employed among its other ufes to denote
the FINAL CAUSE, that being the Caufe
to which all Events, not fortuitous, may be
faid to tend. It is thus ufed in the following inftances, among innumerable others.

———TIBI *fuaveis dædala tellus*
Submittit flores——   Lucret.
———TIBI *brachia contrahit ardens*
Scorpios—   Virg. G. I.
———TIBI *ferviat ultima Thule.*
                             Ibid.

AND fo much for CASES, their Origin
and Ufe; a Sort of Forms, or Terminations,

οἷον ὁ δᾶλ☉ δεσπότε δᾶλ☉, ϰὴ ὁ δεσπότης δελε δεσπότης λέγεται εἶναι, ϰὴ τὸ διπλάσιον ἡμίσε☉ διπλάσιον, ϰὴ τὸ ἥμισυ διπλασίε ἥμισυ. *Omnia vero, quæ funt ad aliquid, referuntur ad ea, quæ reciprocantur. Ut fervus dicitur domini fervus; et dominus, fervi dominus; necnon duplum, dimidii duplum; et dimidium, dupli dimidium.* Categor. C. VII.

Ch. IV. tions, which we could not well pafs over, from their great importance (*h*) both in the *Greek* and *Latin* Tongues; but which however, not being among the Effentials of Language, and therefore not to be found in many particular Languages, can be hardly faid to fall within the limits of our Inquiry.

(*h*) *Annon et illud obfervatione dignum (licet nobis modernis fpiritûs nonnihil redundat) antiquas Linguas plenas declinationum, cafuum, conjugationum, et fimilium fuiffe; modernas, his ferè deftitutas, plurima per præpofitiones et verba auxiliaria fegniter expedire? Sanè facilè quis conjiciat (utcunque nobis ipfi placeamus) ingenia priorum feculorum noftris fuiffe multo acutiora et fubtiliora.* Bacon. *de Augm. Scient.* VI. 1.

CHAP.

CHAP. V.

Concerning Interjections—Recapitulation—Conclusion.

BESIDES the Parts of Speech before mentioned, there remains THE INTERJECTION. Of this Kind among the *Greeks* are ῏Ω, Φεῦ, ῎Αι, &c. among the *Latins*, *Ah! Heu! Hei!* &c. among the *English*, *Ah! Alas! Fie!* &c. These the *Greeks* have ranged among their *Adverbs*; improperly, if we consider the Adverbial Nature, which always co-incides with some Verb, as its Principal, and to which it always serves in the character of an Attributive. Now INTERJECTIONS *co-incide with no Part of Speech, but are either uttered alone, or else thrown into a Sentence, without altering its Form, either in Syntax or Signification.* The *Latins* seem therefore to have done better in † separating

---

† *Vid Servium in Æneid* XII. v. 486.

HERMES.

rating them by themselves, and giving them a name by way of diſtinction from the reſt.

SHOULD it be aſk'd, if not Adverbs, what then are they? It may be anſwered, not ſo properly Parts of Speech, as adventitious Sounds; certain VOICES OF NATURE, rather than Voices of *Art*, expreſſing thoſe Paſſions and natural Emotions, which ſpontaneouſly ariſe in the human Soul, upon the View or Narrative of intereſting Events (*a*).

" AND

(*a*) INTERJECTIONES *a Græcis ad Adverbia referuntur, atque eos ſequitur etiam Boethius. Et recte quidem de iis, quando caſum regunt. Sed quando orationi ſolum inferuntur, ut nota affectûs, velut ſuſpirii aut metûs, vix videntur ad claſſem aliquam pertinere, ut quæ* NATURALES *ſint* NOTÆ; *non, aliarum vocum inſtar, ex inſtituto ſignificant.* Voſſ. de Anal. L. I. c. I. INTERJECTIO *eſt Vox affectum mentis ſignificans, ac citra verbi opem ſententiam complens.* Ibid. c. 3. *Reſtat. claſ. ſium extrema,* INTERJECTIO. *Hujus appellatio non ſimi-*

Ch. V.

" AND thus we have found that ALL
" WORDS ARE EITHER SIGNIFICANT BY
" THEMSELVES, OR ONLY SIGNIFICANT,
"WHEN

---

fimiliter fe habet ac Conjunctionis. Nam cum hæc dicatur Conjunctio, quia conjungat; Interjectio tamen, non quia interjacet, sed quia interjicitur, *nomen accepit. Nec tamen de usia ejus est, ut interjiciatur; cum per se compleat sententiam, nec raro ab eâ incipiat oratio.* Ibid. L. IV. c. 28. INTERJECTIONEM *non esse partem Orationis sic ostendo: Quod naturale est, idem est apud omnes: Sed gemitus & signa lætitiæ idem sunt apud omnes: Sunt igitur naturales. Si vero naturales, non sunt partes Orationis. Nam eæ partes, secundum Aristotelem, ex instituto, non naturâ, debent constare. Interjectionem Græci Adverbiis adnumerant; sed falsò. Nam neque,* &c. Sanct. Miner. I. I. c. 2. INTERJECTIONEM *Græci inter Adverbia ponunt, quoniam hæc quoque vel adjungitur verbis, vel verba ei subaudiuntur. Ut si dicam*—Papæ! quid video?—*vel per se*—Papæ!—*etiamsi non addatur,* Miror; *habet in se ipsius verbi significationem. Quæ res maxime fecit Romanarum artium Scriptores seperatim hanc partem ab Adverbiis accipere; quia videtur affectum habere in sese Verbi, et plenam motûs animi significationem, etiamsi non addatur Verbum, demonstrare. Interjectio tamen non solum illa, quæ dicunt Græci* σχετλιασμον, *significat; sed etiam voces, quæ cujuscunque passionis animi pulsu per exclamationem* interjiciuntur. Prisc. L. XV.

Ch. V. " WHEN ASSOCIATED—*that thofe figni-*
"*ficant by themfelves, denote either* SUB-
" STANCES *or* ATTRIBUTES, *and are call-*
"*ed for that reafon* SUBSTANTIVES *and*
" ATTRIBUTIVES—*that the Subftantives*
"*are either* NOUNS *or* PRONOUNS—*that*
"*the* ATTRIBUTIVES *are either* PRIMARY
"*or* SECONDARY—*that the Primary At-*
"*tributives are either* VERBS, PARTICI-
" PLES, *or* ADJECTIVES; *the Secondary,*
" ADVERBS—*Again, that the Parts of*
"*Speech, only fignificant when affociated, are*
"*either* DEFINITIVES *or* CONNECTIVES
" —*that the Definitives are either* ARTI-
" CULAR, *or* PRONOMINAL—*and that*
"*the Connectives are either* PREPOSITIONS
"*or* CONJUNCTIONS."

AND thus have we refolved LANGUAGE,
AS A WHOLE INTO ITS CONSTITUENT
PARTS, which was the firft thing, that we
propofed, in the courfe of this Inquiry (*b*).
BUT

(*b*) See before, p. 7.

BUT now as we conclude, methinks I Ch. V.
hear some Objector, demanding with an
air of pleasantry, and ridicule—" *Is there*
" *no speaking then without all this trouble?*
" *Do we not talk every one of us, as well*
" *unlearned, as learned; as well poor Pea-*
" *sants, as profound Philosophers?*" We
may answer by interrogating on our part
—Do not those same poor Peasants use
the Levar and the Wedge, and many
other Instruments, with much habitual
readiness? And yet have they any conception of those Geometrical Principles,
from which those Machines derive their
Efficacy and Force? And is the Ignorance
of these Peasants, a reason for others to
remain ignorant; or to render the Subject
a less becoming Inquiry? Think of Animals, and Vegetables, that occur every
day—of Time, of Place, and of Motion
—of Light, of Colours, and of Gravitation—of our very Senses and Intellect,
by which we perceive every thing else—

THAT

Ch. V. THAT they are, we all know, and are perfectly satisfied—WHAT they are, is a Subject of much obscurity and doubt. Were we to reject this last Question, because we are certain of the first, we should banish all Philosophy at once out of the world (c).

BUT a graver Objector now accosts us. "*What* (says he) *is the* UTILITY? "*Whence the Profit, where the Gain?*" Every Science whatever (we may answer) has its Use. Arithmetic is excellent

---

(c) Ἀλλ' ἔστι πολλὰ τῶν ὄντων, ἃ τὴν μὲν ὕπαρξιν ἔχει γνωριμωτάτην, ἀγνωστοτάτην δὲ τὴν ουσίαν· ὥσπερ ἥτε κίνησις, ϗ ὁ τόπος, ἔτι δὲ μᾶλλον ὁ χρόνος. Ἑκάσου γὰρ τούτων τὸ μὲν εἶναι γνώριμον ϗ ἀναμφίλεκτον· τίς δὲ ποτέ ἐστιν αὐτῶν ἡ ουσία, τῶν χαλεπωτάτων ἐραθῆναι. Ἔστι δὲ δὴ τί τῶν τοιούτων ϗ ἡ ψυχή· τὸ μὲν γὰρ εἶναί τι τὴν ψυχὴν, γνωριμώτατον ϗ φανερώτατον· τί δὲ ποτέ ἐστιν, ὲ ῥᾴδιον καταμαθεῖν. Ἀλέξανδ. Ἀφροδ. Περὶ ψυχῆς, Β'. p. 142.

lent for the gauging of Liquors; Geome- Ch. V.
try, for the measuring of Estates; Astro-
nomy, for the making of Almanacks; and
Grammar perhaps, for the drawing of
Bonds and Conveyances.

THUS much to the *Sordid*—If the
Liberal ask for something better than this,
we may answer and assure them from the
best authorities, that every Exercise of the
Mind upon Theorems of Science, like
generous and manly Exercise of the
Body, tends to call forth and strengthen
Nature's original Vigour. Be the Subject itself immediately lucrative or not,
the Nerves of Reason are braced by the
mere Employ, and we become abler Ac-
tors in the Drama of Life, whether our
Part be of the busier, or of the sedater
kind.

Ch. V. PERHAPS too *there is a Pleasure even in Science itself,* distinct from any End, to which it may be farther conducive. Are not Health and Strength of *Body* desirable for their own sakes, tho' we happen not to be fated either for Porters or Draymen; And have not Health and Strength of *Mind* their intrinsic Worth also, tho' not condemned to the low drudgery of sordid Emolument? Why should there not be *a Good* (could we have the Grace to recognize it) *in the mere Energy of our Intellect,* as much as in Energies of lower degree? The Sportsman believes there is Good in his Chace; the Man of Gaiety, in his Intrigue; even the Glutton, in his Meal. We may justly ask of these, *why they pursue such things;* but if they answer, *they pursue them, because they are* GOOD, it would be folly to ask them farther, WHY *they* PURSUE *what is* GOOD. It might well in such case be replied on

their

their behalf (how ſtrange ſoever it may at firſt appear) *that if there was not ſomething* Good, *which was in no reſpect* useful, *even things uſeful themſelves could not poſſibly have exiſtence.* For this is in fact no more than to aſſert, that ſome things are Ends, ſome things are Means, and that if there were no Ends, there could be of courſe no Means.

Ch. V.

It ſhould ſeem then the Grand Queſtion was, what is Good—that is to ſay, *what is that which is deſirable, not for ſomething elſe, but for itſelf;* for whether it be the Chace, or the Intrigue, or the Meal, may be fairly queſtioned, ſince Men in each inſtance are far from being agreed.

In the mean time it is plain from daily experience, there are infinite Pleaſures, Amuſements, and Diverſions, ſome for Summer, others for Winter; ſome for
Country

Ch. V. Country, others for Town; some, easy, indolent, and soft; others, boisterous, active, and rough; a multitude diversified to every taste, and which for the time are enjoyed as PERFECT GOOD, *without a thought of any End, that may be farther obtained*. Some Objects of this kind are at times sought by all men, excepting alone that contemptible Tribe, who, from a love to the Means of life wholly forgetting its End, are truly for that reason called *Misers*, or Miserable.

If there be supposed then a Pleasure, a Satisfaction, a Good, a Something valuable for its self without view to any thing farther, in so many Objects of the *subordinate* kind; shall we not allow the same praise to the *sublimest* of all Objects? Shall THE INTELLECT alone feel no pleasures *in its Energy*, when we allow them to the grossest Energies of Appetite, and Sense? Or if the Reality of all Pleasures and Goods

were

Ch. V.

were to be controverted, may not the *Intellectual* Sort be defended, as rationally as any of them? Whatever may be urged in behalf of the rest (for we are not now arraigning them) we may safely affirm of INTELLECTUAL GOOD, that it is "the "Good of that Part, which is most ex- "cellent within us; that it is a Good ac- "commodated to all Places and Times; "which neither depends on the will of "others, nor on the affluence of external "Fortune; that it is a Good, which de- "cays not with decaying Appetites, but "often rises in vigour, when those are no "more (*d*)."

THERE is a Difference, we must own, between this *Intellectual* Virtue, and *Moral* Virtue. MORAL VIRTUE, from its Em- ployment, may be called more HUMAN,

as

(*d*) See Vol. I. p. 119, 120, &c.

Ch. V. as it tempers our Appetites to the purposes of human Life. But INTELLECTUAL VIRTUE may be surely called more DIVINE, if we consider the Nature and Sublimity of its End.

INDEED for *Moral Virtue*, as it it almost wholly conversant about Appetites, and Affections, either to reduce the natural ones to a proper Mean, or totally to expel the unnatural and vitious, it would be impious to suppose THE DEITY to have occasion for such an Habit, or that any work of this kind should call for his attention. Yet GOD IS, and LIVES. So we are assured from Scripture it self. What then may we suppose the DIVINE LIFE to be? Not a Life of Sleep, as Fables tell us of *Endymion*. If we may be allowed then to conjecture with a becoming reverence, what more likely, than A PERPETUAL ENERGY OF THE PUREST INTELLECT ABOUT THE FIRST, ALL-
COMPREHENSIVE

COMPREHENSIVE OBJECTS OF INTEL-Ch. V.
LECTION, WHICH OBJECTS ARE NO
OTHER THAN THAT INTELLECT IT-
SELF? For in pure INTELLECTION it
holds the reverſe of all Senſation, that
THE PERCEIVER AND THING PER-
CEIVED are ALWAYS ONE AND THE
SAME (e).

IT

(e) Ἐι ἒν ὕτως εὖ ἔχει, ὡς ἡμεῖς ποτὲ, ὁ Θεὸς ἀεὶ, θαυμαστόν· εἰ δὲ μᾶλλον, ἔτι θαυμασιώτερον· ἔχει δὲ ὧδε, ϗ ζωὴ δέ γε ὑπάρχει· ἡ γὰρ Νῦ ἐνέργεια, ζωή· Ἐκεῖνος δέ, ἡ ἐνέργεια· ἐνέργεια δὲ ἡ καθ' αὑτήν, ἐκείνε ζωὴ ἀρίςη ϗ ἀΐδιος. Φαμὲν δὲ τὸν Θεὸν εἶναι ζῶον ἀΐδιον, ἄριστον· ὥστε ζωὴ ϗ αἰὼν συνεχὴς ϗ ἀΐδιος ὑπάρχει τῷ Θεῷ· ΤΟΥΤΟ γὰρ Ο ΘΕΟΣ. Τῶν μετὰ τὰ φυσ· Λ'. ζ'. It is remarkable in Scripture that GOD is peculiarly characterized as A LIVING GOD, in oppoſition to all falſe and imaginary Deities, of whom ſome had no pretenſions to Life at all; others to none higher than that of Vegetables or Brutes; and the beſt were nothing better than illuſtrious Men, whoſe exiſtence was circumſcribed by the ſhort period of Humanity.

To

Ch. V. It was Speculation of this kind concerning THE DIVINE NATURE, which induced one of the wifeſt among the Antients to believe—" That the Man,
" who could live in the pure enjoyment
" of his *Mind,* and who properly culti-
" vated that *divine* Principle, was *happieſt*
" *in himſelf*, and *moſt beloved by the Gods.*
" For if the Gods had any regard to
" what paſt among Men (as it appeared
" they had) it was probable they ſhould
" rejoice in *that which was moſt excellent,*
" and by nature *the moſt nearly allied to*
" *themſelves*; and, as this was MIND,
" that they ſhould requite the Man, who
" moſt loved and honoured *This,* both
" from his regard to that which was
" *dear*

To the paſſage above quoted, may be added another, which immediately precedes it. Ἀυτὸν δὲ νοεῖ ὁ νῆς κατὰ μετάληψιν τῆ νοητῆ· νοητὸς γὰρ γίνεται, θιγγάνων κ᾽ νοῶν· ὥςε ΤΑΥΤΟΝ ΝΟΥΣ ΚΑΙ ΝΟΗΤΟΝ.

"*dear* to themselves, and from his act- Ch. V.
"ing a Part, which was laudable and
"right *(f).*"

AND thus in all SCIENCE there is something *valuable for itself,* because it contains within it something which is *divine.*

(f) Ἠθικ· Νικομαχ· τὸ Κ'. κεφ. ζ.

End of the SECOND BOOK.

HER-

HERMES

OR A PHILOSOPHICAL INQUIRY
CONCERNING UNIVERSAL GRAMMAR.

BOOK III.

CHAP. I.

Introduction—Division of the Subject into its principal Parts.

SOME things the MIND performs thro' the BODY; as for example, the various Works and Energies of Art. Others it performs *without such Medium*; as for example, when it thinks, and reasons, and concludes. Now tho' the Mind, in either case, may be called the Principle or Source, yet are these last

Ch. I. more properly *its own* peculiar Acts, as being immediately referable to its own innate Powers. And thus is MIND *ultimately the Cause of all*; of every thing at least that is *Fair* and *Good*.

AMONG those Acts of Mind more immediately its own, that of *mental Separation* may be well reckoned one. *Corporeal* Separations, however accurate otherwise, are in one respect incomplete, as they may be repeated without end. The smallest Limb, severed from the smallest Animalcule (if we could suppose any instrument equal to such dissection) has still a triple Extension of length, breadth, and thickness; has a figure, a colour, with perhaps many other qualities; and so will continue to have, tho' thus divided to infinity. But (*a*) the *Mind* surmounts all power of *Concretion*,

---

(*a*) *Itaque Naturæ facienda est prorsus Solutio & Separatio ; non per Ignem certe, sed per Mentem, tanquam ignem divinum.* Bacon. Organ. Lib. II. 16.

cretion, and can place in the simplest manner every Attribute by itself; convex without concave; colour without superficies; superficies without Body; and Body without its Accidents; as distinctly each one, as tho' they had never been united.

AND thus it is that it penetrates into the recesses of all things, not only dividing them, as *Wholes*, into their *more conspicuous Parts*, but persisting, till it even separate those *Elementary Principles*, which, being blended together after a more mysterious manner, are united in the *minutest Part*, as much as in the *mightiest Whole* (*b*).

Now if MATTER and FORM are among these Elements, and deserve perhaps to be esteemed as *the principal* among them, it may not be foreign to the Design of this Treatise, to seek whether *these*, or *any things analogous to them*, may be found in

---

(*b*) See below, p. 312.

Ch. I. SPEECH or LANGUAGE (c). This therefore we shall attempt after the following method.

EVERY

(c) See before p. 2. 7. MATTER and FORM (in *Greek* ΥΛΗ and ΕΙΔΟΣ) were Terms of great import in the days of antient Philosophy, when things were scrutinized rather at their beginning than at their End. They have been but little regarded by modern Philosophy, which almost wholly employs itself about the last order of Substance, that is to say, the *tangible, corporeal* or *concrete*, and which acknowledges no separations even in this, but those made by mathematical Instruments or Chemical Process.

The original meaning of the Word ΥΛΗ, was SYLVA, a WOOD. Thus *Homer*,

———Τρέμε δ' ἔρεα μακρὰ κỳ ΥΛΗ,
Ποσσὶν ὑπ' ἀθανάτοισι Ποσειδάωνος ἰόντος.

As Neptune past, the Mountains and the WOOD *Trembled beneath the God's immortal Feet.*

Hence as WOOD was perhaps the first and most useful kind of Materials, the Word ῦλη, which denoted it, came to be by degrees extended, and at length to denote MATTER or MATERIALS in general. In this sense Brass was called the ῦλη or *Matter* of a Statue; Stone, the ῦλη or *Matter* of a Pillar; and so in other instances. The *Platonic Chalcidius*, and other

Authors

Every thing in a manner, whether natural or artificial, is in its constitution com-

Ch. I.

Authors of the latter Latinity use Sylva under the same extended and comprehensive Signification.

Now as the Species of *Matter* here mentioned, (Stone, Metal, Wood, &c.) occur most frequently in common life, and are all nothing more than natural Substances or Bodies, hence by the Vulgar, Matter and Body have been taken to denote the same thing; *Material* to mean *Corporeal*; *Immaterial*, *Incorporeal*, &c. But this was not the Sentiment of Philosophers of old, by whom the Term *Matter* was seldom used under so narrow an acceptation. By these, every thing was called ΥΛΗ, or Matter, whether corporeal or incorporeal, which was *capable of becoming something else*, or *of being moulded into something else*, whether from the operation of Art, of Nature, or a higher Cause.

In this sense they not only called *Brass* the Ὕλη of a Statue, and Timber of a Boat, but Letters and Syllables they called the Ὕλαι of Words; Words or simple Terms, the Ὕλαι of Propositions; and Propositions themselves the Ὕλαι of Syllogisms. The *Stoics* held all things out of our own power ($\tau \grave{\alpha}$ $\mathring{\varepsilon} \kappa$ $\mathring{\varepsilon} \phi$' $\mathring{\eta} \mu \tilde{\iota} \nu$) such as Wealth and Poverty, Honour and Dishonour, Health

Ch. I. compounded of something COMMON, and something PECULIAR; of something *Common*,

---

Health and Sickness, Life and Death, to be the Ὕλαι, or *Materials of Virtue or Moral Goodness*, which had its essence in a proper conduct with respect to all these, (Vid. *Arr. Epict.* L. I. c. 29. Also Vol. the first of these miscellaneous Treatises, p. 187, 309. M. Ant. XII. 29. VII. 29. X. 18, 19. where the Ὑλικὸν and Ἀιτιῶδες are opposed to each other). The *Peripatetics*, tho' they expresly held the Soul to be ἀσώματος, or *Incorporeal*, yet still talked of a Νῦς Ὑλικὸς, *a material Mind* or *Intellect*. This to modern Ears may possibly sound somewhat harshly. Yet if we translate the Words, *Natural Capacity*, and consider them as only denoting that *original* and *native Power* of Intellection, which being previous to all *human* Knowledge, is yet necessary to its *reception*; there seems nothing then to remain, that can give us offence. And so much for the Idea of ΥΛΗ, or MATTER. See *Alex. Aphrod. de Anim.* p. 144. b. 145. *Arist. Metaph.* p. 121, 122, 141. *Edit. Sylb. Procl. in Euclid.* p. 22, 23.

As to ΕΙΔΟΣ, its original meaning was that of FORM or FIGURE, considered as denoting *visible* Symmetry, and Proportion; and hence it had its name from Εἴδω *to see*, Beauty of person being one of the noblest, and most excellent Objects of *Sight*. Thus *Euripides*,

Πρῶτον μὲν Εἶδος ἄξιον τυραννίδος.
Fair FORM *to Empire gave the first pretence.*

Now

mon, and belonging to many other things; and of something *Peculiar*, by which it is

---

Now as the *Form* or *Figure* of visible Beings tended principally to *distinguish* them, and to give to each its Name and Essence; hence in a more general sense, *whatever of any kind (whether corporeal or incorporeal) was peculiar, essential, and distinctive*, so as by its accession to any Beings, as to its ΥΛΗ or *Matter*, to mark them with a Character, which they had not before, was called by the Antients ΕΙΔΟΣ or FORM. Thus not only *the Shape* given to the Brass was called the Εἶδος or *Form* of the Statue; but the *Proportion* assigned to the Drugs was the Εἶδος or *Form* of the Medicine; *the orderly Motion* of the human Body was the Εἶδος or *Form* of the Dance; *the just Arrangement* of the Propositions, the Εἶδος or *Form* of the Syllogism. In like manner *the rational and accurate Conduct of a wise and good man*, in all the various Relations and Occurrences of life, made that Εἶδος or *Form*, described by *Cicero* to his Son,—FORMAM *quidam ipsam, Marce fili, et tanquam faciem* HONESTI *vides: quæ, si oculis cerneretur, mirabiles amores (ut ait Plato) excitaret sapientiæ*, &c. De Offic. I.

We may go farther still—THE SUPREME INTELLIGENCE, which passes thro' all things, and which is the same to our Capacities, as Light is to our Eyes,

Ch. I. is diftinguifhed, and made to be its true and proper felf.

HENCE

this fupreme Intelligence has been called ΕΙΔΟΣ ΕΙΔΩΝ, THE FORM OF FORMS, as being the Fountain of all Symmetry, of all Good, and of all Truth; and as imparting to every Being thofe *effential* and *diftinctive* Attributes, which make it to be *itfelf*, and *not any thing* elfe.

And fo much concerning FORM, as before concerning MATTER. We fhall only add, that it is in the *uniting* of thefe, that every thing generable begins to exift; in their *feparating, to perifh* and *be at an end*—that while the two co-exift, they co-exift not by *juxta-pofition*, like the ftones in a wall, but by a more *intimate Co-incidence*, complete in the minuteft part—that hence, if we were to perfift in dividing any fubftance (for example Marble) to infinity, there would ftill remain after every fection both *Matter* and *Form*, and thefe as perfectly united, as before the Divifion began—laftly, that they are both *pre-exiftent* to the Beings, which they conftitute; the *Matter* being to be found in the world at large; the *Form*, if artificial, pre-exifting within the *Artificer*, or if natural, within the *fupreme Caufe*, the Sovereign Artift of the Univerfe,

—*Pulchrum pulcherrimus ipfe*
Mundum mente gerens, fimilique in imagine formans.

Even

Ch. I.

HENCE LANGUAGE, if compared according to this notion to the murmurs of a

Even without speculating so high as this, we may see among all animal and vegetable Substances, the Form pre-existing in their *immediate generating* Cause; Oak being the parent of Oak, Lion of Lion, Man of Man, &c.

Cicero's account of these Principles is as follows.

MATTER.

Sed subjectam putant omnibus sine ulla specie, atque carentem omni illa qualitate *(faciamus enim tractando usitatius hoc verbum et tritius)* MATERIAM *quandam, ex quâ omnia expressa atque efficta sint: (quæ tota omnia accipere possit, omnibusque modis mutari atque ex omni parte) eôque etiam interire, non in nihilum,* &c. Acad. I. 8.

FORM.

Sed ego sic statuo, nihil esse in ullo genere tam pulchrum, quo non pulchrius id sit, unde illud, ut ex ore aliquo, quasi imago, exprimatur, quod neque oculis, neque auribus, neque ullo sensu percipi potest: cogitatione tantùm et mente complectimur.——HAS RERUM FORMAS *appellat Ideas ille non intelligendi solùm, sed etiam dicendi gravissimus auctor et magister,* Plato: *easque gigni negat, et ait semper esse, ac ratione et intelligentiâ contineri: cætera nasci, occidere, fluere, labi; nec diutiùs esse uno et*

Ch. I. a Fountain, or the dashings of a Cataract, has *in common* this, that like them, *it is a* SOUND. But then on the contrary it has *in peculiar* this, that whereas those Sounds have *no Meaning or Signification*, to Language *a* MEANING *or* SIGNIFICATION *is essential.* Again, *Language*, if compared to the Voice of irrational Animals, has *in common* this, that like them, *it has a Meaning.* But then it has this *in peculiar* to distinguish it from them, that whereas the *Meaning* of those Animal Sounds is derived *from* NATURE, that of Language is derived, not from Nature, but *from* COMPACT (*d*).

FROM

---

eodem statu. Quidquid est igitur, de quo ratione et via disputetur, id est ad ultimam sui generis Formam speciemque redigendum. Cic. ad M. Brut. Orat.

(d) The *Peripatetics* (and with just reason) in all their definitions as well of Words as of Sentences, made it a part of their character to be significant κατὰ συνθήκην, *by Compact.* See *Aristot. de Interp.* c. 2. 4. *Boethius* translates the Words κατὰ συνθήκην, *ad placitum,*

Ch. I.

From hence it becomes evident, that LANGUAGE, taken in the moſt comprehenſive view, *implies certain Sounds, having certain Meanings*; and that of theſe two Principles, the SOUND is as the MATTER, common (like other Matter) to many different things; the MEANING as that peculiar and characteriſtic FORM, by which the Nature or Eſſence of Language becomes complete.

---

tum, or *ſecundum placitum*, and thus explains them in his comment—SECUNDUM PLACITUM *vero eſt, quod ſecundum quandam poſitionem, placitumque ponentis aptatur; nullum enim nomen naturaliter conſtitutum eſt, neque unquam, ſicut ſubjecta res à naturâ eſt, ita quoque a naturâ veniente vocabulo nuncupatur. Sed hominum genus, quod et ratione, et oratione vigeret, nomina poſuit, eaque quibus libuit literis ſyllabiſque conjungens, ſingulis ſubjectarum rerum ſubſtantiis dedit.* Boeth. in Lib. de Interpret. p. 308.

CHAP.

CHAP. II.

Upon the Matter, or common Subject of Language.

Ch. II. THE ΥΛΗ or MATTER OF LANGUAGE comes first to be considered, a Subject, which Order will not suffer us to omit, but in which we shall endeavour to be as concise as we can. Now this ΥΛΗ or Matter is SOUND, and SOUND is *that Sensation peculiar to the Sense of Hearing, when the Air hath felt a Percussion, adequate to the producing such Effect* (a).

As

(a) This appears to be *Priscian's* Meaning when he says of a VOICE, what is more properly true of SOUND in general, that it is—*suum sensibile aurium, id est, quod proprie auribus accidit.* Lib. I p. 537.

The following account of the *Stoics*, which refers the cause of SOUND to an *Undulation in the Air propagated circularly*, as when we drop a stone into a Cistern of water, seems to accord with the modern Hypothesis, and

As the Causes of this Percussion are various, so from hence *Sound* derives the Variety of its Species. Ch. II.

FARTHER, as all these Causes are either Animal or Inanimate, so the two grand Species of Sounds are likewise *Animal* or *Inanimate*.

THERE is no peculiar Name for *Sound Inanimate*; nor even for that of Animals, when made by the trambling of their Feet, the fluttering of their Wings, or any other Cause, which is merely *accidental*. But that,

---

and to be as plausible as any—'Ακούειν δε, τε μεταξυ
τε τι φωνουντος κ τε ακουοντος αερος πληγην σφαι-
ροειδως, ειτα κυματουμενην, κ ταις ακοαις προσπιπτου-
σαν, ως κυματουται το εν τη δεξαμενη υδωρ κατα κυκλους
υπο τε εμβληθεντος λιθε—*Porro audire, cum is, qui me-*
dius inter loquentem, et audientem est, aer verberatur or-
biculariter, deinde agitatus auribus influit, quemadmodum
et cisternæ aqua per orbes injecto agitatur lapide. Diog.
Laert. VII.

Ch. II. that, *which they make by proper Organs, in consequence of some Sensation or inward Impulse, such Animal Sound is called a* Voice.

As Language therefore implies that Sound called Human Voice; we may perceive that *to know the Nature and Powers of the Human Voice,* is in fact *to know* the Matter *or common Subject of Language.*

Now the Voice of Man, and it should seem of all other Animals, is formed by certain Organs between the Mouth and the Lungs, and which Organs maintain the intercourse between these two. The Lungs furnish Air, out of which the Voice is formed; and the Mouth, when the Voice is formed, serves to publish it abroad.

What these Vocal Organs precisely are, is not in all respects agreed by Philo-

sophers

sophers and Anatomists. Be this as it will, it is certain that the *mere primary and simple Voice is completely formed, before ever it reach the Mouth,* and can therefore (as well as Breathing) find a Passage thro' the Nose, when the Mouth is so far stopt, as to prevent the least utterance.

Now *pure* and *simple* VOICE, being thus produced, is (as before was observed) *transmitted to the Mouth.* HERE then, by means of certain *different* Organs, which do not change its primary Qualities, but only superadd others, it receives *the Form or Character of* ARTICULATION. For ARTICULATION is in fact nothing else, than *that Form or Character, acquired to simple Voice, by means of the Mouth and its several Organs, the Teeth, the Tongue, the Lips,* &c. The Voice is not by Articulation made more grave or acute, more loud or soft (which are its *primary* Qualities) but it acquires to these Characters

certain

Ch. II. certain *others additional*, which are perfectly adapted *to exist along with them* (*b*).

THE

(*b*) The several Organs above mentioned not only serve the purposes of *Speech*, but those very different ones likewise of *Mastication* and *Respiration*; so frugal is Nature in thus assigning them double duty, and so careful to maintain her character of *doing nothing in vain*.

He, that would be informed, how much better the Parts here mentioned are framed for *Discourse* in *Man*, *who is a Discursive Animal*, than they are in other Animals, who are not so, may consult *Aristotle* in his Treatise *de Animal. Part.* Lib. II. c. 17. L. III. c. 1. 3. *De Animâ.* L. II. c. 8. § 23, &c.

And here by the way, if such Inquirer be of a Genius truly modern, he may possibly wonder how the Philosopher, considering (as it is modestly phrased) the Age in which he lived, should know so much, and reason so well. But if he have any taste or value for antient literature, he may with much juster cause wonder at the Vanity of his Contemporaries, who dream all Philosophy to be the Invention of their own Age, knowing nothing of those Antients still remaining for their perusal, tho' they are so ready on every occasion to give the preference to *themselves*.

The following account from *Ammonius* will shew whence the Notions in this chapter are taken, and

what

Ch. II.

THE *simplest* of these new Characters are those acquired thro' the *mere Openings of*

---

what authority we have to distinguish VOICE from mere SOUND; and ARTICULATE VOICE from SIMPLE VOICE.

Καὶ ΨΟΦΟΣ μὲν ἐστι πληγὴ ἀέρος αἰσθητὴ ἀκοῇ· ΦΩΝΗ δὲ, ψόφος ἐξ ἐμψύχου γινόμενος, ὅταν διὰ τῆς συστολῆς τοῦ θώρακος ἐκθλιβόμενος ὁ ἐν τοῖς πνεύμοσιν ὁ εἰσπνευθεὶς ἀὴρ προσπίπτῃ ἀθρόως τῇ καλουμένῃ τραχείᾳ ἀρτηρίᾳ, ᾗ ἐπίκειται, ἤτοι τῷ γαργαρεῶνι, καὶ διὰ τῆς πλήγης ἀποτελῇ τινα ἦχον αἰσθητὸν, κατά τινα ὁρμὴν τῆς ψυχῆς· ὅπερ ἐπὶ τῶν ἐμπνευστῶν καλεῖται τοῖς μυσικοῖς καλουμένων ὀργάνων συμβαίνει, οἷον αὐλῶν καὶ συρίγγων· τῆς γλώττης, καὶ τῶν ὀδόντων, καὶ χειλέων πρὸς μὲν ΤΗΝ ΔΙΑΛΕΚΤΟΝ ἀναγκαίων ὄντων, πρὸς δὲ ΤΗΝ ἉΠΛΩΣ ΦΩΝΗΝ οὐδαμῶς συμβαλλομένων.—*Estque* SONUS, *ictus aeris qui auditu percipitur:* VOX *autem est sonus, quem animans edit, cum per thoracis compressionem aer attractus a pulmone, elisus simul totus in arteriam, quam asperam vocant, et palatum, aut gurgulionem impingit, et ex ictu sonum quendam sensibilem pro animi quodam impetu perficit. Id quod in instrumentis quæ quia inflant, ideo* ἐμπνευστὰ *a musicis dicuntur, usu venit, ut in tibiis, ac fistulis contingit, cum lingua, dentes, labiaque ad loquelam necessaria sint, ad vocem vero simplicem non omnino conferant.* Ammon. in Lib. de Intepr. p. 25. b. Vid. etiam *Boerhaave* Institut. Medic. Sect. 626. 630.

Ch. II. *of the Mouth*, as thefe Openings differ in giving the Voice a Paffage. It is the Variety of Configurations in thefe Openings only, which gives birth and origin to the feveral VOWELS; and hence it is they derive their Name, by being thus *eminently Vocal* (c). and *eafy to be founded of themfelves alone.*

THERE are *other articulate Forms,* which the Mouth makes not by mere Openings, but by *different Contacts of its different parts*; fuch for inftance, as it makes by the Junction of the two Lips, of the Tongue with

---

It appears that the *Stoics* (contrary to the notion of the *Peripatetics*) ufed the word ΦΩΝΗ to denote SOUND in general. They defined it therefore to be—Τὸ ἴδιον αἰσθητὸν ἀκοῆς, which juftifies the definition given by *Prifcian,* in the Note preceding. ANIMAL SOUND they defined to be—Ἀὴρ ὑπὸ ὁρμῆς πεπληγμένος, *Air ftruck* (and fo made audible) *by fome animal impulfe*; and HUMAN or RATIONAL SOUND they defined—Ἔναρθρος ὴ ἀπὸ διανοίας ἐκπεμπομένη, *Sound articulate and derived from the difcurfive faculty.* Diog. Laert. VII. 55.

(c) ΦΩΝΗΕΝΤΑ.

with the Teeth, of the Tongue with the Ch. II. Palate, and the like.

Now as all thefe feveral Contacts, unlefs fome Opening of the Mouth either immediately precede, or immediately follow, would rather occafion Silence, than to produce a Voice; hence it is, that with fome fuch Opening, either previous or fubfequent, they are always connected. Hence alfo it is, that the *Articulations fo produced* are called Consonant, becaufe they found not of themfelves, and from their own powers, but *at all times in company with fome auxiliary Vowel* (*d*).

There are other fubordinate Diftinctions of thefe primary Articulations, which to enumerate would be foreign to the defign of this Treatife.

It is enough to obferve, that they are all denoted by the common Name of Ele-

---

(*d*) ΣΥΜΦΩΝΑ.

Ch. II. MENT (*e*), in as much as every Articulation of every other kind is from them derived, and into them refolved. Under their *smallest* Combination they produce a *Syllable*; Syllables properly combined produce a *Word*; Words properly combined produce a *Sentence*; and Sentences properly combined produce an *Oration* or *Discourse*.

AND thus it is that to Principles *apparently* so trivial *(f)*, as about twenty plain ele-

---

(*e*) The *Stoic* Definition of an ELEMENT is as follows—Ἔστι δὲ στοιχεῖον, ἐξ οὗ πρώτου γίνεται τὰ γινόμενα, καὶ εἰς ὃ ἔσχατον ἀναλύεται. *An* ELEMENT *is that, out of which, as their first Principle, things generated are made, and into which, as their last remains, they are resolved.* Diog. Laert. VII. 176. What *Aristotle* says upon ELEMENTS with respect to the Subject here treated, is worth attending to—Φωνῆς στοιχεῖα, ἐξ ὧν σύγκειται ἡ φωνὴ, καὶ εἰς ἃ διαιρεῖται ἔσχατα· ἐκεῖνα δὲ μηκέτ' εἰς ἄλλας φωνὰς ἑτέρας τῷ εἴδει αὐτῶν. *The* ELEMENTS OF ARTICULATE VOICE *are those things, out of which the* VOICE *is compounded, and into which, as its last remains, it is divided: the Elements themselves being no farther divisible into other articulate Voices, differing in Species from them.* Metaph. V. c. 3.

(*f*) The *Egyptians* paid divine Honours to the *Inventor of Letters*, and *Regulator of Language*, whom they

Book the Third.

elementary Sounds, we owe that variety Ch. II.
of articulate Voices, which have been sufficient to explain the Sentiments of so innumerable a Multitude, as all the present
and past Generations of Men.

It

---

they called THEUTH. By the GREEKS he was wor-
shipped under the Name of HERMES, and represented
commonly by a *Head alone without other Limbs*, standing upon *a quadrilateral Basis*. The Head itself was
that of *a beautiful Youth*, having on it a *Petasus*, or
Bonnet, adorned with two Wings.

There was a peculiar reference in this Figure to the
ΕΡΜΗΣ ΛΟΓΙΟΣ, THE HERMES OF LAN-
GUAGE OR DISCOURSE. He possessed no other part
of the human figure but the HEAD, because *no other
was deemed requisite to rational Communication. Words*
at the same time, the medium of this Communication,
being (as *Homer* well describes them) Επεα πτεροέντα,
Winged Words, were represented in their *Velocity* by the
WINGS of his Bonnet.

Let us suppose such a HERMES, having the *Front of
his Basis* (the usual place for Inscriptions) *adorned with
some old Alphabet*, and having *a Veil flung across*, by
which that Alphabet is *partly* covered. Let A YOUTH
be seen *drawing off this Veil*; and A NYMPH, near the
Youth, *transcribing what She there discovers*.

Such a Design would easily indicate its Meaning.
THE YOUTH we might imagine to be THE GENIUS

OF

Ch. II. It appears from what has been said, that THE MATTER or COMMON SUBJECT OF LANGUAGE IS *that Species of Sounds called* VOICES ARTICULATE.

WHAT

OF MAN *(Naturæ Deus humanæ,* as *Horace* stiles him;) THE NYMPH to be ΜΝΗΜΟΣΥΝΗ, or MEMORY; as much as to insinuate that " MAN, for the " Preservation of his *Deeds* and *Inventions, was neces-* " *sarily obliged to have recourse to* LETTERS; and that " MEMORY, *being conscious of her own Insufficiency,* " was glad to avail herself of so valuable an Acquisi- " tion."

MR. STUART, well known for his accurate and elegant Edition of *the Antiquities of* Athens, has adorned this Work with a Frontispiece agreeable to the above Ideas, and that in a Taste truly *Attic* and *Simple*, which no one possesses more eminently than himself.

As to HERMES, his History, Genealogy, Mythology, Figure, &c. Vid. *Platon. Phileb.* T. II. p. 18. *Edit. Serran. Diod. Sic.* L. I. *Horat.* Od. X. L. 1. *Hesiod. Theog.* V. 937. *cum Comment. Joan. Diaconi. Thucyd.* VI. 27. *et Scholiast. in loc. Pighium apud Gronov. Thesaur.* T. IX. p. 1164.

For the *value* and *importance* of *Principles,* and the *difficulty* in attaining them, see *Aristot. de Sophist. Elench.* c. 34.

The

WHAT remains to be examined in the following Chapter, is Language under its characteriſtic and peculiar FORM, that is to ſay, Language conſidered, not with reſpect to *Sound*, but to *Meaning*.

Ch. II.

The following Paſſage, taken from that able Mathematician *Tacquet*, will be found peculiarly pertinent to what has been ſaid in this chapter concerning *Elementary Sounds*, p. 324, 325.

Mille milliones ſcriptorum mille annorum millionibus non ſcribent omnes 24 *literarum alphabeti permutationes, licet ſinguli quotidiè abſolverent* 40 *paginas, quarum unaquæque contineret diverſas ordines litterarum* 24 *Tacquet Arithmeticæ Theor.* p. 381. Edit. Antverp. 1663.

CHAP. III.

Upon the Form, or peculiar Character of Language.

Ch.III. WHEN to any articulate Voice there accedes *by compact* a Meaning or Signification, such Voice by such accession is then called A WORD; and many Words, possessing their Significations (as it were) *under the same Compact* (a), unite in constituting a PARTICULAR LANGUAGE.

IT

(a) See before Note (c) p. 314. See also Vol. I. Treatise II. c. 1. Notes (a) and (c).

The following Quotation from *Ammonius* is remarkable—Καθάπερ ἓν τὸ μὲν κατὰ τόπον κινεῖσθαι, φύσει, τὸ δὲ ὀρχεῖσθαι, θέσει κ̀ κατὰ συνθήκην, κ̀ τὸ μὲν ξύλον, φύσει, ἡ δὲ θύρα, θέσει· ὕτω κ̀ τὸ μὲν φωνεῖν, φύσει, τὸ δὲ δι' ὀνομάτων ἢ ῥημάτων σημαίνειν, θέσει— κ̀ ἔοικε τὴν μὲν φωνητικὴν δύναμιν, ὄργανον ὖσαν τῶν ψυχικῶν ἐν ἡμῖν δυνάμεων γνωστικῶν, ἢ ὀρεκτικῶν, κατὰ φύσιν ἔχειν ὁ ἄνθρωπ☉ παραπλησίως τοῖς ἀλόγοις ζώοις·

IT appears from hence, that A WORD Ch.III.
may be defined *a Voice articulate, and sig-*
nificant by Compact—and that LANGUAGE
may be defined *a System of such Voices, so
significant.*

IT is from notions like these concerning Language and Words, that one may
be

ζώοις· τὸ δὲ ὀνόμασιν, ἢ ῥήμασιν, ἢ τοῖς ἐκ τέτων συγ-
κειμένοις λόγοις χρῆσθαι πρὸς τὴν σημασίαν (ἐκέτι
φύσει ἔσιν, ἀλλὰ θέσει) ἐξαίρετον ἔχειν πρὸς τὰ ἄλογα
ζῶα, διότι κὴ μόνΘ τῶν θνητῶν αὐτοκινήτε μετέχει
ψυχῆς, κὴ τεχνικῶς ἐνεργεῖν δυναμένης, ἵνα κὴ ἐν αὐτῷ
τῷ φωνεῖν ἡ τεχνικὴ αὐτῆς διακρίνηται δύναμις· δηλ ἔσι
δὲ ταῦτα οἱ εἰς κάλλΘ συντιθέμενοι λόγοι μετὰ μέτρων,
ἢ ἄνευ μέτρων. In the *same manner therefore, as local
Motion is from Nature, but Dancing is something positive; and as Timber exists in Nature, but a Door is
something positive; so is the power of producing a vocal
Sound founded in Nature, but that of explaining ourselves
by Nouns, or Verbs, something positive. And hence it is,
that as to the simple power of producing vocal Sound (which
is as it were the Organ or Instrument to the Soul's faculties of Knowlege or Volition) as to this vocal power I say,
Man seems to possess it from Nature, in like manner as*
irra-

Ch. III. be tempted to call LANGUAGE a kind of PICTURE OF THE UNIVERSE, where the Words are as the Figures or Images of all particulars.

AND yet it may be doubted, how far this is true. For if *Pictures* and *Images* are all of them *Imitations*, it will follow, that whoever has natural faculties to know the

---

irrational animals: but as to the employing of Nouns, or Verbs, or Sentences compofed out of them, in the explanation of our Sentiments (the thing thus employed being founded not in Nature, but in Pofition) this he feems to poffefs by way of peculiar eminence, becaufe he alone of all mortal Beings partakes of a Soul, which can move itfelf, and operate artificially; fo that even in the Subject of Sound his artificial Power fhews itfelf; as the various elegant Compofitions both in Metre, and without Metre, abundantly prove. Ammon. de Interpr. p. 51. a.

It muſt be obſerved, that *the operating artificially*, (ἐνεργεῖν τεχνικῶς) of which *Ammonius* here ſpeaks, and which he conſiders as a diſtinctive Mark peculiar to the *Human* Soul, means ſomething very different from the *mere producing works of elegance and defign*; elſe it could never be a mark of Diſtinction between Man, and many other Species of Animals, fuch as the Bee, the Beaver, the Swallow, &c. See Vol. I. p. 8, 9, 10. 158, 159, &c.

BOOK THE THIRD.

the Original, will by help of the same Ch. III. faculties know also its Imitations. But it by no means follows, that he who knows any Being, should know for that reason its *Greek* or *Latin* Name.

THE Truth is, that every Medium, through which we exhibit any thing to another's Contemplation, is either derived from *Natural Attributes,* and then it is an IMITATION; or else from *Accidents quite arbitrary,* and then it is a SYM-BOL (*b*).

Now,

(*b*) Διαφέρει δὲ τὸ ΟΜΟΙΩΜΑ τῦ ΣΥΜΒΟ-ΛΟΥ, καθόσον τὸ μὲν ὁμοίωμα τὴν φύσιν αὐτὴν τῦ πράγματος κατὰ τὸ δυνατὸν ἀπεικονίζεσθαι βύλεται, κ᾽ ἐκ ἔςιν ἐφ᾽ ἡμῖν αὐτὸ μεταπλάσαι· τὸ γὰρ ἐν τῇ εἰκόνι γεγραμμένε τῦ Σωκράτες ὁμοίωμα, εἰ μὴ κ᾽ τὸ φαλακρὸν, κ᾽ τὸ σιμὸν, κ᾽ τὸ ἐξώφθαλμον ἔχει τῦ Σωκράτες, ἐκέτ᾽ ἂν αὐτῦ λέγοιτο εἶναι ὁμοίωμα· τὸ δέ γε σύμβολον, ἤτοι σημεῖον, (ἀμφότερα γὰρ ὁ φιλό-σοφΘ᾽ αὐτὸ ὀνομάζει) τὸ ὅλον ἐφ᾽ ἡμῖν ἔχει, ἄτε κ᾽ ἐκ μόνης ὑφισάμενον τῆς ἡμετέρας ἐπινοίας· οἷον, τῦ πότε δεῖ συμβάλλειν ἀλλήλοις τὺς πολεμῦντας, δύναται

σύμ-

Ch. III. Now, if it be allowed that in far the greater part of things, not any of their *natural* Attributes are to be found in articulate Voices, and that yet thro' such Voices things of every kind are exhibited, it will follow that WORDS *must of necessity be* SYMBOLS, because it appears that they cannot be *Imitations*.

BUT here occurs a Question, which deserves attention—" Why in the common " intercourse of men with men have " Imitations been neglected, and Symbols " pre-

---

σύμβολον εἶναι κỳ σάλπιγΐος ἀπήχησις, κỳ λαμπάδος ῥίψις, καθάπερ φησὶν Εὐριπίδης,

'Επεὶ δ' ἀφείθη πυρσὸς, ὡς τυρσηνικῆς
Σάλπιγΐος ἦχος, σῆμα φοινίου μάχης.

Δύναται δέ τις ὑποθέσθαι κỳ δόρατ☉ ἀνάτασιν, κỳ βέλυς ἄφεσιν, κỳ ἀλλὰ μυρία.—A REPRESENTATION *or* RESEMBLANCE *differs from a* SYMBOL, *in as much as the Resemblance aims as far as possible to represent the very nature of the thing, nor is it in our power to shift or vary it. Thus a* REPRESENTATION *intended for* Socrates *in a Picture, if it have not those circumstances peculiar*

"preferred, although Symbols are only Ch. III.
"known by Habit or Inſtitution, while
"Imitations are recognized by a kind of
"natural Intuition?"—To this it may be
anſwered, that if the Sentiments of the
Mind, like the Features of the Face, were
immediately viſible to every beholder, the
Art of Speech or Diſcourſe would have
been perfectly ſuperfluous. But now,
while our Minds lie inveloped and hid,
and the Body (like a Veil) conceals every
thing but itſelf, we are neceſſarily compelled, when we communicate our Thoughts,

to

---

culiar to Socrates, *the bald, the flat-noſed, and the Eyes projecting, cannot properly be called a Repreſentation of him. But a* SYMBOL *or* SIGN *(for the Philoſopher* Ariſtotle *uſes both names) is wholly in our own pow-er, as depending ſingly for its exiſtence on our imagina-tion. Thus for example, as to the time when two armies ſhould engage, the Symbol or Sign may be the ſounding of a Trumpet, the throwing of a Torch, (according to what* Euripides *ſays,*

But when the flaming Torch was hurl'd, the ſign
Of purple fight, as when the Trumpet ſounds, &c.)

or elſe one may ſuppoſe the elevating of a Spear, the dart-ing of a Weapon, and a thouſand ways beſides. Ammon. in Lib. de Interp. p. 17. b.

Ch. III. to convey them to each other *through a Medium which is corporeal* (c). And hence it is that all Signs, Marks, Imitations, and Symbols muſt needs be *ſenſible*, and addreſſed *as ſuch* to the *Senſes* (d). Now THE SENSES, we know, never exceed their natural Limits; the Eye perceives no Sounds; the Ear perceives no Figures nor Colours. If therefore we were to converſe, not by *Symbols* but by *Imitations*, as far as things are characterized by Figure

---

(c) Αἱ ψυχαὶ αἱ ἡμέτεραι, γυμναὶ μὲν ὖσαι τῶν σωμάτων, ἠδύναντο δι' αὐτῶν τῶν νοημάτων σημαίνειν ἀλλήλαις τὰ πράγματα· Ἐπειδὴ δὲ σώμασι συνδέδενται, δίκην νέφες περικαλύπτουσιν αὐτῶν τὸ νοερόν, ἐδεήθησαν τῶν ὀνομάτων, δι' ὧν σημαίνουσιν ἀλλήλαις τὰ πράγματα. *Animi noſtri a corporis compage ſecreti res viciſſim animi conceptionibus ſignificare poſſent: cum autem corporibus involuti ſint, perinde ac nebulâ, ipſorum intelligendi vis obtegitur: quocirca opus eis fuit nominibus, quibus res inter ſe ſignificarent.* Ammon. in Prædicam. p. 18. a.

(d) *Quicquid ſcindi poſſit in differentias ſatis numeroſas, ad notionum varietatem explicandam (modo differentiæ illæ* ſenſui perceptibiles *ſint) fieri poteſt vehiculum cogitationum de homine in hominem.* Bacon. de Augm. Scient. VI. 1.

BOOK THE THIRD. 335

gure and Colour, our Imitation would be Ch.III.
neceſſarily thro' Figure and Colour alſo.
Again, as far as they are characterized by
Sounds, it would for the ſame reaſon be
thro' the Medium of Sounds. The like
may be ſaid of all the other Senſes, the
Imitation ſtill ſhifting along with the Objects imitated. We ſee then how *complicated* ſuch Imitation would prove.

If we ſet LANGUAGE therefore, as a
Symbol, in oppoſition to *ſuch Imitation*; if
we reflect on the Simplicity of the one, and
the Multiplicity of the other; if we conſider the Eaſe and Speed, with which
Words are formed (an Eaſe which knows
no trouble or fatigue; and a*Speed, which
equals the Progreſs of our very Thoughts)
if we oppoſe to this the difficulty and
length of Imitations; if we remember
that ſome Objects are capable of no Imitations at all, but that all Objects univerſally may be typified by Symbols; we may
plainly

---

* Επεα πτεροέντα—See before p. 325.

Ch. III. plainly perceive an Anfwer to the Queftion here propofed "Why, in the common "intercourfe of men with men, Imita- "tions have been rejected, and Symbols "preferred."

HENCE too we may perceive a Reafon, *why there never was a Language, nor indeed can poſſibly be framed one, to expreſs the Properties and real Eſſences of things*, as a Mirrour exhibits their Figures and their Colours. For if Language of itfelf imply nothing more, than *certain Species of Sounds with certain Motions concomitant*; if to fome Beings Sound and Motion are no Attributes at all; if to many others, where Attributes, they are no way effential (fuch as the Murmurs and Wavings of a Tree during a ftorm) if this be true— it is impoffible the Nature of fuch Beings fhould be expreffed, or the leaft effential Property be any way imitated, while between *the Medium* and *themſelves* there is nothing CONNATURAL (*e*).

It

(*e*) See Vol. I. Treatife II. c. 3. p. 70.

It is true indeed, when *Primitives* were Ch. III. once eſtabliſhed, it was eaſy to follow the Connection and Subordination of Nature, in the juſt deduction of *Derivatives* and *Compounds*. Thus the Sounds, *Water*, and, *Fire*, being once annexed to thoſe two Elements, it was certainly more natural to call Beings participating of the firſt, *Watry*, of the laſt, *Fiery*, than to commute the Terms, and call them by the reverſe. But why, and from what *natural Connections* the Primitives themſelves might not be commuted, it will be found, I believe, difficult to aſſign a Reaſon, as well in the inſtances before us, as in moſt others. We may here alſo ſee the Reaſon, why ALL LANGUAGE IS FOUNDED IN COMPACT, and not in Nature; for ſo are all Symbols, of which Words are a certain Species.

THE Queſtion remains if WORDS are Symbols, then SYMBOLS OF WHAT?—

Ch. III. If it be anſwered, OF THINGS, the Queſtion returns, OF WHAT THINGS?—If it be anſwered, *of the ſeveral Individuals of Senſe, the various particular Beings, which exiſt around us*—to this, it is replied, may be raiſed certain Doubts. In the firſt place every Word will be in fact a *proper Name*. Now if all Words are proper Names, how came Lexicographers, whoſe expreſs buſineſs is to explain Words, either wholly to omit proper Names, or at leaſt to explain them, not from their own Art, but from Hiſtory?

AGAIN, if all *Words* are *proper Names*, then in ſtrictneſs no Word can belong to more than one Individual. But if ſo, then, as *Individuals* are *infinite*, to make a perfect Language, *Words muſt be infinite alſo*. But if infinite, then *incomprehenſible*, and never to be attained by the wifeſt Men; whoſe labours in Language upon this Hypotheſis would be as idle as that ſtudy of infinite written Symbols, which

Miſſion-

Missionaries (if they may be credited) attribute to the *Chinese*.

Ch.III.

AGAIN, *if all Words are proper Names*, or (which is the same) the Symbols of *Individuals*; it will follow, as Individuals are not only *infinite*, but ever *passing*, that the Language of those, who lived ages ago, will be as unknown *now*, as the very Voices of the Speakers. Nay the Language of every Province, of every Town, of every Cottage, must be every where different, and every where changing, since such is the Nature of *Individuals*, which it follows.

AGAIN, *if all Words are proper Names*, the Symbols of *Individuals*, it will follow that in Language there can be no *general Proposition*, because upon the Hypothesis *all Terms are particular*; nor any *Affirmative Proposition*, because *no one Individual in nature is another*. It remains, there can be no Propositions, but *Particular Negatives*.

Ch. III. *tives*. But if so, then is Language incapable of communicating *General Affirmative Truths*—If so, then of communicating *Demonstration*—If so, then of communicating *Sciences*, which are so many Systems of Demonstrations—If so, then of communicating *Arts*, which are the Theorems of Science applied practically—If so, we shall be little the better for it either in Speculation or in Practice (*e*). And so much for this Hypothesis; let us now try another.

IF WORDS are not the Symbols of *external Particulars*, it follows of course, they must be THE SYMBOLS OF OUR IDEAS: For this is evident, if they are not Symbols

---

(*e*) The whole of *Euclid* (whose Elements may be called the basis of Mathematical Science) is founded upon *general Terms*, and *general Propositions*, most of which are *affirmative*. So true are those Verses, however barbarous as to their stile,

Syllogizari non est ex Particulari,
Neve Negativis, recte concludere si vis.

Symbols of things *without,* they can only be Symbols of something *within*.

HERE then the Question recurs, if SYMBOLS OF IDEAS, then of WHAT IDEAS? —OF SENSIBLE IDEAS.—Be it so, and what follows?—Every thing in fact, which has followed already from the supposition of their being the Symbols of *external Particulars*; and that from this plain and obvious reason, because the several *Ideas,* which *Particulars* imprint, must needs be as *infinite* and *mutable,* as they are themselves.

IF then Words are neither the Symbols of *external Particulars,* nor yet of *particular Ideas,* they can be SYMBOLS of nothing else, except of GENERAL IDEAS, because nothing else, except these, remains. —And what do we mean by GENERAL IDEAS?—We mean SUCH AS ARE COMMON TO MANY INDIVIDUALS; not only to Individuals which exist now, but which exifted

Ch. III. exifted in ages paft, and will exift in ages future; fuch for example, as the Ideas belonging to the Words, *Man, Lion, Cedar.* —Admit it, and what follows?—It follows, that *if Words are the Symbols of fuch general Ideas,* Lexicographers may find employ, though they meddle not with *proper Names.*

IT follows that *one Word* may be, not *homonymoufly,* but *truly and effentially common to many Particulars,* paft prefent and future; fo that however thefe Particulars may be *infinite,* and *ever fleeting,* yet Language notwithftanding may be *definite* and *fteady.* But if fo, then attainable even by ordinary Capacities, without danger of incurring the *Chinefe* Abfurdity *.

AGAIN, it follows that the Language of thofe, who lived ages ago, as far as it ftands

---

* See p. 338, 339.

ſtands *for the ſame general Ideas*, may be as Ch.III.
intelligible *now*, as it was *then*. The like
may be ſaid of the ſame Language being
accommodated to diſtant Regions, and
even to diſtant Nations, amidſt all the variety
of *ever new* and *ever changing* Objects.

AGAIN, it follows that Language may
be expreſſive of *general Truths*; and if ſo,
then of Demonſtration, and Sciences, and
Arts; and if ſo, become ſubſervient to
purpoſes of every kind *(f)*.

Now if it be true " that none of theſe
" things could be aſſerted of Language,
" were not Words the Symbols of *general*
" *Ideas*—and it be further true, that theſe
" things may be all undeniably aſſerted
" of Language"—it will follow (and that
neceſſarily) that WORDS ARE THE SYM-
BOLS OF GENERAL IDEAS.

(f) See before Note *(e)*.

Ch. III. AND yet perhaps even here may be an Objection. It may be urged, if Words are the Symbols of *general Ideas*, Language may anfwer well enough the purpofe of Philofophers, who reafon about *general*, and *abſtract* Subjects—but what becomes of the bufinefs of ordinary Life? Life we know is merged in a multitude of *Particulars*, where an Explanation by Language is as requifite, as in the higheſt Theorems. The Vulgar indeed want it to *no other* End. How then can this End in any refpect be anfwered, if Language be expreffive of nothing farther than *general Ideas?*

To this it may be anfwered, that *Arts* furely refpect the bufinefs of ordinary Life; yet fo far are *general Terms* from being an Obſtacle here, that without them no Art can be *rationally* explained. How for inſtance ſhould the meafuring Artiſt afcertain to the Reapers the price of their labours, had not he firſt through *general Terms*

Terms learnt thofe *general Theorems*, that Ch. III. refpect the doctrine and practice of Menfuration?

BUT fuppofe this not to fatisfy a perfevering Objector—fuppofe him to infift, that, admitting this to be true, *there were still a multitude of occafions for minute particularizing, of which it was not poffible for mere Generals to be fufceptible*—fuppofe, I fay, fuch an Objection, what fhould we anfwer?——*That the Objection was juft*; that it was neceffary *to the Perfection and Completion of* LANGUAGE, *that it fhould be expreffive of* PARTICULARS, *as well as of* GENERALS. We muft however add, that its *general* Terms are by far its moft *excellent* and *effential* Part, fince from thefe it derives " that com-
" prehenfive *Univerfality*, that juft pro-
" portion of *Precifion* and *Permanence*,
" without which it could not poffibly
" be either learnt, or underftood, or ap-
" plied to the purpofes of Reafoning and
" Science;"

Ch. III. "Science;"—that *particular* Terms have their Utility and End, and that therefore care too has been taken for a supply of these.

ONE Method of expressing Particulars, is that of PROPER NAMES. This is the least artificial, because *proper Names* being in every district arbitrarily applied, may be unknown to those, who know the Language perfectly well, and can hardly therefore with propriety be considered as parts of it. The other and more artificial Method is that of DEFINITIVES or ARTICLES (*g*), whether we assume the *pronominal*, or those *more strictly* so called. And here we cannot enough admire the exquisite *Art* of Language, which, *without wandering into infinitude, contrives how to denote things infinite*; that is to say in other words, which, by the small Tribe of *Definitives properly applied to general Terms,*

(*g*) See before p. 72, &c. 233, &c.

Terms, knows how to employ thefe laft, Ch.III. tho' in number *finite*, to the accurate expreffion of *infinite* Particulars.

To explain what has been faid by a fingle example. Let the general Term be MAN. I have occafion to apply this Term to the denoting of fome Particular. Let it be required to exprefs this Particular, *as unknown*; I fay, A *Man—known*; I fay, THE *Man—indefinite*; ANY *Man—definite*; A CERTAIN *Man—prefent and near*; THIS *Man—prefent and diftant*; THAT *Man— like to fome other*; SUCH A *Man—an indefinite Multitude*; MANY *Men—a definite Multitude*; A THOUSAND *Men;—the ones of a Multitude, taken throughout*; EVERY *Man—the fame ones, taken with diftinction*; EACH *Man—taken in order*; FIRST *Man*, SECOND *Man*, &c.—*the whole Multitude of Particulars taken collectively*; ALL *Men —the Negation of this Multitude*; NO *Man*. But of this we have fpoken already, when we inquired concerning Definitives.

I THE

Ch. III. THE Sum of all is, that WORDS ARE THE SYMBOLS OF IDEAS BOTH GENERAL AND PARTICULAR; YET OF THE GENERAL, PRIMARILY, ESSENTIALLY, AND IMMEDIATELY; OF THE PARTICULAR, ONLY SECONDARILY, ACCIDENTALLY, AND MEDIATELY.

SHOULD it be asked, " why has Language this *double* Capacity?"—May we not ask, by way of return, Is it not a kind of reciprocal Commerce, or *Intercourse of our Ideas?* Should it not therefore be framed, so as to express *the whole* of our Perception? Now can we call that Perception intire and whole, which implies either INTELLECTION without *Sensation*, or SENSATION without *Intellection?* If not, how should Language explain *the whole* of our Perception, had it not Words to express the Objects, proper to each of the two Faculties?

Ch. III.

To conclude—As in the preceding Chapter we considered Language with a view to its MATTER, so here we have considered it with a view to its FORM. Its MATTER is recognized, when it is considered *as a Voice*; its FORM, as it is *significant of our several Ideas*; so that upon the whole it may be defined—A SYSTEM OF ARTICULATE VOICES, THE SYMBOLS OF OUR IDEAS, BUT OF THOSE PRINCIPALLY, WHICH ARE GENERAL OR UNIVERSAL.

CHAP. IV.

Concerning general or universal Ideas.

Ch.IV. MUCH having been said in the preceding Chapter about GENERAL OR UNIVERSAL IDEAS, it may not perhaps be amiss to inquire, *by what process we come to perceive them,* and *what kind of Beings they are*; since the generality of men think so meanly of their existence, that they are commonly considered, as little better than Shadows. These Sentiments are not unusual even with the Philosopher now a days, and that from causes much the same with those, which influence the Vulgar.

THE VULGAR merged *in Sense* from their earliest Infancy, and never once dreaming any thing to be worthy of pursuit, but what either pampers their Appetite, or fills their Purse, imagine nothing

to

Ch. IV.

to be *real*, but what may be *tasted*, or *touched*. THE PHILOSOPHER, as to these matters being of much the same Opinion, in Philosophy looks no higher, than to *experimental Amusements,* deeming nothing *Demonstration*, if it be not made *ocular*. Thus instead of ascending from *Sense* to *Intellect* (the natural progress of all true Learning) he hurries on the contrary into the midst of Sense, where he wanders at random without any end, and is lost in a Labyrinth of infinite Particulars. Hence then the reason why the sublimer parts of *Science*, the Studies of MIND, INTELLECTION, and INTELLIGENT PRINCIPLES, are in a manner neglected; and, as if the Criterion of all Truth were an Alembic or an Air-pump, what cannot be proved by *Experiment*, is deemed no better than *mere Hypothesis*.

AND yet it is somewhat remarkable, amid the prevalence of such Notions, that there should still remain two Sciences in fashion,

Ch. IV. fafhion, and thefe having their Certainty of all the leaft controverted, *which are not in the minuteft article depending upon Experiment.* By thefe I mean ARITHMETIC, and GEOMETRY (*a*). But to come to our Subject concerning GENERAL IDEAS.

MAN'S

(*a*) The many noble Theorems (fo ufeful in life, and fo admirable in themfelves) with which thefe two SCIENCES fo eminently abound, arife originally from PRINCIPLES, THE MOST OBVIOUS IMAGINABLE; Principles, fo little wanting the pomp and apparatus of EXPERIMENT, that they are *felf-evident* to every one, poffeffed of common fenfe. I would not be underftood, in what I have here faid, or may have faid elfewhere, to undervalue EXPERIMENT; whofe importance and utility I freely acknowlege, in the many curious Noftrums and choice Receipts, with which it has enriched the neceffary Arts of life. Nay, I go farther—I hold *all juftifiable Practice in every kind of Subject* to be founded in EXPERIENCE, which is no more than *the refult of many repeated* EXPERIMENTS. But I muft add withal, that the man who acts *from Experience alone,* tho' he act ever fo well, is but an *Empiric* or *Quack,* and that not only in Medicine, but in every other Subject. It is then only that we recognize ART, and that the EMPIRIC quits his name for the more honourable one of ARTIST, when to his EXPERIENCE he adds SCIENCE,

MAN'S FIRST PERCEPTIONS are thofe Ch.IV.
of the SENSES, in as much as they com-
mence from his earlieft Infancy. Thefe
Perceptions, if not infinite, are at leaft
indefinite, and more *fleeting* and *tranfient*,
than the very Objects, which they exhibit,
becaufe

SCIENCE, and is thence enabled to tell us; not only, WHAT *is to be done*, but WHY *it is to be done*; for ART *is a compofite of Experience and Science*, Experience providing it *Materials*, and Science giving them A FORM.

In the mean time, while EXPERIMENT is thus neceffary to all PRACTICAL WISDOM, with refpect to PURE and SPECULATIVE SCIENCE, as we have hinted already, it has not the leaft to do. For who ever heard of *Logic*, or *Geometry*, or *Arithmetic* being proved *experimentally?* It is indeed by the application of *thefe* that *Experiments* are rendered ufeful; that they are affumed into Philofophy, and in fome degree made a part of it, being otherwife nothing better than puerile amufements. But that thefe Sciences themfelves fhould depend upon the Subjects, on which they work, is, as if the Marble were to fashion the Chizzle, and not the Chizzle the Marble.

Ch. IV. becaufe they not only depend upon the *exiftence* of thofe Objects, but becaufe they cannot fubfift, without their *immediate Prefence*. Hence therefore it is, that there can be *no Senfation of either Paft or Future*, and confequently had the Soul no other Faculties, than the *Senfes*, it never could acquire the leaft Idea of TIME (*b*).

BUT happily for us we are not deferted here. We have in the firft place a Faculty, called IMAGINATION or FANCY, which however as to its *energies* it may be fubfequent to Senfe, yet is truly prior to it both in *dignity* and *ufe*. THIS it is which *retains the fleeting Forms of things*, when Things themfelves are gone, and *all Senfation* at an end.

THAT this Faculty, however connected with Senfe, is ftill perfectly different, may be

---

(*b*) See before p. 105. See alfo p. 112. Note (*f*).

Book the Third.

Ch.IV.

be feen from hence. We have an *Imagination* of things, that are gone and extinct; but no fuch things can be made objects of *Senfation*. We have an eafy command over the Objects of our *Imagination*, and can call them forth in almoft what manner we pleafe; but our *Senfations* are neceffary, when their Objects are prefent, nor can we controul them, but by removing either the Objects, or ourfelves (*c*).

As

(*c*) Befides the diftinguifhing of SENSATION from IMAGINATION, there are two other Faculties of the Soul, which from their nearer alliance ought carefully to be diftinguifhed from it, and thefe are ΜΝΗΜΗ, and ΑΝΑΜΝΗΣΙΣ, MEMORY, and RECOLLECTION.

When we view fome *relict* of fenfation repofed within us, *without thinking of its rife, or referring it to any fenfible Object*, this is PHANSY or IMAGINATION.

When we view fome fuch *relict*, and *refer it withal to that fenfible Object, which in time paft was its caufe and original*, this is MEMORY.

Laftly

Ch. IV. As the Wax would not be adequate to its bufinefs of Signature, had it not a Power to *retain*, as well as to *receive*; the fame holds of the SOUL, with refpect to *Senfe* and *Imagination*. SENSE is its *receptive*

Laftly *the Road, which leads to Memory through a feries of Ideas, however connected whether rationally or cafually,* this is RECOLLECTION. I have added *cafually,* as well as *rationally,* becaufe a cafual connection is often fufficient. Thus from feeing a Garment, I think of its Owner; thence of his Habitation; thence of Woods; thence of Timber; thence of Ships, Sea-fights, Admirals, &c.

If the Diftinction between *Memory* and *Phanfy* be not fufficiently underftood, it may be illuftrated by being compared to the view of a Portrait. When we contemplate a Portrait, *without thinking of whom it is the Portrait,* fuch Contemplation is analogous to PHANSY. When we view it *with reference to the Original, whom it reprefents,* fuch Contemplation is analogous to MEMORY.

We may go farther. IMAGINATION or PHANSY may exhibit (after a manner) even *things that are to come.* It is here that *Hope* and *Fear* paint all their pleafant, and all their painful Pictures of *Futurity*. But MEMORY is confined in the ftricteft manner *to the paft.*

What

ceptive Power; IMAGINATION, its *re-* Ch.IV.
tentive. Had it Senfe without Imagination, it would not be as Wax, but as Water, where tho' all Impreffions may be inftantly made, yet as foon as made they are as inftantly loft.

THUS then, from a view of the two Powers taken together, we may call SENSE (if we pleafe) *a kind of tranfient Imagination*; and IMAGINATION on the contrary *a kind of permanent Senfe* (*d*).

Now

What we have faid, may fuffice for our prefent purpofe. He that would learn more, may confult *Ariftot. de Animâ*, L. III. c. 3, 4. and his Treatife *de Mem. et Reminifc*.

(*d*) Τί τοίνυν ἐςὶν ἡ φαντασία ὧδε ἂν γνωρίσαιμεν· δεῖ νοεῖν ἐν ἡμῖν ἀπὸ τῶν ἐνεργειῶν τῶν περὶ τὰ αἰσθητὰ, ἕιον τύπ]ον (*lege* τύπον) τινὰ κỳ ἀναζωγράφημα ἐν τῷ πρώτῳ αἰσθητηρίῳ, ἐγκατάλειμμά τι τῆς ὑπὸ τȣ̃ αἰσθητȣ̃ γινομένης κινήσεως, ὃ κỳ μηκέτι τȣ̃ αἰσθητȣ̃ παρόντος, ὑπομένει τὲ κỳ σώζεται, ὃν ὥσπερ εἰκών τις αὐτȣ̃, ὃ κỳ

Ch. IV. Now as our Feet in vain venture to walk upon the River, till the Frost bind the Current, and harden the yielding Surface; so does the SOUL in vain seek to exert its higher Powers, the Powers I mean of REASON and INTELLECT, till IMAGINATION first fix the *fluency* of SENSE, and thus provide a proper Basis for the support of its higher Energies.

AFTER

τῆς μνήμης ἡμῖν σωζόμενον ἄιτιον γίνεται· τὸ τοιοῦτον ἐγκατάλειμμα, ᾗ τὸν τοιοῦτον ὥσπερ τύπον, ΦΑΝΤΑΣΙΑΝ καλοῦσιν. *Now what* PHANSY *or* IMAGINATION *is, we may explain as follows. We may conceive to be formed within us, from the operations of our Senses about sensible Subjects, some Impression (as it were) or Picture in our original Sensorium, being a relict of that motion caused within us by the external object; a relict, which when the external object is no longer present, remains and is still preserved, being as it were its Image, and which, by being thus preserved, becomes the cause of our having Memory. Now such a sort of relict and (as it were) Impression they call* PHANSY *or* IMAGINATION. *Alex. Aphrod. de Anima*, p. 135. b. *Edit. Ald.*

Ch. IV.

AFTER this manner, in the admirable Oeconomy of the Whole, are Natures subordinate made subservient to the higher. Were there *no Things external, the Senses* could not operate; were there *no Sensations, the Imagination* could not operate; and were there *no Imagination*, there could be *neither Reasoning* nor *Intellection*, such at least as they are found in *Man*, where they have their Intensions and Remissions in alternate succession, and are at first nothing better, than *a mere* CAPACITY *or* POWER. Whether every Intellect begins thus, may be perhaps a question; especially if there be any one of a nature *more divine*, to which "Intension and Remission " and mere Capacity are unknown (*e*)." But not to digress.

IT

(*e*) See p. 162. The *Life, Energy*, or Manner of MAN's Existence is not a little different from that of the DEITY. THE LIFE OF MAN has its Essence in
MOTION.

Ch. IV. IT is then on these *permanent* Phantasms that THE HUMAN MIND first works, and by

MOTION. This is not only true with respect to that lower and subordinate Life, which he shares in common with Vegetables, and which can no longer subsist than while the Fluids circulate, but it is likewise true in that *Life*, which is peculiar to him as *Man*. Objects from without *first move* our faculties, and thence we move *of ourselves* either to *Practice* or *Contemplation*. But the LIFE or EXISTENCE of GOD (as far as we can conjecture upon so transcendent a Subject) is not only complete throughout Eternity, but complete in every Instant, and is for that reason IMMUTABLE and SUPERIOR TO ALL MOTION.

It is to this distinction that *Aristotle* alludes, when he tells us—Οὐ γὰρ μόνον κινήσεώς ἐστιν ἐνέργεια, ἀλλὰ ϰ ἀκινησίας· ϰ ἡδονὴ μᾶλλον ἐν ἠρεμίᾳ ἐστὶν, ἢ ἐν κινήσει· μεταβολὴ δὲ πάντων γλυκὺ, κατὰ τὸν ποιητὴν, διὰ πονηρίαν τινά· ὥσπερ γὰρ ἄνθρωπος εὐμετάβολος ὁ πονηρὸς, ϰ ἡ φύσις ἡ δεομένη μεταβολῆς· ὺ γὰρ ἁπλῆ, οὐδ' ἐπιεικής. *For there is not only an Energy of* MOTION, *but of* IMMOBILITY; *and* PLEASURE *or* FELICITY *exists rather in* REST *than in* MOTION; *Change of all things being sweet (according to the Poet) from a principle of Pravity in those who believe so. For*

by an Energy as spontaneous and familiar Ch.IV.
to its Nature, as the seeing of Colours is
familiar to the Eye, it discerns at once
what

---

in the same manner as the bad man is one fickle and changeable, so is that Nature bad that requireth Variety, in as much as such Nature is neither simple nor even. Eth. Nicom. VII. 14. & Ethic. Eudem. VI. *sub fin.*

It is to this UNALTERABLE NATURE OF THE DEITY that *Boethius* refers, when he says in those elegant verses,

———*Tempus ab Ævo*
Ire jubes STABILISQUE MANENS *das cuncta moveri.*

From this single principle of IMMOBILITY, may be derived some of the noblest of the *Divine Attributes*; such as that of IMPASSIVE, INCORRUPTIBLE, INCORPOREAL, &c. Vide *Aristot.* Physic. VIII. Metaphys. XIV. c. 6, 7, 9. 10. Edit. *Du Val.* See also Vol. I. of these Treatises, p. 262 to 266—also p. 295, where the Verses of *Boethius* are quoted at length.

It must be remembered however, that tho' we are not *Gods*, yet as *rational* Beings we have within us something *Divine*, and that the more we can become superior to our mutable, variable, and irrational part, and place our welfare in that Good, which is immutable,

per-

Ch. IV. what in MANY is ONE; what in things DISSIMILAR and DIFFERENT is SIMILAR and the SAME *(f)*. By this it comes to behold

---

permanent, and rational, the higher we shall advance in real Happiness and Wisdom. This is (as an antient writer says)—Ὁμοίωσις τῷ Θεῷ κατὰ τὸ δυνατὸν, *the becoming like to* GOD, *as far as in our power.* Τοῖς μὲν γὰρ Θεοῖς πᾶς ὁ βίῳ μακάριῳ· τοῖς δ' ἀνθρώποις, ἐφ' ὅσον ὁμοίωμά τι τῆς τοιαύτης ἐνεργείας ὑπάρχει. *For to* THE GODS (*says another antient*) *the whole of life is one continued happiness; but to* MEN, *it is so far happy, as it rises to the resemblance of so divine an Energy.* See Plat. in Theætet. Arist. Eth. X. 8.

(f) This CONNECTIVE ACT of the Soul, by which it views ONE IN MANY, is perhaps one of the principal Acts of its most excellent Part. It is this removes that impenetrable mist, which renders *Objects of Intelligence* invisible to lower faculties. Were it not for this, even the *sensible* World (with the help of all our Sensations) would appear as unconnected, as the words of an Index. It is certainly not the Figure alone, nor the Touch alone, nor the Odour alone, that makes the Rose, but it is made up of all these, and other attributes UNITED; not an *unknown* Constitution of *insensible* Parts, but a *known* Constitution of *sensible* Parts, unless we chuse to extirpate the possibility of natural Knowledge.

WHAT

behold a kind of *superior* Objects; a new Ch.IV. Race of Perceptions, more comprehensive than

WHAT then perceives this CONSTITUTION or UNION?—Can it be any of the Senses?—No one of these, we know, can pass the limits of its own province. Were the Smell to perceive the union of the Odour and the Figure, it would not only be Smell, but it would be Sight also. It is the same in other instances. We must necessarily therefore recur to some HIGHER COLLECTIVE POWER, to give us a prospect of Nature, even in these her *subordinate Wholes*, much more in that *comprehensive Whole*, whose Sympathy is universal, and of which these smaller Wholes are all no more than Parts.

But no where is this *collecting*, and (if I may be allowed the expression) this *unifying* Power more conspicuous, than in the subjects of PURE TRUTH. By virtue of this power the Mind views *One general Idea*, in *many Individuals*; *One Proposition* in *many general Ideas*; *One Syllogism* in *many Propositions*; till at length by properly repeating and connecting Syllogism with Syllogism, it ascend into those bright and *steady regions of* SCIENCE,

Quas neque concutiunt venti, neque nubila nimbis Adspergunt, &c. Lucr.

Even

Ch. IV. than thofe of Senfe; a Race of Perceptions, *each one of which may be found intire
and*

Even *negative* Truths and *negative* Concluſions cannot ſubſiſt, but by bringing Terms and Propoſitions together, ſo *neceſſary is this* UNITING *Power to every Species of* KNOWLEDGE. See p. 3. 250.

He that would better comprehend the diſtinction between SENSITIVE PERCEPTION, and INTELLECTIVE, may obſerve that, when a Truth is ſpoken, it is *heard* by our Ears, and *underſtood* by our Minds. That theſe two Acts are different, is plain, from the example of ſuch, as *hear* the ſounds, without *knowing* the language. But to ſhew their difference ſtill ſtronger, let us ſuppoſe them to concur in the ſame Man, who ſhall both *hear* and *underſtand* the Truth propoſed. Let the Truth be for example, *The Angles of a Triangle are equal to two right Angles.* That this is ONE Truth, and not *two* or *many* Truths, I believe none will deny. Let me aſk then, in what manner does this Truth become perceptible (if at all) to SENSATION?—The Anſwer is obvious; it is by ſucceſſive Portions of little and little at a time. When the firſt Word is *preſent,* all the ſubſequent are *abſent;* when the laſt Word is *preſent,* all the previous are *abſent;* when any of the middle Words are *preſent,* then are there ſome *abſent,* as well of one ſort as the other, No more exiſts at once than a ſingle Syllable, and the Remainder as much *is not,* (to Senſation at leaſt) as tho'

BOOK THE THIRD.

and whole in the separate individuals of an Ch.IV.
infinite and fleeting Multitude, without de-
parting

tho' it never had been, or never was to be. And so much for the perception of SENSE, than which we see nothing can be more *diffipated, fleeting,* and *detached.* —And is that of the MIND, similar?—Admit it, and what follows?—It follows, that *one* Mind would no more recognize *one* Truth, by recognizing its Terms *succeffively* and *apart,* than *many* diftant Minds would recognize it, were it diftributed among them, a different part to each. The cafe is, every TRUTH is ONE, tho' its TERMS are MANY. It is in no refpect true *by parts at a time,* but it is true of neceffity at *once,* and *in an inftant.*—What Powers therefore recognize this ONENESS or UNITY?—Where even does it refide, or what makes it?—Shall we anfwer with the *Stagirite,* Τὸ δὲ ΕΝ ΠΟΙΟΥΝ ταῦτο ὁ ΝΟΥΣ ἕκαςον—If this be allowed, it fhould feem, where SENSATION and INTELLECTION appear to concur, that Senfation was of MANY, Intellection was of ONE; that Senfation was *temporary, divifible* and *fucceffive*; Intellection, *inftantaneous, indivifible,* and *at once.*

If we confider the Radii of a Circle, we fhall find at the Circumference that they are MANY; at the Center that they are ONE. Let us then fuppofe SENSE and MIND to view the fame Radii, only let Senfe view them at the *Circumference,* Mind at the *Center;*
and

Ch. IV. *parting from the unity and permanence of its own nature.*

AND

and hence we may conceive, how thefe Powers differ, even where they jointly appear to operate in perception of the fame object.

There is ANOTHER ACT OF THE MIND, the very reverfe of that here mentioned; an Act, by which it perceives not *one in many,* but MANY IN ONE. This is that *mental Separation,* of which we have given fome account in the firft Chapter of this Book; that Refolution or Analyfis, which enables us *to invefligate the Caufes, and Principles, and Elements of things.* It is by Virtue of this, that we are enabled to abftract any particular Attribute, and make it *by itfelf* the Subject of philofophical Contemplation. Were it not for this, it would be difficult for *particular Sciences* to exift; becaufe otherwife they would be as much blended, as the feveral Attributes of fenfible Subftances. How, for example, could there be fuch a Science as *Optics,* were we neceffitated to contemplate *Colour concreted with Figure,* two Attributes, which the Eye can never view, but affociated? I mention not a multitude of other fenfible qualities, fome of which ftill prefent themfelves, whenever we look on any *coloured* Body.

Thofe

AND thus we see the *Process by which* Ch. IV.
we arrive at GENERAL IDEAS; for the
Per-

Those two noble Sciences, ARITHMETIC and
GEOMETRY, would have no basis to stand on, were
it not for this *separative* Power. They are both conversant about QUANTITY; *Geometry* about CONTI-
NUOUS Quantity, *Arithmetic* about DISCRETE. Ex-
TENSION is essential to *continuous* Quantity; Mo-
NADS, or UNITS, to *Discrete*. By separating from
the infinite Individuals, with which we are surrounded,
those infinite Accidents, by which they are all *diversified*, we leave nothing but those SIMPLE and PER-
FECTLY SIMILAR UNITS, which being combined
make NUMBER, and are the Subject of ARITHME-
TIC. Again, by separating from *Body* every possible
subordinate Accident, and leaving it nothing but its
triple Extension of Length, Breadth, and Thickness, (of
which were it to be deprived, it would be *Body* no
longer) we arrive at that pure and unmixed MAGNI-
TUDE, the contemplation of whose properties makes
the Science of *Geometry*.

By the same *analytical* or *separative* Power, we investigate DEFINITIONS of all kinds, each one of
which is *a developed Word*, as the same Word is *an inveloped Definition*.

To conclude—IN COMPOSITION AND DIVISION
CONSISTS THE WHOLE OF SCIENCE, COMPOSI-
TION

Ch. IV. Perceptions here mentioned are in fact no other. In thefe too we perceive the objects of SCIENCE and REAL KNOWLEGE, which can by no means be, but *of that which is general, and definite, and fixt* (g).
Here

TION MAKING AFFIRMATIVE TRUTH, AND SHEWING US THINGS UNDER THEIR SIMILIARITIES AND IDENTITIES; DIVISION MAKING NEGATIVE TRUTH, AND PRESENTING THEM TO US UNDER THEIR DISSIMILARITIES AND DIVERSITIES.

And here, by the way, there occurs a Queſtion.— If all Wiſdom be Science, and it be the buſineſs of Science as well to *compound* as to *ſeparate*, may we not ſay that thoſe Philoſophers took *Half* of Wiſdom for the *Whole*, who diſtinguiſhed it from Wit, as if WISDOM only *ſeparated*, and WIT only *brought together?* —Yet ſo held the Philoſopher of *Malmſbury*, and the Author *of the Eſſay on the Human Underſtanding.*

(g) The very Etymologies of the Words ΕΠΙΣΤΗΜΗ, SCIENTIA, and UNDERSTANDING, may ſerve in ſome degree to ſhew the nature of theſe Faculties, as well as of thoſe Beings, their true and proper Objects. ΕΠΙΣΤΗΜΗ ὠνόμαςαι, διὰ τὸ ΕΠΙ ΣΤΑΣΙΝ ἢ ὅρον τῶν πραγμάτων ἄγειν ἡμᾶς,

τῆς

Here too even *Individuals*, however of Ch. IV.
themselves unknowable, become objects of
Knowlege,

τῆς ἀορισίας κỳ μεταβολῆς τῶν ἐπὶ μέρυς ἀπάγυσα· ἡ γὰρ ἐπιςήμη περὶ τὰ καθόλυ κỳ ἀμετάπ]ωτα καταγίνεται· SCIENCE (ΕΠΙΣΤΗΜΗ) *has its name from bringing us* (ΕΠΙ ΣΤΑΣΙΝ) TO SOME STOP *and* BOUNDARY *of things, taking us away from the unbounded nature and mutability of Particulars; for it is conversant about Subjects, that are general, and invariable.* Niceph. Blem. Epit. Logic. p. 21.

This Etymology given by *Blemmides*, and long before him adopted by the *Peripatetics*, came originally from *Plato*, as may be seen in the following account of it from his *Cratylus.* In this Dialogue *Socrates*, having first (according to the *Heraclitean* Philosophy which *Cratylus* favoured) etymologized a multitude of Words with a view to that *Flow* and *unceasing Mutation*, supposed by *Heraclitus* to run thro' all things, at length changes his System, and begins to etymologize from another, which supposed something in nature to be *permanent* and *fixed*. On this principle he thus proceeds —Σκοπῶμεν δή, ἐξ αὐτῶν ἀναλαβόντες πρῶτον μὲν τῦτο τὸ ὄνομα τὴν ΕΠΙΣΤΗΜΗΝ, ὡς ἀμφίβολον ἐςι, κỳ μᾶλλον ἔοικε σημαῖνόν τι ὅτι ΙΣΤΗΣΙΝ ἡμῶν ΕΠΙ τοῖς πράγμασι τὴν ψυχὴν, ἢ ὅτι συμπεριφέρεται. *Let us consider then* (says he) *some of the very*

B b *Words*

Ch. IV. Knowlege, as far as their nature will permit. For then only may *any Particular* be

---

Words already examined ; and in the first place, the Word SCIENCE ; *how disputable is this* (as to its former Etymology) *how much more naturally does it appear to signify, that* IT STOPS THE SOUL AT THINGS, *than that it is carried about with them.* Plat. Cratyl. p. 437. Edit. Serr.

The disputable Etymology, to which he here alludes, was a strange one of his own making in the former part of the Dialogue, adapted to the *flowing* System of *Heraclitus* there mentioned. According to this notion, he had derived ΕΠΙΣΤΗΜΗ from ἕπισθαι and μένειν, as if it *kept along* with things, by perpetually *following* them in their motions. See *Plato* as before, p. 412.

As to SCIENTIA, we are indebted to *Scaliger* for the following ingenious Etymology. RATIOCINATIO, *motus quidam est* ; SCIENTIA, *quies: unde et nomen, tum apud Græcos, tum etiam nostrum.* Παρὰ τὸ ΕΠΙ ΙΣΤΑΣΘΑΙ, ΕΠΙΣΤΗΜΗ. *Sistitur enim mentis agitatio, et fit species in animo. Sic Latinum* SCIENTIA, ὅτι γίνεται ΣΧΕΣΙΣ ΤΟΥ ΟΝΤΟΣ. *Nam Latini, quod nomen entis simplex ab usu abjecerunt atque repudiarunt, omnibus activis participiis idem adjunxerunt.* Audiens, ἀκέων ὤν. Sciens, χῶν ὤν. Scal. in Theophr. de Causis Plant. Lib. I. p. 17.

The

be said to be known, when by asserting it Ch.IV.
to be *a Man*, or *an Animal*, or the like,
we

The *English* Word, UNDERSTANDING, means not so properly *Knowlege*, as that *Faculty of the Soul*, where Knowlege resides. Why may we not then imagine, that the framers of this Word intended to represent it as a kind of firm *Basis*, on which the fair Structure of Sciences was to rest, and which was supposed to STAND UNDER them, as their immoveable Support?

Whatever may be said of these Etymologies, whether they are true or false, they at least prove their Authors to have considered SCIENCE and UNDERSTANDING, not as *fleeting* powers of Perception, like *Sense*, but rather as *steady, permanent*, and *durable* COMPREHENSIONS. But if so, we must somewhere or other find for them certain *steady, permanent*, and *durable* OBJECTS; since if PERCEPTION OF ANY KIND BE DIFFERENT FROM THE THING PERCEIVED, (whether it perceive straight as crooked, or crooked as straight; the moving as fixed, or the fixed as moving) SUCH PERCEPTION MUST OF NECESSITY BE ERRONEOUS AND FALSE. The following passage from a *Greek Platonic* (whom we shall quote again hereafter) seems on the present occasion not without its weight—Εἰ ἐστὶ γνῶσις ἀκριβεστέρα τῆς αἰσθήσεως, ἔτι ἂν ᾖ γνωστὰ ἀληθεστέρα τῶν αἰσθητῶν. *If there be*

Ch.IV. we refer it to some such *comprehensive*, or general *Idea*.

Now it is of these COMPREHENSIVE and PERMANENT IDEAS, THE GENUINE PERCEPTIONS OF PURE MIND, that WORDS of all Languages, however different, are the SYMBOLS. And hence it is, that *as the* PERCEPTIONS *include, so do these their* SYMBOLS

A KNOWLEGE *more accurate than* SENSATION; *there must be certain* OBJECTS *of such knowlege* MORE TRUE THAN OBJECTS OF SENSE.

The following then are Questions worth considering,—*What* these Objects are?—*Where* they reside?—And *how* they are to be discovered?—Not by *experimental Philosophy* it is plain; for that meddles with nothing, but what is tangible, corporeal, and mutable—nor even by the more refined and rational speculation of *Mathematics*; for this, at its very commencement, takes such Objects for granted. We can only add, that *if they reside in our own* MINDS, (and who, that has never looked there, can affirm they do not?) then will the advice of the Satirist be no ways improper,

———NEC TE QUÆSIVERIS EXTRA.

Pers.

Symbols *exprefs, not this or that set of* Ch.IV.
Particulars only, but all indifferently, as
they happen to occur. Were therefore the
Inhabitants of *Salisbury* to be transferred
to *York*, tho' new particular objects would
appear on every fide, they would ftill no
more want a new Language to explain
themfelves, than they would want new
Minds to comprehend what they beheld.
All indeed, that they would want, would
be the *local proper Names*; which Names,
as we have faid already *, are hardly a part
of Language, but muft equally be learnt
both by learned and unlearned, as often
as they change the place of their abode.

It is upon the fame principles we may
perceive the reafon, why the dead Languages (as we call them) are *now* intelligible; and why the Language of *modern
England* is able to defcribe *antient Rome*;
and

---

* Sup. p. 345, 346.

Ch. IV. and that of *antient Rome* to defcribe *modern England* (*h*). But of thefe matters we have fpoken before.

§ 2. AND now having viewed *the Procefs, by which we acquire general Ideas*, let us begin anew from other Principles, and try to difcover (if we can prove fo fortunate) *whence it is that thefe Ideas originally come*. If we can fucceed here, we may difcern perhaps, *what kind of Beings they are*, for this at prefent appears fomewhat obfcure.

LET

(*h*) As far as *Human Nature*, and *the primary Genera* both of *Subftance* and *Accident* are *the fame* in all places, and have been fo thro' all ages: fo far *all Languages* fhare one common IDENTITY. As far as *peculiar fpecies of Subftance* occur in different regions; and much more, as far as *the pofitive Inftitutions of religious and civil Politics are every where different*; fo far each *Language* has its peculiar DIVERSITY. To the Caufes of *Diverfity* here mentioned, may be added *the diftinguifhing Character and Genius of every Nation*, concerning which we fhall fpeak hereafter.

Ch. IV.

LET us suppose any man to look for the first time upon *some Work of Art*, as for example upon a Clock, and having sufficiently viewed it, at length to depart. Would he not retain, when absent, an Idea of what he had seen?—And what is it, *to retain such Idea?—It is to have* A FORM INTERNAL *correspondent to* THE EXTERNAL; only with this difference, that the *Internal Form is devoid of the Matter; the External is united with it*, being seen in the metal, the wood, and the like.

Now if we suppose this Spectator to view *many such Machines*, and not simply to view, but to consider every part of them, so as to comprehend how these parts all operate to one End, he might be then said to possess a kind of INTELLIGIBLE FORM, by which he would not only understand, and know the Clocks, which he had seen *already*, but every Work also of like Sort, which he might see *hereafter*.—

B b 4 Should

Ch. IV. Should it be asked *" which of these Forms* *" is prior, the External and Sensible, or* *" the Internal and Intelligible;"* the Answer is obvious, that *the prior is the Sensible.*

THUS then we see, THERE ARE INTELLIGIBLE FORMS, WHICH TO THE SENSIBLE ARE SUBSEQUENT.

BUT farther still—If these Machines be allowed the Work *not of Chance,* but of *an Artist,* they must be the Work of one, who *knew what he was about.* And what is it, *to work, and know what one is about?* —*It is to have an Idea of what one is doing; to possess* A FORM INTERNAL, *correspondent to the* EXTERNAL, *to which external it serves for an* EXEMPLAR *or* ARCHETYPE.

HERE then we have AN INTELLIGIBLE FORM, WHICH IS PRIOR TO THE SENSIBLE FORM; *which, being truly prior as well in dignity as in time, can no more become subsequent, than Cause can to Effect.*

Thus then, with respect to Works of Art, we may perceive, if we attend, A TRIPLE ORDER OF FORMS; *one* Order, *intelligible* and *previous* to these Works; a *second* Order, *sensible* and *concomitant*; and a *third* again, *intelligible* and *subsequent*. After the first of these Orders the Maker may be said to *work*; thro' the second, the Works themselves *exist*, and are what they are; and in the third they become *recognized, as mere Objects of Contemplation*. To make these Forms by different Names more easy to be understood; *the first* may be called THE MAKER'S FORM; *the second*, that of THE SUBJECT; and the *third*, that of THE CONTEMPLATOR.

Let us pass from hence to Works of NATURE. Let us imagine ourselves viewing some diversified Prospect; "a Plain, "for example, spacious and fertile; a "river

Ch. IV. "river winding thro' it; by the banks "of that river, men walking and cattle "grazing; the view terminated with "diſtant hills, ſome craggy, and ſome "covered with wood." Here it is plain we have plenty of FORMS NATURAL. And could any one quit ſo fair a Sight, and retain no traces of what he had beheld?—And what is it, *to retain traces of what one has beheld?*—It is to have certain FORMS INTERNAL correſpondent to the EXTERNAL, and reſembling them in every thing, *except the being merged in Matter.* And thus, thro' the ſame *retentive* and *collective* Powers, the Mind becomes fraught with *Forms natural,* as before with *Forms artificial.*—Should it be aſked, "*which of theſe natural Forms are* "*prior, the External ones viewed by the* "*Senſes, or the Internal exiſting in the* "*Mind?*" the Anſwer is obvious, that *the prior are the External.*

THUS

Thus therefore in NATURE, as well as Ch.IV.
in ART, THERE ARE INTELLIGIBLE
FORMS, WHICH TO THE SENSIBLE ARE
SUBSEQUENT. Hence then we fee the
meaning of that noted School Axiom, *Nil
eſt in* INTELLECTU *quod non prius fuit in*
SENSU; an Axiom, which we muſt own
to be ſo far allowable, as it reſpects the
Ideas *of a mere Contemplator*.

BUT to proceed ſomewhat farther—Are
natural Productions made BY CHANCE, or
BY DESIGN?—Let us admit *by Deſign*,
not to lengthen our inquiry. They are
certainly * more exquiſite than *any* Works
of ART, and yet *theſe* we cannot bring
ourſelves to ſuppoſe made by *Chance*.—
Admit it, and what follows?—*We muſt of
neceſſity admit a* MIND *alſo, becauſe* DESIGN
implies MIND, *wherever it is to be found*.
—Allowing therefore this, what do we
mean

---

* *Ariſt. de Part. Animal.* L. I. c. 1.

Ch. IV. mean by the Term, MIND?—We mean something, which, when it acts, knows what it is going to do; something stored with Ideas of its intended Works, agreeably to which Ideas those Works are fashioned.

THAT such EXEMPLARS, PATTERNS, FORMS, IDEAS (call them as you please) must *of necessity* be, requires no proving, but follows of course, if we admit the Cause of Nature to be A MIND, as above mentioned. For take away these, and *what a Mind* do we leave without them? CHANCE surely is as knowing, as MIND WITHOUT IDEAS; or rather MIND WITHOUT IDEAS is no less blind than CHANCE.

THE Nature of these IDEAS is not difficult to explain, if we once come to allow a possibility of their Existence. That they are exquisitely *beautiful, various,* and *orderly,* is evident from the exquisite Beauty, Variety, and Order, seen in natural Substances,

Ch. IV.

stances, which are but their *Copies* or *Pictures*. That they are *mental* is plain, as they are *of the Essence of* MIND, and consequently no Objects to any of the *Senses*, nor therefore circumscribed either by *Time* or *Place*.

HERE then, on this System, we have plenty of FORMS INTELLIGIBLE, WHICH ARE TRULY PREVIOUS TO ALL FORMS SENSIBLE. Here too we see that NATURE is not defective in her TRIPLE ORDER, having (like Art) her FORMS PREVIOUS, HER CONCOMITANT, and HER SUBSEQUENT (*i*).

THAT

(*i*) *Simplicius*, in his commentary upon the Predicaments, calls the *first* Order of these intelligble Forms, τὰ πρὸ τῆς μεθέξεως, *those previous to Participation*, and at other times, ἡ ἐξῃρημένη κοινότης, *the transcendent Universality* or *Sameness*; the *second* Order he calls τὰ ἐν μεθέξει, *those which exist in Participation*, that is, those merged in Matter; and at other times, he calls them ἡ κατατεταγμένη κοινότης, *the subordinate Universality* or *Sameness*; lastly, of the *third* Order he says, that

Ch. IV. THAT *the Previous* may be *juftly fo called* is plain, becaufe they are *effentially prior*

that they have no independent exiftence of their own, but that—ἡμεῖς ἀφελόντες αὐτὰ ἐν ταῖς ἡμετέραις ἐννοίαις, καθ' ἑαυτὰ ὑπεςήσαμεν, *we ourfelves abftracting them in our own Imaginations, have given them by fuch abftraction an exiftence as of themfelves.* Simp. in Prædic. p. 17. In another place he fays, in a language fomewhat myfterious, yet ftill conformable to the fame doctrine—Μήποτε ἐν τριτῶν ληπτέον τὸ κοινόν, τὸ μὲν ἐξηρημένον τῶν καθ' ἕκαςα, ᴋ̀ αἴτιον τῆς ἐν αὐτοῖς κοινότητος, κατὰ τὴν μίαν ἑαυτῶ φύσιν, ὥσπερ κ̀ τῆς διαφορότητος κατὰ τὴν πολυειδῆ πρόληψιν—δεύτερον δὲ ἐςι τὸ κοινόν, τὸ ἀπὸ κοινῆς αἰτίας τοῖς διαφόροις εἴδεσιν ἐνδιδόμενον, κ̀ ἐνυπάρχον αὐτοῖς—τρίτον δὲ, τὸ ἐν ταῖς ἡμετέραις διανοίαις ἐξ ἀφαιρέσεως ὑφιςάμενον, ὑςερογενὲς ὄν—*Perhaps therefore we muft admit a* TRIPLE ORDER OF WHAT IS UNIVERSAL AND THE SAME; *that of the firft Order, tranfcendent and fuperior to Particulars, which thro' its uniform nature is the caufe of that Samenefs exifting in them, as thro' its multiform pre-conception it is the caufe of their Diverfity*—*that of the fecond Order, what is infufed from the firft univerfal Caufe into the various Species of Beings, and which has its exiftence in thofe feveral Species*—*that of the third Order, what fubfifts by abftraction in our own Underftandings, being of fubfequent origin to the other two.* Ibid. p. 21.

To

BOOK THE THIRD.   Ch. IV.

prior to all things elſe, The WHOLE VISI-
BLE WORLD exhibits nothing more, than
ſo

To *Simplicius* we ſhall add the two following Quotations from *Ammonius* and *Nicephorus Blemmides*, which we have ventured to tranſcribe, without regard to their uncommon length, as they ſo fully eſtabliſh the Doctrine here advanced, and the works of theſe Authors are not eaſy to be procured.

Ἐννοείσθω τοίνυν δακτύλιός τις ἐκτύπωμα ἔχων, εἰ τύχοι, Ἀχιλλέως, κὴ κηρία πολλὰ παρακείμενα· ὁ δὲ δακτύλι۞ σφραγιζέτω τὰς κηρὰς πάσας· ὕςερον δέ τις εἰσελθὼν κὴ θεασάμεν۞ τὰ κηρία, ἐπιςήσας ὅτι πάντα ἐξ ἑνός εἰσιν ἐκτυπώματ۞, ἐχέτω παρ' αὐτῷ τὸ ἐκτύπωμα τῇ διανοίᾳ. Ἡ τοίνυν σφραγὶς ἡ ἐν τῷ δακτυλίῳ λέγεται ΠΡΟ ΤΩΝ ΠΟΛΛΩΝ εἶναι. ἡ δὲ ἐν τοῖς κηρίοις, ΕΝ ΤΟΙΣ ΠΟΛΛΟΙΣ· ἡ δὲ ἐν τῇ διανοίᾳ τᾶ ἀπομαξαμένε, ΕΠΙ ΤΟΙΣ ΠΟΛΛΟΙΣ, κὴ ὑςερογενής. Τᾶτο ἐν ἐννοείσθω κὴ ἐπὶ τῶν γειῶν κὴ εἰδῶν· ὁ γὰρ Δημιεργὸς, ποιῶν πάντα, ἔχει παρ' ἑαυτῷ τὰ πάντων παραδείγματα· οἷον, ποιῶν ἄνθρωπον, ἔχει τὸ εἶδος παρ' ἑαυτῷ τᾶ ἀνθρώπε, πρὸς ὃ ἀφορῶν, πάντας ποιεῖ. Εἰ δέ τις ἐνςαίη λέγων, ὡς ἐκ ἐςὶ παρὰ τῷ Δημιεργῷ τὰ εἴδη, ἀκείτω ταῦτα, ὡς ὁ Δημιεργὸς δημιεργεῖ, ἢ εἰδὼς τὰ ὑπ' αὐτᾶ δημιεργέμενα, ἢ ἐκ εἰδώς. Ἀλλ' εἰ μὲν μὴ εἰδὼς, ἐκ ἂν δημιεργήσει. Τίς γὰρ, μέλλων ποιήσειν τι, ἀγνοεῖ ὃ μέλλει

Ch. IV. ſo many *paſſing* Pictures of theſe *immutable Archetypes.* Nay thro' theſe it attains even
a

μέλλει ποιεῖν; ἐ γὰρ, ὡς ἡ Φύσις, ἀλόγῳ δυνάμει
ποιεῖ· (ὅθεν κ᾽ ποιεῖ ἡ Φύσις, ἐκ ἐφιςάνεσα γνωςι-
κῶς τῷ γιγνομένῳ) Ἐι δέ τι καθ᾽ ἕξιν λογικὴν ποιεῖ,
οἶδέπε πάντως τὸ γιγνόμενον ὑπ᾽ αὐτῶ. Ἐι τοίνυν μὴ
χεῖρον, ἢ κατὰ ἄνθρωπον, ὁ Θεὸς ποιεῖ, οἶδε τὸ ὑπ᾽
αὐτᾶ γιγνόμενον· εἰ δὲ οἶδεν ὃ ποιεῖ, αὐτόθι δῆλον, ὡς
ἔςιν ἐν τῷ Δημιεργῷ τὰ εἴδη. Ἔςι δὲ τὸ εἶδος ἐν τῷ
Δημιεργῷ, ὡς ὁ ἐν τῷ δακτυλίῳ τύπος· κ᾽ λέγεται
τᾶτο τὸ εἶδος ΠΡΟ ΤΩΝ ΠΟΛΛΩΝ, κ᾽ χωριςὸν
τῆς ὕλης. Ἔςι δὲ τὸ εἶδος τᾶ ἀνθρώπε κ᾽ ἐν τοῖς καθ᾽
ἕκαςον ἀνθρώποις, ὡς τὰ ἐν τοῖς κηροῖς ἐκτυπώματα· κ᾽
λέγεται τὰ τοιαῦτα ΕΝ ΤΟΙΣ ΠΟΛΛΟΙΣ εἶναι,
κ᾽ ἀχώριςα τῆς ὕλης. Θεασάμενοι δὲ τὰς κατὰ μέρος
ἀνθρώπες, ὅτι πάντες τὸ αὐτὸ εἶδος τᾶ ἀνθρώπε ἔχεσιν,
(ὡς ἐπὶ τᾶ ὕςερον ἐλθόντος, κ᾽ θεασαμένε τὰ κηρία)
ἀνεμαξάμεθα αὐτὸ ἐν τῇ διανοίᾳ· κ᾽ λέγεται τᾶτο
ΕΠΙ ΤΟΙΣ ΠΟΛΛΟΙΣ, ἤγουν μετὰ τὰ πολλὰ,
κ᾽ ὑςερογενές. *Intelligatur annulus, qui alicujus, ut-
pote Achillis, imaginem inſculptam habeat: multæ inſuper
ceræ ſint, et ab annulo imprimantur: veniat deinde quiſ-
piam, videatque ceras omnes unius annuli impreſſione for-
matas, annulique impreſſionem in mente contineat: ſigillum
annulo inſculptum,* ANTE MULTA *dicetur: in cerulis
impreſſum, in* MULTIS: *quod vero in illius, qui illo ve-
nerat intelligentiâ remanſerit,* POST MULTA, *et poſte-
rius*

a Semblance of Immortality, and con- Ch.IV.
tinues

---

rius genitum dicetur. Idem in generibus et formis intelligendum censeo: etenim ille optimus procreator mundi Deus, omnium rerum formas, atque exempla habet apud se: ut si hominem efficere velit, in hominis formam, quam habet, intueatur, et ad illius exemplum cæteros faciat omnes. At si quis restiterit, dicatque rerum formas apud Creatorem non esse: quæso ut diligenter attendat: Opifex, quæ facit, vel cognoscit, vel ignorat: sed is, qui nesciet, nunquam quicquam faciet: quis enim id facere aggreditur, quod facere ignorat? Neque enim facultate quâdam rationis experte aliquid aget, prout agit natura (ex quo conficitur, ut natura etiam agat, etsi quæ faciat, non advertat:) Si vero ratione quadam aliquid facit, quodcunque ab eo factum est omnino cognovit. Si igitur Deus non pejore ratione, quam homo, facit quid, quæ fecit cognovit: si cognovit quæ fecit, in ipso rerum formas esse perspicuum est. Formæ autem in opifice sunt perinde ac in annulo sigillum, hæcque forma ANTE MULTA, *et avulsa a materiâ dicitur. Atqui hominis species in unoquoque homine est, quemadmodum etiam sigilla in ceris; et* IN MULTIS, *nec avulsa a materiâ dicitur. At cum singulos homines animo conspicimus, et eandem in unoquoque formam atque effigiem videmus, illa effigies in mente nostrâ insidens* POST MULTA, *et posterius genita dicetur: veluti in illo quoque dicelamus, qui multa sigilla in cerâ uno et eodem annulo impressa conspexerat. Ammon.* in Prophyr. Introduct. p. 29. b.

Λέγεται

Ch.IV. tinues throughout ages to be SPECIFI-
CALLY

Λέγονται δὲ τὰ γένη κὴ τὰ εἴδη ΠΡΟ ΤΩΝ
ΠΟΛΛΩΝ, ΕΝ ΤΟΙΣ ΠΟΛΛΟΙΣ, ΕΠΙ
ΤΟΙΣ ΠΟΛΛΟΙΣ· οἷον ἐννοείσθω τι σφραγιςήριον,
ἔχον κὴ ἐκτύπωμα τὸ τυχὸν, ἐξ ὁ κηρία πολλὰ μετα-
λαβέτω τῦ ἐκτυπώματ©, καί τις ὑπ' ὄψιν ἀγαγέτω
ταῦτα, μὴ προκατιδὼν μηδ' ὅλως τὸ σφραγιςήριον· ἑω-
ρακὼς δὲ τὰ ἐν οἷς τὸ ἐκτύπωμα, κὴ ἐπιςήσας ὅτι
πάντα τῦ αὐτῦ μετέχυσιν ἐκτυπώματ©, κὴ τὰ δοκῦντα πολλὰ τῷ λόγῳ συναθροίσας εἰς ἕν, ἐχέτω τῦτο κατὰ διάνοιαν. Τὸ μὲν ἓν σφραγιςήριον τύπωμα λέγεται ΠΡΟ ΤΩΝ ΠΟΛΛΩΝ· τό δ' ἐν τοῖς κηρίοις,
ΕΝ ΤΟΙΣ ΠΟΛΛΟΙΣ· τὸ δὲ ἐξ αὐτῶν κατα-
ληφθὲν, κὴ κατὰ διάνοιαν ἀΰλως ὑπος̔ὰν, ΕΠΙ ΤΟΙΣ
ΠΟΛΛΟΙΣ. Οὕτως ἓν κὴ τὰ γένη κὴ τὰ εἴδη
ΠΡΟ ΤΩΝ ΠΟΛΛΩΝ μέν εἰσιν ἐν τῷ Δημιυρ-
γῷ, κατὰ τὰς ποιητικὰς λόγυς· ἐν τῷ Θεῷ γὰρ οἱ ἐ-
σιοποιοὶ λόγοι τῶν ὄντων ἑνιαίως προϋφεςήκασι, καθ' ἒς
λόγυς ὁ ὑπερύσι© τὰ ὄντα πάντα κὴ προώρισε κὴ
παρήγαγεν· ὑφεςηκέναι δὲ λέγονται τὰ γένη κὴ τὰ
εἴδη ΕΝ ΤΟΙΣ ΠΟΛΛΟΙΣ, διότι ἐν τοῖς κατὰ
μέρ© ἀνθρώποις τὸ τῦ ἀνθρώπυ εἶδός ἐςι, κὴ τοῖς
κατὰ μέρ© ἵπποις τὸ τῦ ἵππυ εἶδ©· ἐν ἀνθρώποις δὲ,
κὴ ἵπποις, κὴ τοῖς ἄλλοις ζώοις τὸ γέν© εὑρίσκεται
τῶν τοιύτων εἰδῶν, ὅπερ ἐςὶ τὸ ζῶον· κἂν τοῖς ζώοις
ὁμῦ κὴ τοῖς ζωοφύτοις τὸ καθολικώτερον γέν©, τὸ
αἰσθητικὸν, ἐξετάζεται· συναχθέντων δὲ κὴ τῶν φυτῶν,

θεω-

CALLY ONE, amid those infinite particular

θεωρεῖται τὸ ἔμψυχον· εἰ δὲ σὺν τοῖς ἐμψύχοις ἐθέλει τις ἐπισκοπεῖν κὴ τὰ ἄψυχα, τὸ σῶμα σύμπαν κατόψεται· συνδραμουσῶν δὲ τοῖς εἰρημένοις τῶν ἀσωμάτων οὐσιῶν, τὸ πρῶτον γένΘ Φανεῖται κὴ γενικώτατον· κὴ οὕτω μὲν ΕΝ ΤΟΙΣ ΠΟΛΛΟΙΣ ὑφέστηκε τὰ εἴδη κὴ τὰ γένη. Καταλαβὼν δέ τις ἐκ τῶν κατὰ μέρΘ ἀνθρώπων τὴν αὐτῶν φύσιν, τὴν ἀνθρωπότητα, ἐκ δὲ τῶν κατὰ μέρΘ ἵππων αὐτὴν τὴν ἱππότητα, κὴ οὕτω τὸν καθόλου ἄνθρωπον, κὴ τὸν καθόλου ἵππον ἐπινοήσας· κὴ τὸ καθόλου ζῶον ἐκ τῶν καθέκαςα τῷ λόγῳ συναγαγὼν· κὴ τὸ καθόλου αἰσθητικὸν, κὴ τὸ καθόλου ἔμψυχον, κὴ τὸ καθόλου σῶμα, κὴ τὴν καθολικωτάτην οὐσίαν ἐξ ἁπάντων συλλογισάμενΘ, ὁ τοιοῦτΘ ἐν τῇ ἑαυτοῦ διανοίᾳ τὰ γένη κὴ τὰ εἴδη ἀΰλως ὑπέστησεν ΕΠΙ ΤΟΙΣ ΠΟΛΛΟΙΣ, τουτέςι, μετὰ τὰ πολλὰ κὴ ὑστερογενῶς. *Genera vero et Species dicuntur esse* ANTE MULTA, IN MULTIS, POST MULTA. *Ut puta, intelligatur sigillum, quamlibet figuram habens, ex quo multæ ceræ ejusdem figuræ sint participes, et in medium aliquis has proferat, nequaquam præviso sigillo. Cum autem vidisset eas ceras in quibus figura exprimitur, et animadvertisset omnes eandem figuram participare, et quæ videbantur multæ, ratione in unum coegisset, hoc in mente teneat. Nempe sigillum dicitur esse species* ANTE MULTA; *illa vero in ceris,* IN MULTIS; *quæ vero ab iis desumitur, et in mente immaterialiter subsistit,* POST MULTA. *Sic igitur et Genera et Species* ANTE MULTA *in Creatore sunt, secundum rationes efficientes.*

Ch. IV. cular changes, that befal it every moment (k).

MAY

In Deo enim rerum effectrices rationes una et simpliciter præ-existunt; secundum quas rationes ille supra-substantialis omnes res et prædestinavit et produxit. Existere autem dicuntur Genera et Species IN MULTIS, *quoniam in singulis hominibus hominis Species, et in singulis equis equi Species est. In hominibus æque ac in equis et aliis animalibus Genus invenitur harum specierum, quod est animal. In animalibus etiam una cum Zoophytis magis universale Genus, nempe sensitivum exquiritur. Additis vero plantis, spectatur Genus animatum. Si vero una cum animatis quisquam velit perscrutari etiam inanimata, totum Corpus perspiciet. Cum autem entia incorporea conjuncta fuerint iis modo tractatis, apparebit primum et generalissimum Genus. Atque ita quidem* IN MULTIS *subsistunt Genera et Species. Comprehendens vero quisquam ex singulis hominibus naturam ipsam humanam, et ex singulis equis ipsam equinam, atque ita universalem hominem et universalem equum considerans, et universale animal ex singulis ratione colligens, et universale sensitivum, et universale animatum, et universale corpus, et maxime universale ens ex omnibus colligens, hic, inquam, in suâ mente Genera et Species immaterialiter constituit* ΕΠΙ ΤΟΙΣ ΠΟΛΛΟΙΣ, *hoc est,* POST MULTA, *et posterius genita.* Niceph. Blem. Log. Epit. p. 62. Vid. etiam Alcin. in *Platonic.* Philosoph. Introduct. C. IX. X.

(k) The following elegant Lines of *Virgil* are worth attending to, tho' applied to no higher a subject than Bees.

Ergo

BOOK THE THIRD.

MAY we be allowed then to credit thofe Ch.IV.
fpeculative Men, who tell us, " *it is in*
" *thefe*

Ergo ipfas quamvis angufti terminus ævi
Excipiat: (neque enim plus feptima ducitur ætas)
AT GENUS IMMORTALE MANET——G.IV.

The fame *Immortality*, that is, the *Immortality of the Kind*, may be feen in all *perifhable* fubftances, whether animal or inanimate; for tho' *Individuals perifh, the feveral Kinds ftill remain*. And hence, if we take TIME, as denoting *the fyftem of things temporary*, we may collect the meaning of that paffage in the *Timæus*, where the Philofopher defcribes TIME to be——μένοντ@· αἰῶν@· ἐν ἑνὶ κατ' ἀριθμὸν ἰῶσαν αἰώνιον εἰκόνα. *Æternitatis in uno permanentis Imaginem quandam, certis numerorum articulis progredientem. Plat. V. III. p. 37. Edit. Serran.*

We have fubjoined the following extract from *Boethius*, to ferve as a commentary on this defcription of TIME·——ÆTERNITAS *igitur eft, interminabilis vitæ tota fimul et perfecta poffeffio. Quod ex collatione temporalium clarius liquet. Nam quidquid vivit in* TEMPORE, *id præfens à præteritis in futura procedit: nihilque eft in tempore ita conftitutum, quod totum vitæ fuæ fpatium pariter poffit amplecti; fed craftinum quidem nondum apprehendit, hefternum vero jam perdidit. In hodierná quoque vita non amplius vivitis, quam in illo mobili tranfitorioque*

Ch. IV. " *these permanent and comprehensive* FORMS
" *that* THE DEITY *views at once, without*
" *looking abroad, all possible productions*
" *both present, past, and future—that this*
" *great and stupendous View is but a View*
" *of himself, where all things lie inveloped*
" *in their Principles and Exemplars, as be-*
" *ing*

momento. Quod igitur Temporis patitur conditionem, licet illud, sicut de mundo censuit Aristoteles, nec cœperit unquam esse, nec desinat, vitaque ejus cum temporis infinitate tendatur, nondum tamen tale est, ut æternum esse jure credatur. Non enim totum simul infinitæ licet vitæ spatium comprehendit, atque complectitur, sed futura nondum transacta jam non habet. Quod igitur interminabilis vitæ plenitudinem totam pariter comprehendit, ac possidet, cui neque futuri quidquam absit, nec præteriti fluxeret, id ÆTERNUM *esse jure perhibetur: idque necesse est, et sui compos præsens sibi semper assistere, et infinitatem mobilis temporis habere præsentem. Unde quidam non rectè, qui cum audiunt visum Platoni, mundum hunc nec habuisse initium, nec habiturum esse defectum, hoc modo conditori conditum mundum fieri co-æternum putant. Aliud est enim* PER INTERMINABILEM DUCI VITAM, *(quod Mundo Plato tribuit) aliud* INTERMINABILIS VITÆ TOTAM PARITER COMPLEXAM ESSE PRÆSENTIAM, *quod Divinæ Mentis proprium esse manifestum est. Neque enim Deus*

BOOK THE THIRD.

ing essential to the fulness of his universal Ch.IV.
Intellection?"—If so, it will be proper
that we invert the Axiom before mentioned, We must now say——*Nil est in*
SENSU, *quod non prius fuit in* INTELLECTU. For tho' the contrary may be true
with respect to Knowledge *merely human,*
yet never can it be true with respect to Know-

Deus conditis rebus antiquior videri debet temporis quantitate, sed simplicis potius proprietate naturæ. HUNC ENIM VITÆ IMMOBILIS PRÆSENTARIUM STATUM, INFINITUS ILLE TEMPORALIUM RERUM MOTUS IMITATUR; *cumque eum effingere, atque æquare non possit, ex immobilitate deficit in motum; ex simplicitate præsentiæ decrescit in infinitam futuri ac præteriti quantitatem; et, cum totam pariter vitæ suæ plenitudinem nequeat possidere, hoc ipso, quòd aliquo modo nunquam esse desinit, illud, quod implere atque exprimere non potest, aliquatenus videtur æmulari, alligans se ad qualemcunque præsentiam hujus exigui volucrisque momenti: quæ, quoniam* MANENTIS ILLIUS PRÆSENTIÆ QUANDAM GESTAT IMAGINEM, *quibuscunque contigerit, id præstat, ut* ESSE *videantur. Quoniam vero manere non potuit, infinitum Temporis iter arripuit: eoque modo factum est, ut* CONTINUARET VITAM EUNDO, *cujus plenitudinem complecti non valuit* PERMANENDO. *Itaque,* &c. De Consolat. Philosoph. L. V.

Ch. IV. Knowlege univerfally, *unlefs we give Precedence to* ATOMS *and* LIFELESS BODY, making MIND, *among other things, to be ſtruck out by a lucky Concourſe.*

§ 3. IT is far from the defign of this Treatife, to infinuate that Atheifm is the Hypothefis of our latter Metaphyficians. But yet it is fomewhat remarkable, in their feveral Syftems, how readily they admit of the above *Precedence.*

FOR mark the Order of things, according to *their* account of them. Firft comes that huge Body *the ſenſible World.* Then this and its Attributes beget *ſenſible Ideas.* Then out of fenfible Ideas, by a kind of lopping and pruning, are made *Ideas intelligible, whether ſpecific or general.* Thus fhould they admit that MIND was coeval with BODY, yet *till* BODY *gave it Ideas,* and awakened its dormant Powers, it could at beft have been nothing more

more, than *a fort of dead Capacity; for* INNATE IDEAS *it could not poſſibly have* any.

AT another time we hear of *Bodies ſo exceedingly fine,* that their very *Exility* makes them ſuſceptible of *ſenſation* and *knowledge;* as if they ſhrunk into *Intellect* by their exquiſite ſubtlety, which rendered them too delicate to be *Bodies* any longer. It is to this notion we owe many curious inventions, ſuch as *ſubtle Æther, animal Spirits, nervous Ducts, Vibrations,* and the like; Terms, which MODERN PHILOSOPHY, upon parting with *occult Qualities,* has found expedient to provide itſelf, to ſupply their place.

BUT the *intellectual* Scheme, which never forgets Deity, poſtpones every thing *corporeal* to the *primary mental Cauſe.* It is *here* it looks for the origin of *intelligible* Ideas, even of thoſe, which exiſt in *human* Capacities. For tho' *ſenſible* Objects may be

Ch. IV. be the deftined medium, *to awaken* the dormant Energies of *Man's* Underftanding, yet are thofe Energies themfelves no more contained in *Senfe,* than the Explofion of a Cannon, in the Spark which gave it fire (*l*).

IN

(*l*) The following Note is taken from a Manufcript Commentary of the *Platonic Olympiodorus,* (quoted before p. 371) upon the *Phædo* of *Plato*; which tho' perhaps fome may object to from inclining to the Doctrine of *Platonic Reminifcence,* yet it certainly gives a better account how far the *Senfes* affift in the acquifition of *Science,* than we can find given by vulgar Philofophers.

Οὐδέποτε γὰρ τὰ χείρω κỳ δεύτερα ἀρχαὶ ἢ αἰτίαι ἰισὶ τῶν κρειττόνων· εἰ δὲ δεῖ κỳ ταῖς ἐγκυκλίοις ἐξηγήσεσι πείθεσθαι· κỳ ἀρχὴν εἰπεῖν τὴν αἴσθησιν τῆς ἐπιστήμης, λέξομεν αὐτὴν ἀρχὴν ἔχ ὡς ποιητικὴν, ἀλλ' ὡς ἐρεθίζεσαν τὴν ἡμετέραν ψυχὴν εἰς ἀνάμνησιν τῶν καθόλε—κατὰ ταύτην δὲ τὴν ἔννοιαν εἴρηται κỳ τὸ ἐν Τιμαίῳ, ὅτι δι' ὄψεως κỳ ἀκοῆς τὸ τῆς φιλοσοφίας ἐπορισάμεθα γένῳ, διότι ἐκ τῶν αἰσθητῶν εἰς ἀνάμνησιν ἀφικνέμεθα. *Thofe things, which are inferior and fecondary, are by no means the Principles or Caufes of the more excellent; and tho' we admit the common interpretations, and allow* SENSE *to be a Principle of* SCIENCE, *we muft however call it a Principle, not as if it was the*

efficient

BOOK THE THIRD.

In short ALL MINDS, that are, are SI- Ch. IV.
MILAR and CONGENIAL; and so too are
their

*efficient Cause, but as it rouses our Soul to the Recollection
of general Ideas—According to the same way of thinking
is it said in the Timæus, that through the Sight and Hearing we acquire to ourselves Philosophy, because we pass
from Objects of* SENSE *to* REMINISCENCE *or* RE-
COLLECTION.

And in another passage he observes—Ἐπειδὴ γὰρ
πάμμορφον ἄγαλμά ἐστιν ἡ ψυχὴ, πάντων τῶν ὄντων
ἔχουσα λόγους, ἐριθιζομένη ὑπὸ τῶν αἰσθητῶν ἀναμιμ-
νήσκεται ὧν ἔνδον ἔχει λόγων, ᾗ τούτους προβάλλεται.
For in as much as the SOUL, *by containing the Principles of all Beings, is a sort of* OMNIFORM REPRE-
SENTATION *or* EXEMPLAR; *when it is rouzed by
objects of Sense, it recollects those Principles, which it
contains within, and brings them forth.*

Georgius Gemistus, otherwise called *Pletho,* writes
upon the same subject in the following manner. Τὴν
ψυχὴν φασὶν οἱ τὰ εἴδη τιθέμενοι ἀναλαμβάνουσαν ἔσγε
ἐπιστήμην τὰς ἐν τοῖς αἰσθητοῖς λόγους, ἀκριβέστερον αὐτὰς
ἔχοντας ᾗ τελεώτερον ἐν ἑαυτῇ ἴσχειν, ἢ ἐν τοῖς αἰσθητοῖς
ἔχουσι. Τὸ οὖν τελεώτερον τοῦτο ᾗ ἀκριβέστερον ἐκ ἂν
ἀπὸ τῶν αἰσθητῶν ἴσχειν τὴν ψυχὴν, ὅγε μὴ ἐστὶν ἐν αὐτοῖς. Οὐ δ' αὖ μηδαμοῦ ἀλλόθι ὂν αὐτὴν ἐξ αὐτῆς δια-
νοεῖσθαι·

Ch. IV. *their Ideas,* or *intelligible Forms.* Were it otherwife, there could be no intercourfe between

---

νοεῖσθαι· ἐ δὲ γὰρ πεφυκέναι τὴν ψυχὴν μηδαμῆ ὄν, τι διανοεῖσθαι· τὰς γὰρ ψευδεῖς τῶν δοξῶν ἐχὶ μὴ ὄντων ἀλλ' ὄντων μὲν, ἄλλων δὲ κατ' ἄλλων εἶναι συνθέσεις τινὰς, ἐ κατὰ τὸ ὀρθὸν γινομένας. Λείπεσθαι δὲ ἀφ' ἑτέρας τινὸς φύσεως πολλῷ ἔτι κρείτλονός τε κỳ τελεωτέρας ἀφήκειν τῇ ψυχῇ τὸ τελεώτερον τῦτο τῶν ἐν τοῖς αἰσθητοῖς λόγων. *Thofe who fuppofe* IDEAL FORMS, *fay that the Soul, when fhe affumes, for the purpofes of Science, thofe Proportions, which exift in fenfible objects, poffeffes them with a fuperior accuracy and perfection, than that to which they attain in thofe fenfible objects. Now this fuperior Perfection or Accuracy the Soul cannot have from fenfible objects, as it is in fact not in them; nor yet can fhe conceive it herfelf as from herfelf, without its having exiftence any where elfe. For the Soul is not formed fo as to conceive that, which has exiftence no where, fince even fuch opinions, as are falfe, are all of them compofitions irregularly formed, not of mere Non-Beings, but of various real Beings, one with another. It remains therefore that this Perfection, which is fuperior to the Proportions exifting in fenfible objects, muft defcend to the Soul from* SOME OTHER NATURE, WHICH IS BY MANY DEGREES MORE EXCELLENT AND PERFECT. Pleth. de *Ariftotel.* et *Platonic.* Philofoph. Diff. Edit. *Paris* 1541.

The ΛΟΓΟΙ or PROPORTIONS, of which *Gemiftus* here fpeaks, mean not only thofe relative Proportions

Ch. IV.

between Man and Man, or (what is more important) between Man and God.

For portions of *Equality* and *Inequality*, which exist in Quantity, (such as double, sesquialter, &c.) but in a larger sense, they may be extended to mathematical *Lines*, *Angles*, *Figures*, &c. of all which Λόγοι or *Proportions*, tho' we possess in the *Mind* the most clear and precise Ideas, yet it may be justly questioned, whether any one of them ever existed in the *sensible* World.

To these two Authors we may add *Boethius*, who, after having enumerated many acts of the MIND or INTELLECT, wholly distinct from *Sensation*, and independent of it, at length concludes,

> *Hæc est efficiens magis*
> *Longè caussa potentior,*
> *Quam quæ materiæ modo*
> *Impressas patitur notas.*
> *Præcedit tamen excitans,*
> *Ac vires animi movens,*
> *Vivo in corpore passio.*
> *Cùm vel lux oculos ferit,*
> *Vel vox auribus instrepit;*
> *Tum* MENTIS VIGOR *excitus,*
> QUAS INTUS SPECIES TENET,
> *Ad motus simileis vocans,*
> *Notis applicat exteris,*
> INTRORSUMQUE RECONDITIS
> FORMIS *miscet imagines.*
>   De Consolat. Philosoph. L. V.

Ch. IV. FOR what is Converſation between Man and Man?—It is a mutual intercourſe of *Speaking* and *Hearing*.—To the Speaker, it is *to teach*; to the Hearer, it is *to learn*.—To the Speaker, it is *to deſcend* from *Ideas* to *Words*; to the Hearer, it is *to aſcend* from *Words* to *Ideas*.—If the Hearer, in this aſcent, can arrive at *no* Ideas, then is he ſaid *not to underſtand*; if he aſcend to Ideas diſſimilar and heterogeneous, then is he ſaid *to miſunderſtand*.—What then is requiſite, that he may be ſaid *to underſtand?* —That he ſhould aſcend to certain Ideas, treaſured up *within himſelf*, correſpondent and ſimilar to thoſe *within the Speaker*. The ſame may be ſaid of a *Writer* and a *Reader*; as when any one reads to day or to morrow, or here or in *Italy*, what *Euclid* wrote in *Greece* two thouſand years ago.

Now is it not marvelous, there ſhould be *ſo exact an Identy of our Ideas*, if they

were

were only generated from *sensible* Objects, Ch.IV. infinite in number, ever changing, distant in Time, distant in Place, and no one Particular the same with any other?

AGAIN, do we allow it possible for GOD to signify his *will* to Men; or for MEN to signify their *wants* to GOD?—In both these cases there must be *an Idenity of Ideas*, or else nothing is done either one way or the other. Whence then do these COMMON IDENTIC IDEAS come?—Those of *Men*, it seems, come all from *Sensation*. And whence come *God's Ideas*?—Not surely from *Sensation* too; for this we can hardly venture to affirm, without giving to *Body* that *notable Precedence of being prior to the Intellection of even God himself.*—Let them then be *original*; let them be *connate, and essential to the divine Mind.*—If this be true, is it not a fortunate Event, that *Ideas of corporeal rise, and others of mental, (things derived from subjects so totally distinct) should*

so

Ch. IV. *ſo happily co-incide in the ſame wonderful Identity?*

HAD we not better reaſon thus upon ſo abſtruſe a Subject?—Either all MINDS have their Ideas *derived;* or all have them *original;* or *ſome have them original, and ſome derived.* If all Minds have them derived, they muſt be derived from ſomething, *which is itſelf not Mind,* and thus we fall inſenſibly into a kind of Atheiſm. If all have them original, *then are all Minds divine,* an Hypotheſis by far more plauſible than the former. But if this be not admitted, than muſt *one* Mind (at leaſt) have *original* Ideas, and the reſt have them *derived.* Now ſuppoſing this laſt, whence are thoſe Minds, whoſe Ideas are derived, moſt likely to derive them?—From MIND, or from BODY?—From MIND, a thing *homogeneous;* or from BODY, a thing *heterogeneous?* From MIND, ſuch as (from the Hypotheſis) has

original

BOOK THE THIRD.

original Ideas; or from BODY, which we Ch.IV.
cannot difcover to have any Ideas at all? (*l*)
—An Examination of this kind, purfued
with accuracy and temper, is the moſt
probable method of folving thefe doubts.
It is thus we ſhall be enabled with more
affurance to decide, whether we are to
admit the Doctrine of *the Epicurean
Poet,*

CORPOREA NATURA *animum conſtare,
animamque;*

or truſt *the Mantuan Bard,* when he ſings
in divine numbers,

Igneus eſt ollis vigor, et CÆLESTIS ORIGO
Seminibus.———

BUT

(*l*) ΝΟΥΝ δὲ ἐδὲν ΣΩΜΑ γεννᾶ· πῶς γὰρ ἂν
τὰ ΑΝΟΗΤΑ ΝΟΥΝ γεννήσοι; *No* BODY *produces* MIND: *for how ſhould* THINGS DEVOID OF
MIND *produce* MIND? *Salluſt de Diis et Mundo,* c. 8.

D d

Ch.IV. But it is now time, to quit thefe Speculations. Thofe, who would trace them farther, and have leifure for fuch ftudies, may perhaps find themfelves led into regions of Contemplation, affording them profpects both interefting and pleafant. We have at prefent faid as much as was requifite to our Subject, and fhall therefore pafs from hence to our concluding chapter.

CHAP. V.

Subordination of Intelligence—Difference of Ideas, both in particular Men, and in whole Nations—Different Genius of different Languages — Character of the English, *the* Oriental, *the* Latin, *and the* Greek Languages—*Superlative Excellence of the Last—Conclusion.*

ORIGINAL TRUTH (*a*), having the most intimate connection with the *supreme Intelligence,* may be said (as it were) to

---

(*a*) Those Philosophers, whose Ideas of *Being* and *Knowlege* are derived from *Body* and *Sensation*, have a short method to explain the nature of TRUTH. It is a *factitious* thing, made by every man for himself; which comes and goes, just as it is remembered and forgot; which in the order of things makes its appearance *the last* of any, being not only subsequent to *sensible* Objects, but even to our *Sensations* of them. According to this Hypothesis, there are many Truths, which have been, and are no longer; others, that will be, and have not

Ch. V. to shine with unchangeable splendor, enlightening throughout the Universe every possible Subject, by nature susceptible of its benign influence. Passions and other obstacles may prevent indeed its efficacy, as clouds and vapours may obscure the Sun; but it self neither admits *Diminution*, nor *Change*, because the Darkness respects only particular Percipients. Among *these* therefore we must look for ignorance and

---

not been yet; and multitudes, that possibly may never exist at all.

But there are other Reasoners, who must surely have had very different notions; those I mean, who represent TRUTH not as the *last*, but the *first* of Beings; who call it *immutable, eternal, omnipresent*; Attributes, that all indicate something more than human. To these it must appear somewhat strange, how men should imagine, that a crude account of the method *how they perceive* Truth, was to pass for an account of *Truth itself*; as if to describe the road to *London*, could be called a Description of that Metropolis.

For my own part, when I read the detail about Sensation and Reflection, and am taught the process at large how my Ideas are all generated, I seem to view

and errour, and for that *Subordination of* Ch. V.
Intelligence, which is their natural confequence.

We have daily experience in the Works
of Art, that a *partial Knowlege* will fuffice for *Contemplation*, tho' we know not
enough, to profefs ourfelves Artifts. Much
more is this true, with refpect to Nature; and well for mankind is it found

to the human Soul in the light of a Crucible, where Truths are produced by a kind of logical Chemiftry. They may confift (for aught we know) of *natural* materials, but are as much *creatures of our own*, as a Bolus or Elixir.

If *Milton* by his Urania intended to reprefent Truth, he certainly referred her to a much more an-tient, as well as a far more noble origin.

— ———*Heav'nly born!*
Before the hills appear'd, or fountains flow'd,
Thou with eternal Wifdom didft converfe,
Wifdom thy Sifter; and with her didft play
In prefence of th' almighty Father, pleas'd
With thy celeftial Song.——   P. L. VII.

See *Proverbs* VIII. 22, &c. *Jeremiah*. X. 10. *Marc. Antonin.* IX. 1.

Ch. V. to be true, elfe never could we attain any *natural* Knowlege at all. For if the *conſtitutive Proportions of a Clock* are ſo ſubtle, that few conceive them truly, but the Artiſt himſelf; what ſhall we ſay to *thoſe ſeminal Proportions,* which make the eſſence and character of every *natural Subject?*—Partial views, the Imperfections of Senſe; Inattention, Idleneſs, the turbulence of Paſſions; Education, local Sentiments, Opinions, and Belief, conſpire in many inſtances to furniſh us with Ideas, ſome *too general,* ſome *too partial,* and (what is worſe than all this) with many that are *erroneous,* and contrary to Truth. Theſe it behoves us to correct as far as poſſible, by cool ſuſpence and candid examination.

Νῆφε, κỳ μέμνησ᾿ ἀπιςεῖν, ἄρθρα ταῦτα
τῶν φρενῶν.

And thus by a connection perhaps little expected, the Cauſe of Letters, and
that

that of VIRTUE appear to co-incide, it being the bufinefs of both *to examine our Ideas, and to amend them by the Standard of Nature and of Truth* (*b*).

Ch. V.

IN this important Work, we fhall be led to obferve, how Nations, like fingle Men, have their *peculiar* Ideas; how thefe *peculiar* Ideas become THE GENIUS OF THEIR LANGUAGE, fince the *Symbol* muft of courfe correfpond to its *Archetype* (*c*);

how

(*b*) How ufeful to ETHIC SCIENCE, and indeed to KNOWLEGE in general, a GRAMMATICAL DISQUISITION into the *Etymology* and *Meaning* of WORDS was efteemed by the chief and ableft Philofophers, may be feen by confulting *Plato* in his *Cratylus*; *Xenoph. Mem.* IV. 5. 6. *Arrian. Epict.* I. 17. II. 10. *Marc. Anton.* III. 11. V. 8. X. 8.

(*c*) ΠΘΟΥΣ ΧΑΡΑΚΤΗΡ ἐςὶ τ' ἀνθρώπε ΛΟΓΟΣ. Stob. *Capiuntur Signa haud levia, fed obfervatu digna (quod fortaffe quifpiam non putarit) de ingeniis et moribus populorum et nationum ex linguis ipforum.* Bacon. de Augm. Scient. VI. 1. Vid. etiam *Quinctil.* L. XI. p. 675. *Edit. Capperon.* Diog. L. I. p. 58. et *Menag. Com. Tufc. Difp.* V. 16.

Ch. V. how the *wifeſt* Nations, having the *moſt* and *beſt Ideas*, will confequently have the *beſt* and *moſt copious Languages*; how others, whofe Languages are motley and compounded, and who have borrowed from different countrys different Arts and Practices, difcover by WORDS, to whom they are indebted for THINGS.

To illuſtrate what has been faid, by a few examples. WE BRITONS in our time have been remarkable borrowers, as our *multiform* Language may fufficiently fhew. Our Terms in *polite Literature* prove, that this came from *Greece*; our Terms in *Muſic* and *Painting*, that thefe came from *Italy*; our Phrafes in *Cookery* and *War*, that we learnt thefe from the *French*; and our Phrafes in *Navigation*, that we were taught by the *Flemings* and *Low Dutch*. Thefe many and very different Sources of our Language may be the caufe, why it is fo deficient in *Regularity* and *Analogy*. Yet we have this advantage to compenfate the defect,

defect, that what we want in *Elegance*, we gain in *Copiousness*, in which last respect few Languages will be found superior to our own.

Ch. V.

LET us pass from ourselves to the NATIONS OF THE EAST. The (*d*) Eastern World, from the earliest days, has been at all times the Seat of enormous Monarchy. On its natives fair Liberty never shed its genial influence. If at any time civil Discords arose among them (and arise there did innumerable) the contest was never about *the Form of their Government*; (for this was an object, of which the Combatants had no conception;) it was all from the poor motive of, *who should be their* MASTER, whether

---

(*d*) Διὰ γὰρ τὸ δυλικώτεροι εἶναι τὰ ἤθη οἱ μὲν Βάρβαροι τῶν Ἑλλήνων, οἱ δὲ περὶ τὴν Ἀσίαν τῶν περὶ τὴν Εὐρώπην, ὑπομένουσι τὴν δεσποτικὴν ἀρχὴν, οὐδὲν δυσχεραίνοντες. *For the* Barbarians *by being more slavish in their Manners than the* Greeks, *and those of* Asia *than those of* Europe, *submit to despotic Government without murmuring or discontent.* Arist. Polit. III. 4.

Ch. V. whether a *Cyrus* or an *Artaxerxes*, a *Mahomet* or a *Muſtapha*.

SUCH was their Condition, and what was the conſequence?—Their Ideas became conſonant to their ſervile State, and their Words became conſonant to their ſervile Ideas. The great Diſtinction, for ever in their ſight, was that of *Tyrant* and *Slave*; the moſt unnatural one conceivable, and the moſt ſuſceptible of pomp, and empty exaggeration. Hence they talked of Kings as Gods, and of themſelves, as the meaneſt and moſt abject Reptiles. Nothing was either great or little in moderation, but every Sentiment was heightened by incredible Hyperbole. Thus tho' they ſometimes aſcended into *the Great* and *Magnificent* (*e*), they as frequently degenerated

---

(*e*) The trueſt Sublime of the Eaſt may be found in the Scriptures, of which perhaps the principal cauſe is the intrinſic Greatneſs of the Subjects there treated; the Creation of the Univerſe, the Diſpenſations of divine Providence, &c.

nerated into the *Tumid* and *Bombaſt*. The Ch. V.
Greeks too of Aſia became infected by their
neighbours, who were often at times not
only their neighbours, but their maſters;
and hence that Luxuriance of the *Aſiatic
Stile*, unknown to the chaſte eloquence
and purity of *Athens*. But of the *Greeks* we
forbear to ſpeak now, as we ſhall ſpeak of
them more fully, when we have firſt conſidered the Nature or Genius of the *Romans*.

AND what ſort of People may we pro-
nounce the ROMANS?—A Nation engaged
in wars and commotions, ſome foreign,
ſome domeſtic, which for ſeven hun-
dred years wholly engroſſed their thoughts.
Hence therefore their LANGUAGE became, *like their Ideas*, copious in all Terms
expreſſive of things *political*, and well
adapted to the purpoſes both of *Hiſtory*
and *popular Eloquence.*—But what was
their *Philoſophy?*—As a Nation, it was
none, if we may credit their ableſt Writers.
And hence the Unfitneſs of their Language

Ch. V. to this Subject; a defect, which even *Cicero* is compelled to confess, and more fully makes appear, when he writes Philosophy himself, from the number of terms, which he is obliged to invent *(f)*. *Virgil* seems

---

(f) See *Cic. de Fin.* I. C. 1, 2, 3. III. C. 1, 2, 4, &c. but in particular *Tusc. Disp.* l. 3. where he says, PHILOSOPHIA *jacuit usque ad hanc ætatem, nec ullum habuit lumen* LITERARUM LATINARUM; *quæ illustranda et excitanda nobis est; ut si*, &c. See also *Tusc. Disp.* IV. 3. and *Acad.* I. 2. where it appears, that 'till CICERO applied himself to the writing of *Philosophy*, the *Romans* had nothing of the kind in their language, except some mean performances of *Amafanius* the *Epicurean*, and others of the same sect. How far the *Romans* were indebted to *Cicero* for Philosophy, and with what industry, as well as eloquence, he cultivated the Subject, may be seen not only from the titles of those Works that are now lost, but much more from the many noble ones still fortunately preserved.

The *Epicurean* Poet LUCRETIUS, who flourished nearly at the same time, seems by his silence to have over-looked the *Latin* writers of his own sect; deriving all his Philosophy, as well as *Cicero*, from *Grecian* Sources; and, like him, acknowleging the difficulty of writing *Philosophy in Latin*, both from the *Poverty* of the Tongue, and from the *Novelty* of the Subject.

Nec

seems to have judged the moſt truly of his Ch. V.
Countrymen, when admitting their infe-
riority in the more elegant Arts, he concludes at laſt with his uſual majeſty,

Tu

Nec me animi fallit, GRAIORUM *obſcura reperta*
Difficile inluſtrare LATINIS *verſibus eſſe,*
(Multa novis rebus præſertim quom ſit agendum,)
Propter EGESTATEM LINGUÆ *et* RERUM NO-
   VITATEM:
Sed tua me virtus tamen, et ſperata voluptas
Suavis amicitiæ quemvis perferre laborem
Suadet———   Lucr. I. 137.

In the ſame age, VARRO, among his numerous
works, wrote ſome in the way of *Philoſophy*; as did the
Patriot BRUTUS, a Treatiſe *concerning Virtue*, much
applauded by *Cicero*; but theſe Works are now loſt.

Soon after the Writers above-mentioned came HO-
RACE, ſome of whoſe Satires and Epiſtles may be juſtly
ranked among the moſt valuable pieces of *Latin Philo-*
ſophy, whether we conſider the purity of their Stile, or
the great Addreſs, with which they treat the Subject.

After *Horace*, tho' with as long an interval as from
the days of *Auguſtus* to thoſe of *Nero*, came the Satiriſt
PERSIUS, the friend and diſciple of the Stoic *Cornutus*;
to whoſe precepts as he did honour by his virtuous Life,

ſo

Ch. V. *Tu* REGERE IMPERIO POPULOS, *Romane, memento,*
(Hæ tibi erunt artes) pacisque imponere morem,
Parcere subjectis, et debellare superbos.

FROM

---

so his works, tho' small, shew an early proficiency in the Science of Morals. Of him it may be said, that he is almost the single *difficult* writer among the *Latin* Classics, whose meaning has sufficient merit, to make it worth while to labour thro' his obscurities.

In the same degenerate and tyrannic period, lived also SENECA; whose character, both as a Man and a Writer, is discussed with great accuracy by the noble Author of the *Characteristics,* to whom we refer.

Under a milder Dominion, that of *Hadrian* and the *Antonines,* lived AULUS GELLIUS, or (as some call him) AGELLIUS, an entertaining Writer in the miscellaneous way; well skilled in Criticism and Antiquity; who tho' he can hardly be entitled to the name of a *Philosopher,* yet deserves not to pa's unmentioned here, from the curious fragments of Philosophy interspersed in his works.

With *Aulus Gellius* we range MACROBIUS, not because a Contemporary, (for he is supposed to have lived under

FROM considering *the Romans*, let us Ch. V.
pass to THE GREEKS. THE GRECIAN
COMMON-

---

under *Honorius* and *Theodosius*) but from his near resemblance, in the character of a Writer. His Works, like the other's, are miscellaneous; filled with Mythology and antient Literature, some Philosophy being intermixed. His Commentary upon the *Somnium Scipionis* of *Cicero* may be considered as wholly of the *philosophical* kind.

In the same age with *Aulus Gellius*, flourished APULEIUS of *Madaura* in *Africa*, a *Platonic* Writer, whose Matter in general far exceeds his perplexed and affected Stile, too conformable to the false Rhetoric of the Age when he lived.

Of the same Country, but of a later Age, and a harsher Stile, was MARTIANUS CAPELLA, if indeed he deserve not the name rather of a *Philologist*, than of a *Philosopher*.

After *Capella*, we may rank CHALCIDIUS the *Platonic*, tho' both his Age, and Country, and Religion are doubtful. His manner of writing is rather more agreeable than that of the two preceding, nor does he appear to be their inferior in the knowlege of Philosophy, his work being a laudable Commentary upon the *Timæus* of *Plato*.

The

Ch. V. COMMONWEALTHS, while they maintained their Liberty, were the moſt heroic Confederacy, that ever exiſted. They were the

---

The laſt *Latin* Philoſopher was BOETHIUS, who was deſcended from ſome of the nobleſt of the *Roman* Families, and was Conſul in the beginning of the ſixth Century. He wrote many philoſophical Works, the greater part in the *Logical* way. But his *Ethic* piece, *On the Conſolation of Philoſophy*, and which is partly proſe, and partly verſe, deſerves great encomiums both for the Matter, and for the Stile; in which laſt he approaches the Purity of a far better age than his own, and is in all reſpects preferable to thoſe crabbed *Africans* already mentioned. By command of *Theodoric* king of the *Goths*, it was the hard fate of this worthy Man to ſuffer death; with whom the *Latin Tongue*, and the laſt remains of *Roman Dignity*, may be ſaid to have ſunk in the weſtern World.

There were other *Romans*, who left *Philoſophical* Writings; ſuch as MUSONIUS RUFUS, and the two Emperors, MARCUS ANTONINUS and JULIAN; but as theſe preferred the uſe of the *Greek* Tongue to their own, they can hardly be conſidered among the number of *Latin* Writers.

And ſo much (by way of ſketch) for THE LATIN AUTHORS OF PHILOSOPHY; a ſmall number for ſo vaſt an Empire, if we conſider them as all the product of near ſix ſucceſſive centuries.

the politeſt, the braveſt, and the wiſeſt of men. In the ſhort ſpace of little more than a Century, they became ſuch Stateſ-men, Warriors, Orators, Hiſtorians, Phy-ſicians, Poets, Critics, Painters, Sculptors, Architects, and (laſt of all) Philoſophers, that one can hardly help conſidering THAT GOLDEN PERIOD, as a Providential Event in honour of human Nature, to ſhew to what perfection the Species might aſ-cend (g).

Now

(g) If we except *Homer*, *Heſiod*, and the *Lyric* Poets, we hear of few *Grecian* Writers before the ex-pedition of *Xerxes*. After that Monarch had been de-feated, and the dread of the *Perſian* power was at an end, the EFFULGENCE OF GRECIAN GENIUS (if I may uſe the expreſſion) broke forth, and ſhone till the time of *Alexander the Macedonian*, after whom it diſappeared, and never roſe again. This is that *Golden Period* ſpoken of above. I do not mean that *Greece* had not many writers of great merit ſubſequent to that period, and eſpecially of the philoſophic kind; but the *Great*, the *Striking*, the *Sublime* (call it as you pleaſe) attained at that time to a height, to which it never could aſcend in any after age.

Ch. V. Now the Language of these Greeks was truly like themſelves, it was con-

---

The ſame kind of fortune befel the people of *Rome*. When the *Punic* wars were ended, and *Carthage* their dreaded Rival was no more, then (as *Horace* informs us) they began to cultivate the politer arts. It was ſoon after this, their great Orators, and Hiſtorians, and Poets aroſe, and *Rome*, like *Greece*, had her *Golden Period*, which laſted to the death of *Octavius Cæſar*.

I call theſe two Periods, from the two greateſt Geniuſes that flouriſhed in each, one THE SOCRATIC PERIOD, the other THE CICERONIAN.

There are ſtill farther analogies ſubſiſting between them. Neither Period commenced, as long as ſollicitude for the common welfare engaged men's attentions, and ſuch wars impended, as threatened their deſtruction by Foreigners and Barbarians. But when once theſe fears were over, a general ſecurity ſoon enſued, and inſtead of attending to the arts of defence and ſelf-preſervation, they began to cultivate thoſe of Elegance and Pleaſure. Now, as theſe naturally produced a kind of wanton inſolence (not unlike the vitious temper of high fed animals) ſo by this the bands of union were inſenſibly diſſolved. Hence then among

the

conformable to their transcendent and universal Genius. Where Matter so abounded, Ch. V.

---

the *Greeks* that fatal *Peloponnesian* War, which together with other wars, its immediate consequence, broke the confederacy of their Commonwealths; wasted their strength; made them jealous of each other; and thus paved a way for the contemptible kingdom of *Macedon* to enslave them all, and ascend in a few years to universal Monarchy.

A like luxuriance of prosperity sowed discord among the *Romans*; raised those unhappy contests between the *Senate* and the *Gracchi*; between *Sylla* and *Marius*; between *Pompey* and *Cæsar*; till at length, after the last struggle for Liberty by those brave Patriots *Brutus* and *Cassius* at *Philippi*, and the subsequent defeat of *Antony* at *Actium*, the *Romans* became subjects to the dominion of a FELLOW-CITIZEN.

It must indeed be confessed, that after *Alexander* and *Octavius* had established their Monarchies, there were many bright Geniuses, who were eminent under their Government. *Aristotle* maintained a friendship and epistolary correspondence with *Alexander*. In the time of the same Monarch lived *Theophrastus*, and the Cynic, *Diogenes*. Then also *Demosthenes* and *Æschines* spoke their two celebrated Orations. So likewise in the time of *Octavius*, *Virgil* wrote his *Eneid*, and with

Ch. V. abounded, Words followed of courſe, and thoſe exquiſite in every kind, as the Ideas for which they ſtood. And hence it followed, there was not a Subject to be found, which could not with propriety be expreſſed in *Greek*.

HERE were Words and Numbers for the Humour of an *Ariſtophanes*; for the native

---

Horace, *Varius*, and many other fine Writers, partook of his protection and royal munificence. But then it muſt be remembered, that theſe men were bred and educated in the principles of a free Government. It was hence they derived that high and manly ſpirit, which made them the admiration of after-ages. The Succeſſors and Forms of Government left by *Alexander* and *Octavius*, ſoon ſtopt the growth of any thing farther in the kind. So true is that noble ſaying of *Longinus*—Θρέψαι τε γὰρ ἱκανὴ τὰ φρονήματα τῶν μεγαλοφρόνων ἡ ΕΛΕΥΘΕΡΙΑ, κὴ ἐπελπίσαι, κὴ ἅμα διωθεῖν τὸ πρόθυμον τῆς πρὸς ἀλλήλους ἔριδος, κὴ τῆς περὶ τὰ πρωτεῖα φιλοτιμίας. *It is* LIBERTY *that is formed to nurſe the ſentiments of great Geniuſes; to inſpire them with hope; to puſh forward the propenſity of conteſt one with another, and the generous emulation of being the firſt in rank.* De Subl. Sect. 44.

native Elegance of a *Philemon* or *Me-* Ch. V.
nander; for the amorous Strains of a *Mim-*
nermus or *Sappho*; for the rural Lays of a
Theocritus or *Bion*; and for the sublime
Conceptions of a *Sophocles* or *Homer*. The
same in Prose. Here *Isocrates* was enabled
to display his Art, in all the accuracy of
Periods, and the nice counterpoise of
Diction. Here *Demosthenes* found materials for that nervous Composition, that
manly force of unaffected Eloquence,
which rushed, like a torrent, too impetuous to be withstood.

WHO were more different in exhibiting their *Philosophy*, than *Xenophon*,
Plato, and his disciple, *Aristotle?* Different, I say, in their character of *Composition*; for as to their *Philosophy itself*,
it was in reality *the same*. *Aristotle*,
strict, methodic, and orderly; subtle in
Thought; sparing in Ornament; with
little address to the Passions or Imagination; but exhibiting the whole with
such

Ch. V. such a pregnant brevity, that in every sentence we seem to read a page. How exquisitely is this all performed *in Greek*? Let those, who imagine it may be done as well in another Language, satisfy themselves either by attempting to translate him, or by perusing his translations already made by men of learning. On the contrary, when we read either *Xenophon* or *Plato*, nothing of this *method* and strict *order* appears. The *Formal* and *Didactic* is wholly dropt. Whatever they may teach, it is without professing to be teachers; a train of Dialogue and truly polite Address, in which, as in a Mirrour, we behold human Life, adorned in all its colours of Sentiment and Manners.

AND yet though these differ in this manner from the *Stagirite*, how different are they likewise in character from each other?——*Plato*, copious, figurative, and majeftic; intermixing at times Ch. V. the facetious and fatiric; enriching his Works with Tales and Fables, and the myftic Theology of ancient times. *Xenophon*, the Pattern of perfect fimplicity; every where fmooth, harmonious, and pure; declining the figurative, the marvelous, and the myftic; afcending but rarely into the Sublime; nor then fo much trufting to the colours of Stile, as to the intrinfic dignity of the Sentiment itfelf.

THE Language in the mean time, in which *He* and *Plato* wrote, appears to fuit fo accurately with the Stile of both, that when we read either of the two, we cannot help thinking, that it is he alone, who has hit its character, and that it could not have appeared fo elegant in any other manner.

AND thus is THE GREEK TONGUE, *from its Propriety and Univerfality, made*
for

for all that is great, and all that is beautiful, in every Subject, and under every Form of writing.

> GRAIIS *ingenium,* GRAIIS *dedit ore rotundo*
> *Musa loqui.*

IT were to be wished, that those amongst us, who either write or read, with a view to employ their liberal leisure (for as to such, as do either from views more sordid, we leave them, like Slaves, to their destined drudgery) it were to be wished, I say, that the liberal (if they have a relish for letters) would inspect the finished Models of *Grecian Literature;* that they would not waste those hours, which they cannot recall, upon the meaner productions of the *French* and *English* Press; upon that fungous growth of Novels and of Pamphlets, where, it is to be feared, they rarely find

any

any rational pleasure, and more rarely still, any solid improvement.

To be *competently* skilled in antient learning, is by no means a work of such insuperable pains. The very progress itself is attended with delight, and resembles a Journey through some pleasant Country, where every mile we advance, new charms arise. It is certainly as easy to be a Scholar, as a Gamester, or many other Characters equally illiberal and low. The same application, the same quantity of habit will fit us for one, as completely as for the other. And as to those who tell us, with an air of seeming wisdom, that *it is Men*, and *not Books*, we must study to become knowing; this I have always remarked from repeated Experience, to be the common consolation and language of Dunces. They shelter their ignorance under a few bright Examples, whose transcendent abilities, without the common

Ch. V. common helps, have been sufficient *of themselves* to great and important Ends. But alas!

Decipit exemplar vitiis imitabile—

In truth, each man's Understanding, when ripened and mature, is a composite of *natural Capacity*, and of *super-induced Habit*. Hence the greatest Men will be necessarily those, who possess *the best* Capacities, cultivated with *the best* Habits. Hence also moderate Capacities, when adorned with valuable Science, will far transcend others the most acute by nature, when either neglected, or applied to low and base purposes. And thus for the honour of CULTURE *and* GOOD LEARNING, *they are able to render a man, if he will take the pains, intrinsically more excellent than his natural Superiors.*

AND

Ch. V.

AND so much at present as to GENERAL IDEAS; *how we acquire them; whence they are derived; what is their Nature; and what their connection with Language.* So much likewise as to the Subject of this Treatise, UNIVERSAL GRAMMAR.

End of the THIRD BOOK.

A D-

ADVERTISEMENT.

THE following Notes are either Tran-flations of former Notes, or Additions to them. The additional are chiefly Extracts from Greek Manufcripts, which (as the Author has faid already concerning others of the fame kind) are valuable both for their Rarity, and for their intrinfic Merit.

ADDITIONAL NOTES.

PAG. 95.——TO STOP, &c.] The Quotation from *Proclus* in the Note may be thus rendered —THAT THING IS AT REST, *which* FOR A TIME PRIOR AND SUBSEQUENT IS IN THE SAME PLACE, *both itself, and its Parts.*

P. 105. In the Note, for γιγνόμενον read γενόμενον, and render the passage thus—*For by this faculty* (namely the faculty of Sense) *we neither know the Future, nor the Past, but the Present only.*

P. 106. NOTE (*d*)] The passage of *Philoponus* here referred to, but by mistake omitted, has respect to the notion of beings *corporeal* and *sensible,* which were said *to be nearly approaching to Non-Entitys.* The Author explains this among other reasons, by the following—Πῶς δὲ τοῖς μὴ ἔσι γειτνιάζει; Πρῶτον μὲν, ἐπειδὴ ἐνταῦθα τὸ παρελθὸν ἔςι κỳ τὸ μέλλον, ταῦτα δὲ μὴ ὄντα· τὸ μὲν γὰρ ἠφάνιςαι κỳ ἐκ ἔτι ἐςὶ, τὸ δὲ ἐπώ ἐςι· συμπαραθίει δὲ τῷ χρόνῳ τὰ φύσικα πάνʆα, μᾶλλον δὲ τῆς κινήσεως αὐτῶν παρακολέθημά ἐςι ὁ χρόνος. *How therefore is it that they approach nearly to Non-Entitys? In the first place, because* HERE (*where they exist*) *exists* THE PAST *and* THE FUTURE, *and these are* NON-ENTITYS; *for the one is vanished, and is no more, the other is not as yet. Now all natural Substances pass away along with* TIME, *or rather it is upon their Motion that* TIME *is an Attendant.*

P.

ADDITIONAL NOTES.

P. 119—in the Note here subjoined mention is made of the REAL NOW, or INSTANT, and its efficacy. To which we may add, that there is not only a *necessary* Connection between *Existence* and *the Present Instant*, because *no other Point* of Time can properly be said *to be*, but also between *Existence* and *Life*, because whatever *lives*, by the same reason necessarily *Is*. Hence *Sophocles*, speaking of *Time present*, elegantly says of it—

——χρόνῳ τῷ ζῶντι, κ̀ παρόντι νῦν·
THE LIVING, *and Now present* TIME.
Trachin. V. 1185.

P. 227.—The Passage in *Virgil*, of which *Servius* here speaks, is a description of *Turnus*'s killing two brothers, *Amycus* and *Diores*; after which the Poet says of him,

——*curru abscissa* DUORUM
Suspendit capita————

This, literally translated, is—*he hung up on his chariot the heads of* TWO *persons, which were cut off*, whereas the Sense requires, *of* THE *Two persons*, that is to say, of *Amycus* and *Diores*. Now this by *Amborum* would have been exprest properly, as *Amborum* means THE *Two*; by *Duorum* is exprest improperly, as it means only Two *indefinitely*.

P. 259.—The Passage in Note (*o*) from *Themistius*, may be thus rendered—*Nature in many instances appears to make her transition by little and little, so that in some Beings it may be doubted, whether they are Animal, or Vegetable.*

P.

P. 294. Note (c)—*There are in the number of things many, which have a most known* EXISTENCE, *but a most unknown* ESSENCE ; *such for example as* Motion, Place, *and more than either of them,* Time. *The* EXISTENCE *of each of these is known and indisputable, but what their* ESSENCE *is, or Nature, is among the most difficult things to discern.* The Soul *also is in the same Class: that it is something, is most evident ; but what it is, is a matter not so easy to learn.* Alex. Aphrod. p. 142.

P. 340.—LANGUAGE—INCAPABLE OF COMMUNICATING DEMONSTRATION.] See Three Treatises, or Vol. I. p. 220, and the additional note on the words, *The Source of infinite Truths,* &c.

P. 368.—in the Note—*yet so held the Philosopher of* Malmesbury, *and the Author of the Essay,* &c.]

Philoponus, from the Philosophy of *Plato* and *Pythagoras,* seems to have far excelled *these Moderns* in his account of WISDOM or PHILOSOPHY, and its *Attributes,* or *essential Characters.*—Ἴδιον γὰρ φιλοσοφίας τὸ ἐν τοῖς πολλοῖς ἔχυσι διαφορὰν δεῖξαι τὴν κοινωνίαν, ᾗ τὸ ἐν τοῖς πολλοῖς ἔχυσι κοινωνίαν δεῖξαι τίνι διαφέρυσιν· ἐ γὰρ δυσχερὲς τὸ δεῖξαι φάτνης *(lege* φάτλης*)* ᾗ περιστερᾶς κοινωνίαν, *(*παντὶ γὰρ πτηνόν*)* ἀλλ' ἐ *(lege* ὅπυ*)* τὸ διάφορον τέτων εἰπεῖν· ἐδὲ κυνὸς ᾗ ἵππυ διαφορὰν, ἀλλὰ τί κοινὸν ἔχυσιν. IT IS THE PROPER BUSINESS OF PHILOSOPHY TO SHEW IN MANY THINGS, WHICH HAVE DIFFERENCE, WHAT IS THEIR COMMON CHARACTER ; *and* IN MANY THINGS, WHICH HAVE A COMMON CHARACTER, THRO' WHAT IT IS THEY DIFFER. *It* *is indeed no difficult matter to shew the common Character of a Wood-Pigeon and a Dove, (for this is evident to every one) but rather to tell where lies the Difference; nor to tell the Difference between a Dog and a Horse, but rather to shew, what they possess in common.* Philop. Com. MS. in Nicomach. Arithm.

P. 379—THEY ARE MORE EXQUISITE THAN, &c.] The Words of *Aristotle*, here referred to, are these— μᾶλλον δ' ἐςι τὸ οὗ ἕνεκα κὴ τὸ καλὸν ἐν τοῖς τῆς φύσεως ἔργοις, ἢ ἐν τοῖς τῆς τέχνης. THE PRINCIPLES OF DESIGN *and* BEAUTY *are more in the Works of* NATURE, *than they are in those of* ART.

P. 379.—WE MUST OF NECESSITY ADMIT A MIND, &c.] The following quotation, taken from the third book of a *manuscript Comment of* Proclus *on the* Parmenides *of* Plato, is here given for the sake of those, who have curiosity with regard to the doctrine of IDEAS, as held by antient Philosophers.

Εἰ δὲ δεῖ συντόμως εἰπεῖν τὴν αἰτίαν τῆς τῶν ἰδεῶν ὑποθέσεως, δι' ἣν ἐκείνοις ἤρεσε, ῥητέον ὅτι ταῦτα πάντα ὅσα ὁρατὰ, ὀράνια κὴ ὑπὸ σελήνην, ἢ ἀπὸ ταὐτομάτε ἐςὶν, ἢ κατ' αἰτίαν· ἀλλ' ἀπὸ ταὐτομάτε ἀδύνατον· ἔςι γὰρ ἐν τοῖς ὑςέροις τὰ κρείττονα, νῦς, κὴ λόγος, κὴ αἰτία, κὴ τὰ αἰτίας, κὴ ὅτω τὰ ἀποτελέσματα κρείτω τῶν ἀρχῶν, πρὸς τῷ κὴ ὅ φησιν ὁ Ἀριςοτέλης· δεῖ πρὸ τῶν κατὰ συμβεβηκὸς αἰτίων εἶναι τὰ καθ' αὑτά, τάτων γὰρ ἔκβασις τὸ κατὰ συμβεβηκός· ὥςε τὰ ἀπὸ ταὐτομάτε πρεσβύτερον ἂν ἦν τὸ κατ' αἰτίαν, εἰ κὴ ἀπὸ ταὐτομάτε τὰ Θειότατα ἦν τῶν φανερῶν. *If there-*

ADDITIONAL NOTES. 435

therefore we are to relate concisely the Cause, why THE HYPOTHESIS OF IDEAS *pleased them* (namely *Parmenides, Zeno, Socrates,* &c.) *we must begin by observing that all the various visible objects around us, the heavenly as well as the sublunary, are either from* CHANCE, *or according to a* CAUSE. FROM CHANCE IS IMPOSSIBLE; *for then the more excellent things (such as Mind, and Reason, and Cause, and the Effects of Cause) will be among those things that come last, and so the* ENDINGS *of things will be more excellent than their* BEGINNINGS. *To which too may be added what* Aristotle *says; that* ESSENTIAL CAUSES OUGHT TO BE PRIOR TO ACCIDENTAL, *in as much as* EVERY ACCIDENTAL CAUSE IS A DEVIATION FROM THEM; *so that whatever is the Effect of such essential Cause* [as is indeed every work of Art and human Ingenuity] *must needs be prior to that which is the Effect of Chance, even tho' we were to refer to Chance the most divine of visible objects,* [the Heavens themselves].

The Philosopher, having thus proved a *definite Cause* of the World in opposition to *Chance*, proceeds to shew that from the Unity and concurrent Order of things this Cause must be ONE. After which he goes on, as follows.———

———'Ει μὲν ἓν ἄλογον τῦτο, ἄτοπον. ἔςαι γάρ τι πάλιν τῶν ὑςέρων τῆς τάτων αἰτίας κρεῖτlον, τὸ κατὰ λόγον καὶ γνῶσιν ποιῶν, εἴσω τῶ Παντὸς ὂν, καὶ τῶ Ὅλυ μέρος, ὃ ἐςιν ἀπ' αἰτίας ἀλόγυ τοῦτο. Ἐι δὲ λόγον ἔχον, καὶ αὐτὸ γινώσκιν, οἶδεν ἑαυτὸ δήπυ τῶν πάντων αἴτιον ὂν, ἢ τῶτο ἀγνοῶν, ἀγνοήσει τὴν ἑαυτῶ φύσιν. Ἐι δὲ οἶδεν, ὅτι κατ' ἐσίαν ἐςὶ τῶ παντὸς αἴτιον, τὸ

δὲ ὡρισμένως εἰδὸς θάτερον, κỳ θάτερον οἶδεν ἐξ ἀνάγκης, οἶδεν ἄρα κỳ ὗ ἔςιν αἴτιον ὡρισμένως· οἶδεν ἂν κỳ
τὸ Πᾶν, κỳ πάντα ἐξ ὧν τὸ Πᾶν, ὧν ἐςι κỳ αἴτιον.
Καὶ ἐι τῦτο, ἤτοι εἰς ἑαυτὸ ἄρα βλέπον, κỳ ἑαυτὸ γι-
νῶσκον, οἶδε τὰ μετ' αὐτό. Λόγοις ἄρα κỳ ἔιδεσιν ἀΰ-
λοις οἶδε τὰς Κοσμικὰς Λόγυς, κỳ τὰ ἔιδη, ἐξ ὧν τὸ
Πᾶν, κỳ ἔςιν ἐν αὐτῷ τὸ Πᾶν, ὡς ἐν αἰτίῳ, χωρὶς τῆς
ὕλης.——*Now if this Cause be void of Rea-*
son, that indeed would be absurd; for then again there
would be something among those things, which come last
in order, more excellent than their Principle or Cause. I
mean by more excellent, something operating according to
Reason and Knowlege, and yet within that Universe, and
a Part of that Whole, which is, what it is, from a Cause
devoid of Reason.

But if, on the contrary, THE CAUSE OF THE UNI-
VERSE BE A CAUSE, HAVING REASON *and know-*
ing itself, it of course knows itself to be the Cause of all
things; else being ignorant of this, it would be ignorant
of its own nature. But if it know, that from ITS VERY
ESSENCE IT IS THE CAUSE OF THE UNIVERSE,
and if that, which knows one part of a Relation definite-
ly, knows also of necessity the other, it knows for this rea-
son definitely the thing of which it is the Cause. IT
KNOWS THEREFORE THE UNIVERSE, *and all*
things out of which the Universe is composed, of all which
also it is the Cause. But if this be true, it is evident that
BY LOOKING INTO ITSELF, AND BY KNOWING
ITSELF, IT KNOWS WHAT COMES AFTER IT-
SELF, AND IS SUBSEQUENT. *It is therefore, through*
certain REASONS *and* FORMS DEVOID OF MATTER
that

that it knows *those mundane Reasons and Forms, out of which the Universe is composed, and that the Universe is in it, as in a Cause, distinct from and without the Matter.*

P. 380—AGREEABLE TO WHICH IDEAS THESE WORKS ARE FASHIONED, &c.] It is upon these Principles that *Nicomachus* in his *Arithmetic*, p. 7. calls *the Supreme Being an Artist*—ἐν τῇ τῦ τεχνίτυ Θεῦ διανοίᾳ, *in Dei artificis mente.* Where *Philoponus*, in his *manuscript Comment*, observes as follows —τεχνίτην φησὶ τὸν Θεὸν, ὡς πάντων τὰς πρώτας αἰτίας κ) τὰς λόγυς αὐτῶν ἔχοντα. *He calls* GOD *an* ARTIST, *as possessing within himself the first Causes of all things, and their Reasons or Proportions.* Soon after speaking of those Sketches, after which Painters work and finish their Pictures, he subjoins——ὥσπερ ἐν ἡμεῖς, εἰς τὰ τοιαῦτα σκιαγραφήματα βλέποντες, ποιοῦμεν τόδέ τι, ὕτω κ) ὁ δημιυργὸς, πρὸς ἐκεῖνα ἀποβλέπων, τὰ τῆδε πάντα κεκόσμηκεν· ἀλλ' ἰςέον, ὅτι τὰ μὲν τῆδε σκιαγραφήματα ἀτελῆ εἰσιν, ἐκεῖνοι δὲ οἱ ἐν τῷ Θεῷ λόγοι ἀρχέτυποι κ) παντέλειοί εἰσιν. *As therefore we, looking upon such Sketches as these, make such and such particular things, so also the Creator, looking at those Sketches of his, hath formed and adorned with beauty all things here below. We must remember however, that the Sketches here are imperfect; but that the others, those* REASONS *or* Proportions, *which exist in* GOD, *are* ARCHETYPAL *and* ALL-PERFECT.

It is according to this Philosophy, that *Milton* represents *God*, after he had created this visible World, contemplating

―――― *how it show'd*
In prospect from his throne, how good, how fair,
ANSW'RING HIS GREAT IDEA――――
P. Loft, VII. 556.

Proclus proves the Existence of these GENERAL IDEAS or UNIVERSAL FORMS by the following Arguments.―――― εἰ τοίνυν ἐςὶν αἰτία τῦ παντὸς αὐτῷ τῷ ἔιναι ποιῦσα, τὸ δὲ αὐτῷ τῷ ἔιναι ποιῦν ἀπὸ τῆς ἑαυτῦ ποιεῖ ὐσίας τῦτό ἐςι πρώτως, ὅπερ τὸ ποιύμενον δευτέρως κỳ ὅ ἐςι πρώτως, δίδωσι τῷ ποιυμένῳ δευτέρως· οἷον τὸ πῦρ κỳ δίδωσι θερμότητα ἄλλῳ, κỳ ἔςι θερμὸν, ἡ ψυχὴ δίδωσι ζωὴν, κỳ ἔχει ζωὴν, κỳ ἐπὶ πάντων ἴδοις ἂν ἀληθῆ τὸν λόγον, ὅσα αὐτῷ τῷ ἔιναι ποιεῖ. κỳ τὸ ἄιτιον ἓν τῦ παντὸς αὐτῷ τῷ ἔιναι ποιῦν τῦτό ἐςι πρώτως, ὅπερ ὁ κόσμος δευτέρως. εἰ δὴ ὁ κόσμος πλύρωμα ἰδῶν ἐςὶ παντοίων, εἴη ἂν κỳ ἐν τῷ ἀιτίῳ τῦ κόσμυ ταῦτα πρώτως· τὸ γὰρ αὐτὸ ἄιτιον κỳ ἥλιον, κỳ σελήνην, κỳ ἄνθρωπον ὑπέςησε, κỳ ἵππον, κỳ ὅλως τὰ ἔιδη, τὰ ἐν τῷ παντί. ταῦτα ἄρα πρώτως ἐςὶν ἐν τῆ ἀιτία τῦ παντὸς, ἄλλος ἥλιος παρὰ τὸν ἐμφανῆ, κỳ ἄλλος ἄνθρωπος, κỳ τῶν ἐιδῶν ὁμοίως ἕκαςον. ἔςιν ἄρα τὰ ἔιδη πρὸ τῶν ἀισθητῶν, κỳ ἄιτια αὐτῶν τὰ δημιυργικὰ κατὰ τὸν εἰρημένον λόγον, ἐν τῆ μιᾷ τῦ κόσμυ παντὸς ἀιτία προϋπάρχοντα. *If therefore* THE CAUSE OF THE UNIVERSE *be a Cause which operates merely by existing, and if that which operates merely by existing, operate from its own proper Essence,* SUCH CAUSE IS PRIMARILY, WHAT ITS EFFECT IS SECONDARILY, *and that, which it is primarily, it giveth to its Effect secondarily. It is thus that Fire both giveth Warmth to something else, and is itself warm; that the Soul giveth Life, and possesseth Life; and this reasoning you may perceive to be true in all things whatever, which operate merely by existing.* It follows therefore, THAT THE CAUSE OF THE UNIVERSE, *operating after this manner,* IS THAT PRIMARILY, WHICH THE WORLD IS SECONDARILY. *If therefore the* WORLD *be the plenitude of* FORMS *of all Sorts, these* FORMS MUST ALSO BE PRIMARILY IN THE CAUSE OF THE WORLD, *for it was the same Cause, which constituted the Sun, and the Moon, and Man, and Horse, and in general all the Forms existing in the Universe. These therefore exist primarily in the Cause of the Universe; another Sun besides the apparent, another Man, and so with respect to every Form else. The* FORMS *therefore,* PREVIOUS *to the sensible and external Forms, and which according to this reasoning are their* ACTIVE *and* EFFICIENT CAUSES, *are to be found* PRE-EXISTING IN THAT ONE AND COMMON CAUSE OF ALL THE UNIVERSE. *Procli* Com. MS. in Plat. Parmenid. L. 3.

We have quoted the above passages for the same reason, as the former; for the sake of those, who may have a curiosity to see a sample of this *antient* Philosophy, which (as some have held) may be traced up from *Plato* and *Socrates* to *Parmenides, Pythagoras,* and *Orpheus* himself.

If the Phrase, *to operate merely by existing,* should appear questionable, it must be explained upon a supposition, that *in the Supreme Being* no Attributes are *secondary, intermittent,* or *adventitious,* but all *original, ever perfect* and *essential.* See p. 162, 359.

That we should not therefore think of a *blind uncon-
scious* operation, like that of Fire here alluded to, the
Author had long before prepared us, *by uniting Knowlege with natural Efficacy*, where he forms the Character
of these *Divine* and *Creative* Ideas.

But let us hear him in his own Language.—ἀλλ'
εἴπερ ἐθέλοιμεν τὴν ἰδιότητα αὐτῶν (sc. Ἰδεῶν) ἀφορί-
σασθαι διὰ τῶν γνωριμωτέρων, ἀπὸ μὲν τῶν φυσικῶν
λόγων λάβωμεν τὸ αὐτῷ τῷ εἶναι ποιητικὸν, ὧν δὴ κỳ
ποιῦσι· ἀπὸ δὲ τῶν τεχνικῶν τὸ γνωστικὸν, ὧν ποιῦσιν,
εἰ κỳ μὴ αὐτῷ τῷ εἶναι ποιῦσι, κỳ ταῦτα ἑνώσαντες φῶ-
μεν αἰτίας εἶναι τὰς Ἰδέας δημιουργικὰς ἅμα κỳ νοερὰς
πάντων τῶν κατὰ φύσιν ἀποτελουμένων. *But if we
should chuse to define the peculiar character of* IDEAS *by
things more known to us than themselves, let us assume
from* NATURAL PRINCIPLES THE POWER OF EF-
FECTING, MERELY BY EXISTING, *all the things that
they effect; and from* ARTIFICIAL PRINCIPLES THE
POWER OF COMPREHENDING *all that they effect,
although they did not effect them merely by existing; and
then uniting those two, let us say that* IDEAS *are at once
the* EFFICIENT *and* INTELLIGENT CAUSES *of all
things produced according to Nature*. From book the second of the same Comment.

The Schoolman, *Thomas Aquinas*, a subtle and acute
writer, has the following sentence, perfectly cor-
responding with this Philosophy. *Res omnes comparan-
tur ad Divinum Intellectum, sicut artificiata ad Artem.*

The Verses of *Orpheus* on this subject may be found in the tract *De Mundo*, ascribed to *Aristotle*, p. 23. Edit. Sylburg.

Ζεὺς ἄρσην γένετο, Ζεὺς κ. τ. λ.

P. 391—WRERE ALL THINGS LIE INVELOPED, &c.]

—ὅσα περ ἐστι ΤΑ ΠΟΛΛΑ κατὰ δή τινα μερισμὸν, τοσαῦτα κὶ ΤΟ ΕΝ ἐκεῖνο πρὸ τῦ μερισμῦ κατὰ τὸ πάντη ἀμερές· ὐ γὰρ ἕν, ὡς ἐλάχιςον, καθάπερ ὁ Σπεύσιππος ἔδοξε λέγειν, ἀλλ' ΕΝ, ΩΣ ΠΑΝΤΑ. *As numerous as is* THE MULTITUDE OF INDIVIDUALS *by* Partition, *so numerous also is that* PRINCIPLE OF UNITY *by universal* Impartibility. *For it is not* ONE, *as a* MINIMUM *is one,* (*according to what* Speucippus *seemed to say,*) *but it is* ONE, *as being* ALL THINGS. Damascius περὶ Ἀρχῶν, MS.

P. 408—THE WISEST NATIONS—THE MOST COPIOUS LANGUAGES.] It is well observed by *Muretus*——*Nulli unquam, qui res ignorarent, nomina, quibus eas exprimerent, quæsierunt.* Var. Lect. VI. 1.

P. 411.——BUT WHAT WAS THEIR PHILOSOPHY?] The same *Muretus* has the following passage upon the ROMAN TASTE FOR PHILOSOPHY.——*Beati autem illi, et opulenti, et omnium gentium victores* ROMANI, *in petendis honoribus, et in prensandis civibus, et in exteris nationibus verbo componendis, re compilandis occupati, philosophandi curam servis aut libertis suis, et Græculis esurientibus relinquebant. Ipsi, quod ab avaritia,*

tia, quod ab ambitione, quod a voluptatibus reliquum erat temporis, ejus si partem aliquam aut ad audiendum Græcum quempiam philosophum, aut ad aliquem de philosophia libellum vel legendum vel scribendum contulissent, jam se ad eruditionis culmen pervenisse, jam victam a se et profligatam jacere Græciam somniabant. Var. Lect. VI. 1.

INDEX.

A.

ADJECTIVE, how it differs from other Attributives, such as the Verb, and the Participle, 186. verbal, 187. pronominal, 189. strictly speaking can have no Genders, — — — 190

ADVERBS, their character and use, 192 to 194. Adverbs of Intension and Remission, 195. of Comparison, 196 to 199. of Time, and Place, and Motion, 204, 205. made out of Prepositions, 205. Adverbs of Interrogation, 206. affinity between these last, and the Pronoun relative, 206 to 208. Adverbs derived from every Part of Speech, 209. found in every Predicament, 210. called by the *Stoics* Πανδέκτης, — — — — *ibid.*

ÆSCHINES, — — — 419

ALEXANDER APHRODISIENSIS, 294, 310, 433. his account of Phansy or Imagination. — 357

ALEXANDER and THAIS, 71. his influence upon the *Greek* Genius, — — 419, 420

AMAFANIUS, — — — 412

AMMONIUS, his account of Speech, and its relations, 4. of the progress of human Knowlege from Complex to Simple, 10. of the Soul's two principal Powers, 17. of the Species of Sentences, *ibid.* his notion of GOD, 55. quoted, 59. his notion of a Verb, 87, 193. his notion of Time, 100. illustrates from *Homer* the Species of Modes or Sentences, 145. quoted, 154. his notion of conjunctive Particles, and of the Unity which they produce, 241. quoted, 278. his account of Sound, Voice, Articulation, &c. 321, 328.

INDEX.

328. of the diftinction between a Symbol and a Re-
femblance, 331. what he thought the human Body
with refpect to the Soul, 334. his triple order of
Ideas or Forms, — — — 382
Analyfis and *Synthefis*, 2, 3, 367. analyfis of Cafes,
275, 276, 285
ANAXAGORAS — — — 269
ANTHOLOGIA GR. — — 47, 50
ANTONINUS, — 183, 310, 405, 407, 416
APOLLONIUS, *the Grammarian*, explains the Species
of Words by the Species of Letters, 27. his elegant
name for the Noun and Verb, 33. quoted, 63. his
idea of a Pronoun, 65, 67. quoted, 70. explains the
Diftinction and Relation between the Article and
the Pronoun, 73, 74. his two Species of Δεῖξις or
Indication, 77. holds a wide difference between the
Prepofitive and Subjunctive Articles, 78. explains
the nature of the Subjunctive Article, 80. corrects
Homer from the doctrine of Enclitics, 84, 85. his
notion of that Tenfe called the *Præteritum perfectum*, 129. holds the Soul's difpofition peculiarly explained by Verbs, 141. his notion of the Indicative
Mode, 151. of the Future, implied in all Imperatives, 155. explains the power of thofe paft Tenfes,
found in the *Greek* Imperatives, 156. his Idea of the
Infinitive, 165. his name for it, 166. quoted, 168,
175. his notion of middle Verbs, 176. quoted, 179,
181, 195. explains the power and effect of the *Greek
Article*, 217 to 222. holds it effential to the Pronoun
not to coalefce with it, 225 to 228. fhews the different force of the Article when differently placed in
the fame Sentence, 231. quoted, 238, 239. his idea
of the Prepofition, — — — 261

APU-

INDEX.

APULEIUS, short account of him, — 415
AQUINAS, THOMAS, quoted, — 440
Argument a priori & a posteriori, 9, 10. which of the two more natural to Man, — — *ibid.*
ARISTOPHANES, — — — 420
ARISTOTLE, his notion of Truth, 3. quoted, 8. his notion of the difference between things absolutely prior, and relatively prior, 9, 10. quoted, 15. his Definition of a Sentence, 19. of a Word, 20. of Substance, 29. divides things into Substance and Accident, 30. how many Parts of Speech he admitted, and why, 32, 33, 34, &c. his notion of Genders, 42. his account of the metaphorical use of Sex, 48. quoted, 55, 56, 89. his Definition of a Verb, 96. his notion of a Now or Instant, 102. of Sensation limited to it, 104, 105, 431. of Time, 106, 107. of Time's dependence on the Soul, 112. quoted, 119, 193. his notion of Substance, 202. calls *Euripides* ὁ ποιητής, 223. himself called *the Stagirite*, why, *ibid.* a distinction of his, 224. his definition of a Conjunction, 239. a passage in his Rhetoric explained, 240. his account of Relatives, 286. his notion of the divine Nature, 301. whom he thought it was probable the Gods should love, 302. his notion of Intellect and intelligible Objects, *ibid.* held Words founded in Compact, 314, 315. quoted, 310, 320. his account of the Elements or Letters, 324. his high notion of Principles, 325. quoted, 357, 379, 434. his notion of the difference between moveable and immoveable Existence, 360. between intellectual or divine Pleasure, and that which is subordinate, *ibid.* quoted, 361. his notion of the divine Life or Existence, compared with that of Man, 362. of the difference between

INDEX.

tween the *Greeks* and the *Barbarians*, 409. his character as a Writer, compared with *Plato* and *Xenophon*, 421. correfponds with *Alexander*, 419

Arithmetic, founded upon what Principles, 352. (See *Geometry*.) its fubject, what, 367. owes its Being to the Mind, how, — — — *ibid.*

Art, what, and Artift, who, — 111, 352.

ARTICLES, 31. their near alliance with Pronouns, 73. of two kinds, 214. the firft kind, 214 to 232. the fecond kind, 233 to 236. *Englifh* Articles, their difference and ufe, 215. *Greek* Article, 219. Articles denote pre-acquaintance, 218, 220. thence eminence and notoriety, 222 to 224. with what words they affociate, with what not, 224 to 229. *Greek* Article marks the Subject in Propofitions, 230. Articles, inftances of their effect, 231, 232. Articles pronominal, 72, 73, 233. inftances of their effect, 235, 236, 347. Subjunctive Article, fee *Pronoun* relative or fubjunctive.

Articulation, fee *Voice*.

ASCONIUS, — — — 132

ATTRIBUTIVES, 30, 31. defined, 87. of the firft order, 87 to 191. of the fecond order, 192 to 211. *See* VERB, PARTICIPLE, ADJECTIVE, ADVERB.

AULUS GELLIUS, fhort account of him as a Writer, 414

B

BACON, his notion of *Univerfal* Grammar, 2. of *antient* Languages and Geniufes, compared to *modern*, 283. of *mental* Separation or Divifion, 306. of Symbols, to convey our thoughts, 334. of the Analogy be-

INDEX.

between the Geniuses of Nations and their Languages, — — — 407
Being, or *Existence*, mutable, immutable, 90, 371. temporary, superior to Time, 91, 92. See *Truth*, God.
BELISARIUS, — — — 150
BLEMMIDES, NICEPHORUS, his notion of Time present, 119. his Etymology of Ἐπιϛήμη, 368. his triple order of Forms or Ideas, — 386
Body, Instrument of the Mind, 305. chief Object of modern Philosophy, 308. confounded with Matter, 309. human, the Mind's veil, 333. Body, that, or Mind, which has precedence in different Systems, 392, 393
BOERHAAVE, — — — 321
BOETHIUS, how many Parts of Speech he admitted as necessary to *Logic*, 33. his idea of GOD's Existence, 92. illustrates from *Virgil* the Species of Modes or Sentences, 146. quoted, 312. held Language founded in Compact, 315. refers to the Deity's unalterable Nature, 361. his notion of original, intelligible Ideas, 397. of the difference between Time (however immense) and Eternity, 389. short account of his Writings, and character, — 416
Both, differs from *Two*, how, — 227
BRUTUS, — — — — 413, 419

C.

CÆSAR, C. JULIUS, his Laconic Epistle, 178
CÆSAR, OCTAVIUS, influence of his Government upon the *Roman* Genius, — 419, 420
CALLIMACHUS, — — — 52

CASES,

INDEX.

CASES, scarce any such thing in modern Languages, 273. name of, whence, 277. Nominative, 279 to 282 Accusative, 282, 283. Genitive and Dative, 284 to 287. Vocative, why omitted, 276. Ablative, peculiar to the *Romans*, and how they employed it, — — — 276, 277

Causes, Conjunctions connect the four Species of, with their effects, 248. final Cause, first in Speculation, but last in Event, *ibid*. has its peculiar Mode, 142. peculiar Conjunction, 248. peculiar Case, 287

CHALCIDIUS, 301. short account of him, 415

Chance, subsequent to Mind or Reason, 434, 435

CHARISIUS, SOSIPATER, — 205, 210

CICERO, 132, 170, 269, 272, 311, 313, 407. compelled to allow the unfitness of the *Latin* Tongue for Philosophy, 411. one of the first that introduced it into the *Latin* Language, 412. *Ciceronian* and *Socratic* Periods, — — — 418

City, Feminine, why, — — 48

CLARK, *Dr.* SAM. —— —— 128

COMPARISON, degrees of, 197 to 199. why Verbs admit it not, 200. why incompatible with certain Attributives, *ibid*. why with all Substantives, 201

CONJUNCTION, 32. its Definition, 238. its two kinds, 240, 241. Conjunctions Copulative, 242. Continuative, *ibid*. Suppositive, Positive, 244. Causal, Collective, 245, 246. Disjunctive Simple, 252. Adversative, *ibid*. Adversative absolute, 254. of Comparison, 255. Adequate, *ibid*. Inadequate, 256. Subdisjunctive, 258. Some Conjunctions have an obscure Signification, when taken alone, 259

CONNECTIVE, 30, 31. its two kinds, 237. its first kind, *ibid* to 260. its second, 261 to 274. *See* CONJUNCTION, PREPOSITION.

INDEX.

CONSENTIUS, his notion of the Neuter Gender, 43. of middle Verbs, 177. of the positive Degree, 198
Consonant, what, and why so called, — 323
Contraries, pass into each other, 132. destructive of each other, — — — 251
Conversation, what, — — 398
Conversion, of Attributives into Substantives, 38. of Substantives into Attributives, 182, 189. of Attributives into one another, 187. of Interrogatives into Relatives, and *vice versâ,* 206, 207. of Connectives into Attributes, — — 205, 272
CORN. NEPOS, — — 212
Country, Feminine, why. — — 48

D.

DAMASCIUS, his notion of Deity, — 441
Death, Masculine, why, 51. Brother to sleep, 52
Declension, the name, whence, — 278
DEFINITIVE, 30, 31, 214. *See* ARTICLES.
Definitions, what, — — 367
Δεῖξις, — — — 64, 76
DEMOSTHENES, — 49, 419, 421
Derivatives, more rationally formed than Primitives, why, — — — 336
Design, necessarily implies Mind, 379, 434
DIOGENES, *the Cynic,* — — 419
DIOGENES LAERTIUS, 34, 145, 154, 317, 322, 324, 407
DIONYSIUS of *Halicarnassus,* — 34, 35
Diversity, its importance to Nature, 250. heightens by degrees, and how, — *ibid.* to 252
DONATUS, — — 74, 272

G g   E.

INDEX.

E.

Earth, Feminine, why, — — 47
ECCLESIASTICUS, — — 56
Element, defined, 324. primary Articulations or Letters so called, why, *ibid.* their extensive application, 325. See *Letters.*
Empiric, who, — — 352
Enclitics, among the Pronouns, their character, 84, 85
ENGLISH *Tongue*, its rule as to Genders, 43. a peculiar privilege of, 58. expresses the power of contradistinctive and enclitic Pronouns, 85. its poverty as to the expression of Modes and Tenses, 148. its analogy in the formation of Participles, 185, 186. neglected by illiterate Writers, *ibid.* force and power of its Articles, 215 to 233. shews the Predicate of the Proposition by position, as also the Accusative Case of the Sentence, 26, 274, 276. its character, as a Language, — — 408
EPICTETUS, — — 310, 407
Επιϛήμη, its Etymology, — — 368
Ether, Masculine, why, — — 46
EUCLID, a difference between him and *Virgil*, 69. his Theorems founded upon what, — 340
EURIPIDES, — — 52, 310, 331
Existence, differs from *Essence* how, 294, 433
Experience, founded on what, — 352
Experiment, its utility, 352. conducive to Art, how, *ibid.* beholden to Science, tho' Science not to that, 353

F.

Form and *Matter*, 2, 7, elementary Principles, 307. mysteriously blended in their co-existence, *ibid* and 312.

INDEX.

312. Form, its original meaning, what, 310. transferred from lower things to the highest, 311. preexistent, where, 312. described by *Cicero*, 311, 313, in Speech, what, 315, 326, 327, &c. Form of Forms, 312. triple order of Forms in Art, 374. in Nature, 377. intelligible or specific Forms, their peculiar character, 364, 365, 372, 380, 396, 436, 438
Fortune, Feminine, why, —— —— 57
FULLER, —— —— —— 183

G.

GAZA, THEODORE, his Definition of a Word, 21. explains the Persons in Pronouns, 67. hardly admits the Subjunctive for an Article, 78. his account of the Tenses, 129. of Modes, 140. quoted, 151. calls the Infinitive the Verb's Noun, 165. quoted, 181. his Definition of an Adverb, 195. arranges Adverbs by classes according to the Order of the Predicaments, 210. explains the power of the Article, 218. quoted, 225. explains the different powers of conjunctive Particles, 245. of disjunctive, 249. his singular explanation of a Verse in *Homer*, 253. quoted, —— —— 262, 271
GEMISTUS, *Georgius*, otherwise *Pletho*, his doctrine of Ideas or intelligible Forms, —— 395
Genders, their origin, 41. their natural number, 42. (See *Sex*.) why wanting to the first and second Pronoun, —— —— —— 69
Genus and *Species*, why they (but not Individuals) admit of Number, —— —— 39
Geometry, founded on what Principles, 352. that and Arithmetic independent on Experiment, *ibid*. (See *Science*.)

INDEX.

Science.) its Subject, what, 367. beholden for it to the Mind, how, —— —— *ibid.*

GOD, expressed by Neuters such as τὸ θεῖον, *Numen*, &c. why, 54, 55. as Masculine, why, *ibid.* immutable, and superior to Time and its Distinctions, 92. allwise, and always wise, 301. immediate objects of his Wisdom, what, *ibid.* whom among men he may be supposed to love, 302. Form of Forms, sovereign Artist, 312, 313, 437. above all Intensions and Remissions, 162, 359, 439. his Existence different from that of Man, how, 360, 362. his divine Attributes, 361. his Existence necessarily infers that of Ideas or exemplary Forms, 379, 380, 436. exquisite Perfection of these divine Ideas or Forms, 380, 437. his stupendous view of all at once, 389, 390, 442. region of Truth, 162, 391, 403, 405. in Him Knowlege and Power unite, —— 440

Good, above all utility, and totally distinct from it, 297. sought by all men, 296, 298. considered by all as valuable for itself, *ibid.* intellectual, its character, 299. See *Science,* GOD.

GORGIAS, —— —— —— 52

Grammar, philosophical or universal, 2. how essential to other Arts, 6. how distinguished from other Grammars, —— —— —— 11

Grammarians, error of, in naming Verbs Neuter, 177. in degrees of Comparison, 198. in the Syntax of Conjunctions, —— —— 238

GREEKS, their character, as a Nation, 415, &c. *Asiatic Greeks,* different from the other *Greeks,* and why, 410. *Grecian* Genius, its maturity and decay, 417, &c.

GREEK

INDEX.

GREEK *Tongue*, how perfect in the expreſſion of Modes and Tenſes, 147. force of its imperatives in the paſt tenſes, 156. wrong in ranging Interjections with Adverbs, 289. its character, as a Language, 418, 423
GROCINUS, his Syſtem of the Tenſes, —— 128

H.

HERACLITUS, Saying of, 8. his Syſtem of things, what, —— —— —— 369, 370
HERMES, his Figure, Attributes, and Character, 324, 325, 326. Authors, who have writ of him, 326
HESIOD, called ὁ ποιητής, *the* Poet, by *Plato*, 223
HOADLY's Accidence, —— —— 128
HOMER, 50, 52, 82, 84, 145, 149, 221, 223, 235, 253, 273, 285, 308, 417, 421
HORACE, 57, 80, 125, 142, 163, 169, 178, 199, 207, 232, 260, 413, 424, 425

I.

Ideas, of what, Words the Symbols, 341 to 347. if only particular were to exiſt, the conſequence what, 337 to 339. general, their importance, 341, 342. undervalued by whom, and why, 350. of what faculty the Objects, 360. their character, 362 to 366, 390, the only objects of Science and real Knowlege, why, 368. acquired, how, 353 to 374. derived whence, 374, &c. their triple Order in Art, 376. the fame in Nature, 381. eſſential to Mind, why, 379, 380. the firſt and higheſt Ideas, character of, 380, 440. Ideas, their different Sources, ſtated, 400. their real ſource, 434, 438

INDEX.

JEREMIAH, — — 405

Imagination, what, 354. differs from Senfe, how, 355. from Memory and Recollection, how, *ibid.*

Individuals, why fo called, 39, 40. quit their character how and why, 40, 41. their infinity, how expreffed by a finite number of Words, 214 to 217, 234, 346. become objects of Knowlege, how, 369

INSTANT, *See* Now.

Intellect, See *Mind.*

INTERJECTIONS, their application and effect, 289. no diftinct Part of Speech with the *Greeks*, though with the *Latins*, 289. their character and defcription, — — — 290

Interrogation, its fpecies explained and illuftrated, 151 to 154. Interrogatives refufe the Article, why, 228

JOANNES GRAMMAT. *See* PHILOPONUS.

ISOCRATES, — — — 421
JULIAN. — — —, 416

K.

KUSTER, — — — 176

Knowlege, if any more excellent than Senfation, the confequence, — — 371, 372

L.

LANGUAGE, how conftituted, 327. defined, 329. founded in compact, 314, 327. (See *Speech.*) fymbolic, not imitative, why, 332 to 355. impoffible for it to exprefs the real Effences of things, 335. its double capacity why neceffary, 348. its Matter, what, 349. its Form, what, *ibid.* its Precifion and Permanence derived whence, 345. particular Languages,

INDEX.

guages, their Identity, whence, 374. their Diversity, whence, *ibid.* See *English, Greek, Latin, Oriental.*

LATIN *Tongue,* deficient in Aorists, and how it supplies the defect, 125. its peculiar use of the *Præteritum Perfectum,* 131. has recourse to Auxiliars, for some Modes and Tenses, 148. to a Periphrasis for some Participles, 185. in what sense it has Articles, 233. the Ablative, a Case peculiar to it, 276. right in separating Interjections from the other Parts of Speech, 289, 290. its character, as a Language, 411. not made for Philosophy, *ibid.* 412. sunk with *Boethius,* ——— ——— 416

Letters, what *Socrates* thought of their inventor, 325. divine honours paid him by the *Egyptians, ibid.* See *Element.*

Liberty, its influence upon Mens Genius, 420
Life, connected with Being, — 300, 301, 432
LINNÆUS, ——— ——— ——— 44
Literature, its cause and that of Virtue, connected, how, 407. antient, recommended to the Study of the liberal, 424. its peculiar effect with regard to a man's character, ——— ——— 425, 426
Logic, what, ——— ——— 3, 4
LONGINUS, noble remark of, ——— 420
LUCIAN, ——— ——— ——— 41
LUCILIUS, ——— ——— ——— *ibid.*

M.

MACROBIUS, short account of him, 414. quoted 127, 157, 168

INDEX.

Man, rational and social, 1, 2. his peculiar ornament, what, 2. first or prior to Man, what, 9, 269. his Existence, the manner of, what, 359. how most likely to advance in happiness, 362. has within him something divine, 302. his Ideas, whence derived, 393 to 401. Medium, thro' which he derives them, what, 359, 393. his errors, whence, 406, to be corrected, how, ——   ——   ibid.

Manuscripts quoted, of OLYMPIODORUS, 371, 394, 395. of PHILOPONUS, 431, 433, 437. of PROCLUS, 434, 435, 438, 440. of DAMASCIUS, 441

MARCIANUS CAPELLA, short account of him, 415

Master Artist, what forms his character, —   111

Matter joined with *Form*, 2, 7. its original meaning, confounded by the Vulgar, how, 309. its extensive character according to antient Philosophy, 308. described by *Cicero*, 313. of Language, what, 315. described at large, ——   316, &c.

MAXIMUS TYRIUS, his notion of the Supreme Intellect, ——   ——   ——   162

Memory and *Recollection*, what, 355. distinguished from Imagination or Phansy, how, —   ibid.

Metaphor, its use, ——   ——   269

Metaphysicians modern, their Systems, what, 392

MILTON, 13, 14, 44, 45, 47, 49, 51, 53, 56, 59, 60, 112, 124, 147, 207, 267, 268, 404, 437

MIND (n t *Sense*) recognizes time, 107 to 112. universal, 162, 311, 312, 359. differs not (as *Sense* does) from the objects of its perception, 301. acts in part through the body, in part without it, 305. its high power of separation, 306, 366. penetrates into all things, 307. Νοῦς Ὑλικός, what, 310. Mind differs from Sense, how, 364, 365. the source

INDEX.

of Union by viewing One in Many, 362 to 365. of Diſtinction by viewing Many in One, 366. without Ideas, reſembles what, 380. region of Truth and Science. 371, 372. that or Body, which has precedence, 302, &c. Mind human how ſpontaneous and eaſy in its Energies, 361, 362. all Minds ſimilar and congenial, why, ——— 395

MODES or MOODS, whence derived, and to what end deſtined, 140. Declarative or Indicative, 141. Potential, 142. Subjunctive, 143. Interrogative, *ibid*. Inquiſitive, *ibid*. Imperative, 144. Precative or Optative, *ibid*. the ſeveral Species illuſtrated from *Homer*, *Virgil*, and *Milton*, 145 to 147. Infinitive Mode, its peculiar character, 162, 163. how dignified by the *Stoics*, 164. other Modes reſolvable into it, 166. its application and coaleſcence, 167. Mode of Science, of Conjecture, of Proficiency, of Legiſlature, 168 to 170. Modes compared and diſtinguiſhed, 149 to 160. *Greek* Imperatives of the Paſt explained, and illuſtrated, ——— 156, 157

Moon, Feminine, why, ——— ——— 45

Motion, and even its Privation neceſſarily imply Time, 95

MURETUS, quoted, 441, 442. his notion of the *Romans*, ——— ——— ——— *ibid*.

MUSONIUS RUFUS, ——— ——— 416

N.

Names, proper, what the conſequence if no other words, 337 to 339. their uſe, 345. hardly parts of Language, ——— ——— 346, 373

NATHAN and DAVID, ——— ——— 232

Na-

INDEX.

Nature, first to Nature, first to Man, how they differ, 9, 10. frugality of, 320. Natures subordinate subservient to the higher, —— 359
NICEPHORUS, *See* BLEMMIDES.
NICOMACHUS, —— —— 437
NOUN, or Substantive, its three Sorts, 37. what Nouns susceptible of Number, and why, 39. only Part of Speech susceptible of Gender, 41, 171.
A Now or INSTANT, the bound of Time, but no part of it, 101, 102. analogous to a Point in a geometrical Line, *ibid.* its use with respect to Time, 104. its minute and transient presence illustrated, 117. by this Presence Time made present, 116, 117, 118. See *Time, Place, Space*.
Number, to what words it appertains, and why, 39, 40

O.

Objectors, ludicrous, 293. grave, —— 294
Ocean, Masculine, why, —— —— 49
OLYMPIODORUS, quoted from a Manuscript, —— his notion of Knowlege, and its degrees, 371, 372. of general Ideas, the objects of Science, 394, 395
ONE, by natural co-incidence, 162, 173, 192, 241, 262 to 265. by the help of external connectives, 241, 265
Oriental Languages, number of their Parts of Speech, 35. their character and Genius, —— 409
ORPHEUS, —— —— —— 441
OVID, —— —— 132, 141, 206

P.

INDEX.

P.

PARTICIPLE, how different from the Verb, 94, 184. its essence or character, 184. how different from the Adjective, 186. See *Attributive,* LATIN and ENGLISH *Tongues.*
Particulars, how though infinite, expressed by Words which are finite, 346. consequence of attaching ourselves wholly to them, —— 351
PAUSANIAS, —— —— 285
Perception and *Volition,* the Soul's leading Powers, 15, 17. Perception two-fold, 348. In Man what first, 9, 10, 353, 359. sensitive and intellective differ, how, 364, 365. if not correspondent to its objects, erroneous, —— —— 371
Period. See *Sentence.*
PERIPATETIC *Philosophy,* in the latter ages commonly united with the *Platonic,* 160. what species of Sentences it admitted, 144. its notion of Cases, 277. held words founded in Compact, 314
PERIZONIUS, his rational account of the Persons in Nouns and Pronouns, —— —— 171
PERSIUS, 76, 163, 372. short account of his character, —— —— 413
Persons, first, second, third, their Origin and Use, 65 to 67
Phansy, See *Imagination.*
PHILOPONUS, his notion of Time, 431. of the business of Wisdom or Philosophy, 433. of God, the Sovereign Artist, —— —— 437
Philosophy, what would banish it out of the World, 293, 294. its proper business, what, 433. antient differs

INDEX.

differs from modern, how, 308. modern, its chief object, what, —— —— *ibid.*

Philosophers, ancient, who not qualified to write or talk about them, 270. provided words for new Ideas, how, —— —— 269

Philosophers, modern, their notion of Ideas, 350. their employment, 351. their Criterion of Truth, *ibid.* deduce all from Body, 392. supply the place of occult Qualities, how. —— 393

Place, mediate and immediate, 118. applied to illustrate the present Time, and the present Instant, *ibid.* its various relations denoted, how, 266, 271. its Latitude and Universality, — 266

PLATO, 21. how many Parts of Speech he admitted, 32. his account of Genius and Species, 39. quoted, 92. his Style abounds with Particles, why, 259. new-coined Word of, 269. quoted, 325. in what he placed real happiness, 362. his two different, and opposite Etymologies of Ἐπιςήμην, 369, 370. his Idea of Time, 389. quoted, 407. his character, as a Writer, compared with *Zenophon* and *Aristotle*, 422

PLETHO, See GEMISTUS.

PLINY, his account how the antient artists inscribed their names upon their Works, —— 136

PLUTARCH, —— —— 33
Poetry, what, —— —— 5, 6
PORPHYRY, —— —— 39
Position, its force in Syntax, 26, 274, 276, 230
PREPOSITIONS, 32. defined, 261. their use, 265. their original Signification, 266. their subsequent and figurative, 268. their different application, 270, 271. force in Composition, 271, 272. change into Adverbs, —— —— 272, 205

Prin-

INDEX.

Principles, to be eftimated from their confequences, 7, 232, 236, 325. of Union and Diverfity, their different ends and equal importance to the Univerfe, 250. (*See* ONE, *Union*, *Diverfity*) elementary Principles myfterioufly blended, 307. their invention difficult, why, 325. thofe of Arithmetic and Geometry how fimple, ——— — 352
PRISCIAN, defines a Word, 20. explains from Philofopy the Noun and Verb, 28, 33. quoted, 34. explains how Indication and Relation differ, 63. the nature of the Pronoun, 65. of pronominal Perfons, 67. his reafon why the two firft Pronouns have no Genders, 70. why but one Pronoun of each fort, 71. ranges Articles with Pronouns according to the *Stoics*, 74. a pertinent obfervation of his, 88. explains the double Power of the *Latin Præteritum*, 125, 131. his doctrine concerning the Tenfes, 130. defines Moods or Modes, 141. his notion of the Imperative, 155. of the Infinitive, 165, 166. of Verbs which naturally precede the Infinitive, 168. of Imperfonals, 175. of Verbs Neuter, 177. of the Participle, 194. of the Adverb, 195. of Comparatives, 202. quoted, 210. his reafon why certain Pronouns coalefce not with the Article, 225, 226. explains the different powers of Connectives which conjoin, 243, 244, 245. of Connectives which disjoin, 250. quoted, 262. his notion of the Interjection, 291. of Sound or Voice, ——— 316
PROCLUS, his Opinion about Reft, 95, 431. quoted, 310. explains the Source of the Doctrine of Ideas, 434, 435, 436, 438
PRONOUNS, why fo called, 65. their Species, or Perfons, 65, 66. why the firft and fecond have no Sex, 69.

INDEX.

69, 70. refemble Articles, but how diftinguifhed, 73. their coalefcence, 74, 75. their importance in Language, 77. relative or fubjunctive Pronoun, its nature and ufe, 78 to 83. thofe of the firft and fecond perfon when expreffed, when not, 83. Ἐγκλιίικαὶ and ὀρθοτονυμέναι, how diftinguifhed, 84. Primitives, refufe the Article, why, 225
PROTAGORAS, his notion of Genders, 42. a Sophifm of his, —— —— 144
Proverbs of *Solomon*, —— —— 405
PUBLIUS SYRUS, —— —— 124

Q.

QUINTILIAN, —— — 154, 233, 407
Qualities occult, what in modern Philofophy fupplies their place, —— —— 393

R.

Relatives, mutually infer each other, 251, 286. their ufual Cafe, the Genitive, —— *ibid.*
Rhetoric, what, —— —— 5, 6
ROMANS, their character as a Nation, 411. *Roman Genius*, its maturity and decay, — 418, &c.

S.

SALLUSTIUS PHILOSOPH. —— — 401
SANCTIUS, his elegant account of the different Arts refpecting Speech, 5. quoted, 36, 163, 171. rejects Imperfonals, 175. quoted, 202. his notion of the Conjunction, after *Scaliger*, 238. of the Interjection, — — — 291

SCA-

INDEX.

SCALIGER, his Etymology of *Quis*, 82. his notion of Tenfes from *Grocinus*, 128. his elegant obfervation upon the order of the Tenfes, 138. upon the pre-eminence of the Indicative Mode, 169. his account how the *Latins* fupply the place of Articles, 233. his notion of the Conjunction, 238. his fubtle explication of its various powers, 242 to 247, 258. his reafon from Philofophy why Subftantives do not coalefce, 264. his origin of Prepofitions, 266. his Etymology of *Scientia*, —— 370

Science, 5. its Mode the Indicative, and Tenfe the Prefent, why, 159. its Conjunction the Collective, why, 246. defended, 295. valuable for its confequences, *ibid*. for itfelf, 296 to 303. (See GOD) pure and fpeculative depends on Principles the moft fimple, 352. not beholden to Experiment, though Experiment to it, 353. whole of it feen in Compofition and Divifion, 367. its Etymology, 369. refidence of itfelf and it's objects, where, 372. See *Mind*.

Scriptures, their Sublimity, whence, — 410
SENECA, — — 47, 139, 414
Senfation, of the Prefent only, 105, 107, 139. none of Time, 105. each confined to its own Objects, 333, 369. its Objects infinite, 338, 353. Man's firft Perception, *ibid*. confequence of attaching ourfelves wholly to its objects, 351. how prior to Intellection, 379. how fubfequent, — 391
Sentence, definition of, 19, 20. its various Species inveftigated, 14, 15. illuftrated from *Milton*, 147, &c. connection between Sentences and Modes, 144
Separation, corporeal inferior to mental, why, 306
SERVIUS, —— — 132, 227, 432

Sex,

INDEX.

Sex, (See *Gender*.) transferred in Language to Beings, that in Nature want it, and why, 44, 45. Substances alone susceptible of it, — 171

SHAKESPEAR, — 12, 13, 23, 41, 47, 51, 53

Ship, Feminine, why, — — 48

SIMPLICIUS, his triple Order of Ideas or Forms, 381, 382

SOPHOCLES, — — 432

Soul, its leading Powers, — 15, &c.

Sound, species of, 314, 317. the Ὕλη, or Matter of Language, 315. defined, 316. See *Voice*.

Space, how like, how unlike to Time, 100. See *Place*.

Speech, peculiar Ornament of Man, 1, 2. how resolved or analyzed, 2. its four principal Parts, and why these, and not others, 28 to 31. its Matter and Form taken together, 307 to 315. its Matter taken separately, 316 to 326. its Form taken separately, 327 to 359. necessity of Speech, whence, 332, 333. founded in Compact, — 314, 327

SPENCER, — — 134, 164

Spirits animal, subtle Ether, nervous Ducts, Vibrations, &c. their use in modern Philosophy. See *Qualities occult*.

STOICS, how many Parts of Speech they held, 34. ranged Articles along with Pronouns, 74. their account of the Tenses, 130. multiplied the number of Sentences, 144. allowed the name of Verb to the infinitive only, into which they supposed all other Modes resolvable, 164 to 166. their logical view of Verbs, and their Distinctions subsequent, 179 to 181. their notion of the Participle, 194. of the Adverb, 195. called the Adverb πανδέκτης, and why, 210.

INDEX.

210. called the Prepofition σύνδεσμος προθετικός, 261. invented new Words, and gave new Significations to old ones, 269. their notion of Cafes, 278. of the Ὕλη or Matter of Virtue, 309, 310. of Sound, 316. of the Species of Sound, 322. their Definition of an Element, ——— 324
Subject and *Predicate*, how diftinguifhed in *Greek*, 230. how in *Englifh*, ibid. analogous to what in nature, 279
Subftance and *Attribute*, 29. the great Objects of natural Union, 264. Subftance fufceptible of Sex, 171, 41. of Number, 40. co-incides, not with Subftance, 264. incapable of Intenfion, and therefore of Comparifon, — — 201, 202
SUBSTANTIVE, 30, 31. defcribed, 37. primary, *ibid.* to 62. fecondary, 63 to 67. (See NOUN, PRONOUN.) *Subftantive* and *Attributive*, analogous in Nature to what, —— — 279
Σύμβαμα, Παρασύμβαμα, &c. — 180
Sun, Mafculine, why, — — 45
Sylva, a peculiar Signification of, — 308, 309
Symbol, what, 330. differs from Imitation, how, *ibid.* preferred to it in conftituting Language, why, 332

T.

Tenfes, their natural Number, and why, 119, 120. Aorifts, 123. Tenfes either paffing or compltive, what authorities for thefe Diftinctions, 128 to 130. *Præteritum perfectum* of the *Latins*, peculiar ufes of, 131 to 134. *Imperfectum*, peculiar ufes of, 135 to 137. order of Tenfes in common Grammars not fortuitous, ——— — 138

H h TERENCE,

INDEX.

TERENCE, — — 205, 206, 272
THE and A. See ARTICLE.
THEMISTIUS, 9. his notion how the Mind gains the idea of Time, 108. of the dependance of Time on the Soul's exiftence, 112. of the latent tranfition of Nature from one Genus to another, 259, 432
THEODECTES, — — 35
THEOPHRASTUS, his notion of Speech under its various Relations, 4. mentioned, — 419
THEUTH, inventor of Letters, 324. See HERMES.
TIBULLUS, — — 76, 132, 133
Time, Mafculine, why, 50. why implied in every Verb, 95, 96. gave rife to Tenfes, *ibid.* its moft obvious divifion, 97. how like, how unlike to Space, 100 to 103. ftrictly fpeaking no Time prefent, 105. in what fenfe it may be called prefent, 116, 117, 432. all Time divifible and extended, 118, 100, 101. no object of Senfation, why, 105. how faint and fhadowy in exiftence, 106, 431. how, and by what power we gain its idea, 107. Idea of the paft, prior to that of the future, 109. that of the future, how acquired, 109, 110. how connected with Art and Prudence, 111. of what faculty, Time the proper Object, 112. how intimately connected with the Soul, *ibid.* order and value of its feveral Species, 113. what things exift in it, what not, 160 to 162. its natural effect on things exifting in it, 161, 50. defcribed by *Plato*, as the moving Picture of permanent Eternity, 389. this account explained by *Boethius*, *ibid.* See NOW or INSTANT.
Truth, neceffary, immutable, fuperior to all diftinctions of prefent, paft, and future, 90, 91, 92, 159, 160, 404, 405. (See *Being*, GOD) its place or region, 162,

INDEX.

162, 372. feen in Compofition and Divifion, 3, 367. even negative, in fome degree fynthetical, 3, 250, 364. every Truth One, and fo recognized, how, 364, 365. factitious Truth, — 403

V.

VARRO, — — 56, 61, 74, 413
VERB, 31. its more loofe, as well as more ſtrict acceptations, 87, 193. Verb ſtrictly fo called, its character, 93, 94. diſtinguiſhed from Participles, 94. from Adjectives, *ibid* implies Time, why, 95. Tenſes, 98, 119. Modes or Moods, 140, 170. Verbs, how fuſceptible of Number and Perſon, 170. Species of Verbs, 173. active, 174. paſſive, *ibid*. middle, 175, 176. tranſitive, 177 neuter, *ibid*. inceptive, 126, 182. deſiderative or meditative, 127. formed out of Subſtantives, 182, 183. (See *Time, Tenſes*, MODES.) Imperſonals rejected, 175
Verbs Subſtantives, their pre-eminence, 88. eſſential to every Propoſition, *ibid*. implied in every other Verb, 90, 93. denote exiſtence, 88. vary, as varies the exiſtence or Being, which they denote, 91, 92. See *Being, Truth*, GOD.
Verſes, logical, — — 340
Vice, Feminine, why, — — 56
VIRGIL, 46, 47, 48, 49, 57, 68, 83, 132. his peculiar method of coupling the paſſing and completive Tenſes, 133 to 136. quoted, 141, 182, 198, 199, 206, 235, 286, 287, 389, 401, 432. his idea of the *Roman* Genius, — 235, 412
Virtue, Feminine, why, 55. moral and intellectual differ, how, 299, 300. its Matter, what, 309, 310.

INDEX.

its Form, what, 311. connected with Literature, how, — — — 407

Understanding, its Etymology, 369. human Understanding, a composite of what, — 425

Union, natural, the great objects of, 264, 279. perceived by what power, 363. in every truth, whence derived, — — — 365

Universe. See *World*.

Voice, defined, 318. simple, produced how, 318, 319. differs from articulate, how, *ibid*. articulate, what, 319 to 324. articulate, species of, 321 to 323. See *Vowel, Consonant, Element*.

Volition. See *Perception*.

VOSSIUS, — — 35, 75, 290

Vowel, what, and why so called, — 321, 322

Utility, always and only sought by the sordid and illiberal, 294, 295, 298. yet could have no Being, were there not something beyond it, 297. See *Good*.

W.

Whole and *Parts*, — — — 7

Wisdom, how some Philosophers thought it distinguished from Wit, — — 368, 433

WORDS, defined, 20, 21, 328. the several Species of, 23 to 31. significant by themselves, significant by Relation, 27. variable, invariable, 24. significant by themselves and alone, 37 to 211. by Relation and associated, 213 to 274. significant by Compact, 314, 327. Symbols, and not Imitations, 332. Symbols, of what not, 337 to 341. Symbols, of what, 341 to 349, 372. how, though in Number finite, able to express infinite Particulars, 346, 372, 373

INDEX.

World, visible and external, the passing Picture of what, 383, 437. preserved one and the same, though ever changing, how, 384, 385. its Cause not void of Reason, — — — 436

Writers, antient polite differ from modern polite, in what and why, — — 259, 260

X.

XENOPHON, 56, 407. his character as a Writer, compared with *Plato* and *Aristotle*, — 422, 423

Y.

Ὕλη, 308. See *Matter, Sylva*.

F I N I S.

E R R A T A.

Page 4. *for* περιτιθέλαι, *read*, προτιθέλαι. P. 8. line 15. *for* philosopical, *read* philosophical. P. 29. *for* Prisc. L. IX. *read*, Prisc. L. XI. P. 30. Note (*f*) *for* an, *read*, and. P. 74. Note, line 22. *for* Voscius, *read*, Vossius. Line 23. *for* analogi, *read*, analogia. P. 78. Note, line 13. *for* γεμην, *read*, γε μην. P. 87. *for* καχηγορυμενιν, *read*, κατηγορούμενον. P. 96. *for* Proposition, *read*, Preposition. P. 128. line 8. *for* Illiad, *read*, Iliad. P. 165. Note, line 4. *for* frequentur, *read*, frequenter. P. 181. Note, line 2. *for* ῆ, *read*, ἡ. P. 244. line ult. *for* Ευπαπτικοι, *read*, Συναπτικοι. P. 262. line 6. *for* ofters, *read*, others. P. 290. Note, line 9 *for* restat. class. ium, *read*, restat classium. P. 292. line 15. *for* er, *read*, or. P. 300. line 6. *for* it it, *read*, it is. P. 306. line 16. *for* figufe, *read*, figure. P. 317. line. 10. *for* trambling, *read*, trampling. P. 311. Note, line 5. *for* distinctive, *read*, distinctive. P. 384. Note, line 4. *for* οἱδιπε, *read*, ωδε πε. P. 399. *for* idenity, *read*, identity. P. 417. Note, line 14. *for* subjects, *read*, subject. P. 421. line 5 *for* WRERE, *read*, WHERE.

ADVERTISEMENT.

The Reader is desired to take notice, that as often as the author quotes V. I. p. *&c. he refers to Three Treatises published first in one Volume, Octavo, in the year* 1745.

www.ingramcontent.com/pod-product-compliance
Lightning Source LLC
Chambersburg PA
CBHW021425300426
44114CB00010B/645